What Do We Tell the Children?
Critical Essays on Children's Literature

What Do We Tell the Children?
Critical Essays on Children's Literature

Edited by

Ciara Ní Bhroin and Patricia Kennon

CAMBRIDGE SCHOLARS
PUBLISHING

What Do We Tell the Children?
Critical Essays on Children's Literature,
Edited by Ciara Ní Bhroin and Patricia Kennon

This book first published 2012

Cambridge Scholars Publishing

12 Back Chapman Street, Newcastle upon Tyne, NE6 2XX, UK

British Library Cataloguing in Publication Data
A catalogue record for this book is available from the British Library

ISBN (10): 1-4438-3788-1, ISBN (13): 978-1-4438-3788-0

CONTENTS

Part IV: What was told to children in the past?

Part V: What are the children hearing and what are they telling us?

PREFACE

What Do We Tell the Children? Critical Essays on Children's Literature is the fifth publication of the Irish Society for the Study of Children's Literature (ISSCL). It follows the Society's publication of *Studies in Children's Literature 1500-2000* (Dublin: Four Courts Press, 2004), *Treasure Islands: Studies in Children's Literature* (Dublin: Four Courts Press, 2006), *Divided Worlds: Studies in Children's Literature* (Dublin: Four Courts Press, 2007) and *Young Irelands: Studies in Children's Literature* (Dublin: Four Courts Press, 2011). The editors of this collection of essays would like to express their sincere gratitude to the following for their support and encouragement: the president of the Irish Society for the Study of Children's Literature, Marian Thérèse Keyes; the members of the ISSCL committee, Nora Maguire, Anne Markey, Áine McGillicuddy, Beth Rodgers and Julie Anne Stevens; and past committee members Keith O'Sullivan and Pádraic Whyte. A particular debt of gratitude is due to the members of the ISSCL editorial review board whose expert advice was invaluable: Evelyn Arizpe, Matthew Grenby, Peter Hunt, Vanessa Joosen, Celia Keenan, Emer O' Sullivan, Pat Pinsent and David Rudd. We would also like to thank Carol Koulikourdi and Amanda Millar from Cambridge Scholars Press.

Introduction

Ciara Ní Bhroin and Patricia Kennon

It is over a quarter of a century since Jacqueline Rose (1984) drew attention to the power imbalance in the ideologically fraught relation of adult writer to child reader. Rose's argument, that children's literature perpetuates adult fantasies about childhood purity rather than reflecting the desires, characteristics or interests of actual children, exposed for analysis the inconsistencies in a system of texts written for and about children but by adults: "if children's fiction builds an image of the child inside the book, it does so in order to secure the child who is outside the book, the one who does not come so easily within its grasp" (1984, 2). As evidenced by the 2010 Fall themed edition of *Children's Literature Association Quarterly*, Rose's controversial rejection of the possibility of children's literature continues to challenge children's literature criticism. Concepts of childhood and children's status within socio-cultural regimes of power have been problematized as part of this subsequent interrogation of issues of authority and power between the generations. However, as John Stephens (2002) has argued, "the adult's domination over the child appears so complete and so seamless—so a part of the obviousness of childhood—that for some even raising the issue of the child's subjugation seems ridiculous" (xviii). Following Rose, critics such as Karín Lesnik-Oberstein (1994) deny the existence of children's literature and its criticism as anything other than adult constructs based on a false view of children as a homogenous group that can be easily defined and addressed.

While acknowledgement of the gap between writer and reader peculiar to children's literature is now commonplace, the contention that children's literature primarily serves adult needs and interests has been contested (Watson 1992; Rudd 2004, 2010; Reynolds 2007; Griswold 2011). The imbalance between adult writer and child reader need not necessarily be malign and young people are far from powerless in the reading process. Even so, there is now a widespread acknowledgment that all texts are ideological and that those produced by adults for children are especially so (Sutherland 1985; Hollindale 1988; Stephens 1992).

"Since a culture's future is, to put it crudely, invested in its children, children's writers often take upon themselves the task of trying to mould audience attitudes into 'desirable' forms, which can mean either an attempt to perpetuate certain values or to resist socially dominant values which particular writers oppose" (Stephens 1992, 3).

There is a potential tension between the subjectivity of child readers and the implicit authorial control which Peter Hunt (1988) identified as a characteristic marker of the discourse of children's fiction. This tension is suggested by the title of this volume of critical essays which aims to interrogate what adult writers "tell" their child readers about the world, the power relations informing society and what adults consider to be young people's appropriate place in these regulatory systems. Its focus is on fiction addressed at readers from mid-childhood to young adulthood.

Peter Hollindale has argued that "to write books for children, and to write about them, is a political act" (1997, 11). However, this political endeavour is problematized by the elusive nature of the figure of the child and a deep adult ambivalence around how to interpret and mediate the fluidity of childhood experience:

"Often, in our rhetoric, the child embodies change, its threat and its potential. The child, both literally and metaphorically, is always in the process of becoming something else" (Jenkins 1998, 5).

Thus, a central concern of this volume is investigating how concepts of childhood operate within a field of adult anxieties, desires and hopes which propel the utilization of children's literature as a powerful means of socializing and acculturating its target audience, conveying, overtly or covertly, normalizing messages about how to behave, conform and interact with the world around them.

What kinds of knowledge and experience are considered to be appropriate, desirable and even necessary for young audiences? Who is involved in this decision-making process? How are these attitudes and ideologies produced, managed and circulated? Adult writers, publishers and critics "construct children variously as readers, consumers, producers of meaning, as gendered and class-inflected, as politicized or as its opposites, erased, unspoken and passive" (Thompson 2004, 10). While the conceptualization of childhood as a space and time of innocence has saturated many mechanisms for the socialization and regulation of young people—not least, the powerful instrument of story—the power of the media, the marketplace and the flow of consumer culture in today's globalized world have led to a commodification of childhood that problematizes the notion of innocence (Zipes 2001; Pattee 2006; Bullen 2009; Napoli 2012). The essays in this collection aim to interrogate how regimes of power and adult authority inscribe norms and notions of belonging, difference and autonomy for young audiences. The various sections address a range of experiences and ways of knowing: the treatment and mediation of relationship between self and gendered embodiment, the configuration of attitudes around representing mortality and pain for young audiences, the power dynamics informing concepts of national identity and global citizenship, the conditioning forces at work in educational and recreational texts for children and, ultimately, the potential for young people to exercise agency and autonomy in critically interpreting media produced by adults and speaking for themselves as equals in the participatory culture of the twenty-first century.

The first section of the collection focuses on performances and government of gender identity and the body in children's fiction. The recognition of children's embodiment and the acceptance of the consequences of the attendant experiences of materiality, sexuality and mortality, are difficult for many adults to accommodate in relation to concepts of childhood innocence and purity. The chapters in this section examine how youth literature and popular culture contribute to the inscription of particular gender ideologies on young people. The commodification of children's literature and its appropriation as an instrument of capitalism and of cultural homogenization are also addressed. Kerry Mallan examines the configurations of gender and sexuality in recent children's fiction in light of the regulatory pressures of heteronormativity and considers the potential for expanding and enriching concepts of masculinity and femininity for young readers. Analyzing a range of texts including the commercially successful *Go Girl*! and *Totalgirl* series directed at "tweens", Mallan considers the role and accountability of the publishing and culture industries in this arena of socialization and emphasizes the importance of providing counter narratives to hegemonic systems of being gendered and ways of knowing gender. While there has been significant research investigating the strategies, ideologies and material practices of the commodification of childhood through the socializing medium of literature (Pattee 2006; Bullen 2009; Napoli 2012), "the trick with and tension around consuming children always returns to their uneasy status as knowing, choosing subjects" (Cook 2004, 69).

Michele Gill addresses the controversial issue of teenage prostitution and the commodification of the male body in her study of agency, Otherness and authenticity in realistic fiction for young adults. She notes how this genre is situated within tensions and ambiguities about youth sexuality and the subversive roles that young people can play: while the young male protagonists may ultimately be casualties of their circumstances, they also actively collude in their sexualization and are therefore neither passive nor wholly victims. She concludes that this ambivalence ultimately allows complex, multi-dimensional portrayals of young males involved in sex work, thus affording readers the potential to review their expectations about the innocence and experience of youth. Norma Clarke continues this investigation regarding ideologies of "suitability" and "appropriate content" in her discussion of Melvin Burgess's writing for teenagers and the popular and critical reception to his contentious, uncompromising and unflinching depiction of adolescent sexual activity and experimentation. Considering the question of whether children's authors and publishers have a special responsibility to society and their young readers, she probes the generic boundaries of children's literature and the conventional classification of childhood as an asexual space, arguing instead that what is truly needed and appropriate is the realistic, complex and authentic representation of adolescent sexual activity and experience.

The second section of the volume addresses a demanding challenge for children's writers: how to mediate an uncomfortable and often taboo territory—suffering, bereavement and death—for young audiences. While a well-intentioned tendency of adults can be to shield children in their care from potentially upsetting kinds of knowledge of pain and violence, this protective impulse is situated within a constellation of concepts and assumptions about children's state of innocence and their attendant vulnerability to what might be considered "dark" ideas and experiences. Nora Maguire raises thought-provoking questions about the representation of trauma and cultural memory in children's historical fiction in her investigation of how John Boyne portrays the Holocaust in his 2006 crossover novel, *The Boy in the Striped Pyjamas*. Reading this narrative as a text of childhood as well as a children's text, she examines the nature of the book's addresses to adult and to child readers and investigates, not only "what we tell the children", but also "what we adults tell ourselves" about the Holocaust through childhood. In her discussion of the novel's historical inaccuracies and problematic reliance on stereotypes of Jewish and German identity, she emphasizes the text's systematic misrepresentation of this traumatic period, its mythologizing of childhood innocence and the troubling political and ethical dimensions of its sanitization and homogenization of history. Continuing this study of the simplifying and reifying impulse of some adult-produced texts for young audiences, Jane Suzanne Carroll draws upon Susan Cooper's fantasy novel, *The Dark Is Rising* (1973), and its subsequent adaptations for cinema and radio in her analysis of how the medium of landscape can provide a valuable space for young people to reflect on the complex interdependence of life and death. Drawing upon theories of topography, Caroll considers the ideological shifts regarding the representation of death across the various versions of this text. She ultimately argues that the film adaptation's silencing and mitigation of death fail to sufficiently problematize the relationship between good and evil and thus fail to appropriately support its transitional audience's emotional and psychological needs.

Essays in the third section of the volume address issues of inclusion and exclusion regarding concepts of nation, sameness and difference in the world of children's literature. The "imagined communities" of nation (Anderson 1983) play out their dramas of power relationships, belonging and segregation across the imaginative landscape of diverse storyworlds. Postcolonial critics such as Homi Bhabha (1990) have challenged concepts of a unique, hegemonic and stable national identity and instead emphasized concepts of hybridity, mimicry, ambivalence and displacement. Shehrazade Emmambokus thus considers the representation of Muslim characters and culture in a post-9/11 mediascape, exploring the negotiation of the global, the national and the personal in recent teenage fiction from the South Asian Diaspora. Considering the bibliotherapeutic impact of these novels and their potential for reassuring and inspiring their adolescent readers to feel valued as equal citizens, she stresses the importance of recognizing the ways in which the international media industry and the children's book world produce, inscribe and circulate conservative notions about cultural identity. Emmambokus emphasizes the value of texts which not only respect the complexity of how young people learn and negotiate ideas of cultural sameness, difference and plurality but which celebrate these young global citizens' right to choose who they want to be during this enculturation process. Anne Markey investigates how the Irish writers, Kate Thompson and Éilís Ní Dhuibhne, invoke tropes of fantasy, traditional storytelling and folklore as strategies for their respective negotiation and construction of concepts of Irishness for contemporary Irish and international children. Markey identifies a duality in twenty-first-century Irish children's literature's deployment of the English and Irish languages and its construction and representation of modern Irish society. Tracking the placement of recent works by these two authors within the trajectory and agendas of the international marketplace and adult perceptions of national identity, she concludes that Thompson's endorsement of an essential Irish identity neglects the shifting divisions of history and the complicated realities of contemporary Ireland. However, she argues that Ní Dhuibhne's work emphasizes the construction of identity as a dynamic process that meaningfully and richly blends allegiances to the past with an empowering orientation towards the future. In her study of the treatment of Japanese-Canadian internment in Joy Kogawa's historical narrative *Obasan* (1981) and its subsequent adaptations for children, Eimear Hegarty probes the processes of appropriation and reclamation of the past and the transmission of cultural memory from the adult generation to children through the socializing mechanism of children's fiction. Tracing the relationship between young people's self-invention and self-reflection, Hegarty discusses the various versions of Kogawa's autobiographical story and how the child reader is respectively positioned regarding concepts of cultural memory, national inheritance and the constitution of Canadian identity

The history of children's literature has been bound up with the agendas of various stakeholders to manage children's literature for their respective ideological purposes. The next section of the volume explores how childhood was constituted and managed through the cultural practices of children's fiction and print media in nineteenth and early twentieth-century Irish and British society. In her exploration of issues of gender, nation and class in the works of L.T. Meade and Raymond Jacberns, Beth Rodgers investigates the tensions between the didactic and the empowering in school stories for girls in late-Victorian Britain and Ireland and considers the genre's potential for developing young readers' sense of self and agency. Despite this genre's reputation for conservatism, Rodgers argues that girls' school stories offer their young readers an alternative mode of self-identification and that the stories' focus on creating successful female communities should be read within the wider feminist discourse and context of the late-nineteenth-century Woman Question. Marnie Hay addresses the political ideologies and politicizing agenda around issues of gender, nation and citizenship in early-twentieth-century propaganda material generated for Irish children by advanced nationalist groups such as the Inghinidhe na hÉireann. Exploring the strategies deployed by such organizations in cultivating particular concepts of national identity and patriotism, Hay investigates how these media and cultural products were designed to cultivate and recruit the political sympathies and loyalties of Irish youth for the services of the Irish nation at a time of increasing nationalism and political transformation.

The final section of the collection is dedicated to the possibility of recognizing and supporting children's own voices, responses and perspectives in contemporary children's literature. While the didactic impulse of texts for young audiences is indeed powerful, reading is a dialectic process in which young people construct their own meanings. Kay Sambell poses provocative questions about the impact of today's surveillance culture, the allure of celebrity and the immersive nature of consumer culture on young people's capacity for understanding themselves and also their potential for self-invention in her study of Melvin Burgess's novel, *Sara's Face* (2006). In contrast to the saturating tendencies of contemporary adult media and society to position the figure of the teenage girl as consumed by the controlling gaze of the outside world, Sambell argues that Burgess's novel explicitly contests this passive model of victimhood through an ambitious and successful relocation of the act of surveillance, so that the watched, not the watchers, are offered new forms of control and power. The final chapter turns the question of "what do we tell the children?" in a child-centred and inclusive direction: "what do the children hear?" Kimberley Reynolds explores the frictions between telling and hearing, adult authority and adolescent meaning-making, in relation to two recent plays for adolescents, and ultimately questions the credibility of children's literature itself in the eyes of its intended audience. Emphasizing the importance of young people's capacity to speak for themselves, rather than being spoken for by adult writers and the media, Reynolds considers the provision of open-ended, non-hierarchical and discursive forums for dialogue between the generations in contemporary society. She stresses the need for opportunities for adolescents to construct independently images of themselves and affirms the potential of the internet for enabling young people's active experimentation with different voices and ideas.

The stories children are directed towards, given access to and that they encounter provide them with the crucial instruments of "images, vocabularies, attitudes and structures to think about themselves, what happens to them and how the world around them operates" (Reynolds 2005, 3). However, since ideology is "an inevitable, untameable and largely uncontrollable factor in the transaction between books and children" (Hollindale 1988, 10), child readers need to be equipped to recognize and interrogate the ideology of fictional texts. In particular, they need to be made aware of narrative point of view, since this serves to construct subject positions and inscribe ideological assumptions (Stephens 1992, 56). While some fictions construct a passive subject position for child readers (as suggested by this volume's title) others, such as the carnivalesque texts identified by Stephens or the radical fiction explored by Reynolds (2007), encourage a fuller dialectic. The project of sufficiently honouring the equity of youth experience and the integrity of their perspective still remains an ongoing challenge for the adult status quo, requiring as it does a reconceptualization of childhood and the associated power relations between adults and young people. We hope that this collection illuminates how texts may serve to perpetuate and also to question regimes of childhood and adulthood and that the following essays provide valuable insights into the processes of interpretation, negotiation, reflection, construction of norms and modes of surveillance which saturate encounters between adult storytellers, storytelling and young audiences.

References

Anderson, Benedict. 1983. *Imagined Communities: Reflections on the Origin and Spread of Nationalism*. London: Verso.

Bhabha, Homi. 1990. *Nation and Narration*. New York and London: Routledge.

Bullen, Elizabeth. 2009. Inside Story: Product Placement and Adolescent Consumer Identity in Young Adult Fiction. *Media, Culture and Society* 31(3): 497-507.

Cook, Daniel. 2004. *The Commodification of Childhood: The Children's Clothing Industry and the Rise of the Child Consumer*. Durham, NC: Duke University Press.

Griswold, Jerry. 2011. The Art of Children's Literature Criticism. Unpublished lecture given at St. Patrick's College, Dublin 19th October 2011.

Hollindale, Peter. 1988. *Ideology and the Children's Book*. Stroud: Thimble Press.

—. 1997. *Signs of Childness in Children's Books*. Stroud: Thimble Press.

Hunt, Peter. 1988. Degrees of Control: Stylistics and the Discourse of Children's Literature. *Styles of Discourse*, ed. Nikolas Coupland, 163-82. London: Croom Helm.

Jenkins, Henry. 1998. Introduction: Childhood Innocence and Other Modern Myths. *The Children's Culture Reader,* ed. Henry Jenkins, 1-37. New York: New York University Press.

Lesnik-Oberstein, Karín. 1994. *Children's Literature: Criticism and the Fictional Child*. Oxford: Clarendon Press.

Napoli, Mary. 2012. *Selling the Perfect Girl: Girls as Consumers, Girls as Commodities*. London: Routledge.

Pattee, Amy. 2006. Commodities in Literature, Literature as Commodities: A Close Look at the Gossip Girl Series. *Children's Literature Association Quarterly* 31(2): 154-175.

Reynolds, Kimberley. 2005. Introduction. *Modern Children's Literature: An Introduction,* ed. Kimberley Reynolds, 1-7. London: Palgrave Macmillan.

—. 2007. *Radical Children's Literature: Future Visions and Aesthetic Transformations in Juvenile Fiction.* Basingstoke: Palgrave Macmillan.

Rose, Jacqueline. 1984. *The Case of Peter Pan, Or The Impossibility of Children's Literature.* London: Macmillan.

Rudd, David. 2004. Theories and Theorising: The Conditions of Possibility of Children's Literature. *International Companion Encyclopedia of Children's Literature,* ed. Peter Hunt, 29-43. 2nd ed. Volume 1. London: Routledge.

—. 2010. Children's Literature and the Return to Rose. *Children's Literature Association Quarterly* 35(3): 290-310.

Rudd, David, and Anthony Pavlik. 2010. The (Im)Possibility of Children's Fiction: Rose Twenty-Five Years On. *Children's Literature Association Quarterly* 35 (3): 223-229.

Stephens, John. 1992. *Language and Ideology in Children's Fiction.* London: Longman.

—. 2002. *Ways of Being Male: Representing Masculinities in Children's Literature and Film,* ed. John Stephens. New York: Routledge.

Sutherland, R.D. 1985. Hidden Persuaders: Political Ideologies in Literature for Children. *Children's Literature in Education* 16(3):143-158.

Thompson, Mary Shine. Introduction. *Studies in Children's Literature 1500-2000,* eds. Celia Keenan and Mary Shine Thompson, 9-19. Dublin: Four Courts Press.

Watson, Victor. 1992. The Possibilities of Children's Fiction. *After Alice: Exploring Children's Literature,* eds. Morag Styles, Eve Bearne and Victor Watson, 11-24. London: Cassell.

Zipes, Jack. 2001. *Sticks and Stones: The Troublesome Success of Children's Literature from Slovenly Peter to Harry Potter.* New York: Routledge.

PART I

WHAT DO WE TELL THE CHILDREN ABOUT SEXUALITY AND THE BODY?

(Un)doing Gender:
Ways of Being in an Age of Uncertainty

Kerry Mallan

Children's literature has conventionally and historically been concerned with identity and the often tortuous journey to becoming a subject who is generally older and wiser, a journey typically characterized by mishap, adventure, and detours. Narrative closure in children's and young adult novels and films typically provides a point of self-realization or self-actualization, whereby the struggles of finding one's "true" identity have been overcome. In this familiar coming-of-age narrative, there is often an underlying premise of an essential self that will emerge or be uncovered. This kind of narrative resolution provides readers with a reassurance that things will work for the best in the end, which is an enduring feature of children's literature, and part of liberal-humanism's project of harmonious individuality. However, uncertainty is a constant that has always characterized the ways lives are lived, regardless of best-laid plans. Children's literature provides a field of narrative knowledge whereby readers gain impressions of childhood and adolescence, or more specifically, knowledge of ways of being at a time in life, which is marked by uncertainty. Despite the prevalence of children's texts which continue to offer normative ways of being, in particular, normative forms of gender behaviour, there are texts which resist the pull for characters to be "like everyone else" by exploring alternative subjectivities. Fiction, however, cannot be regarded as a source of evidence about the material realities of life, as its strength lies in its affective and imaginative dimensions, which nevertheless can offer readers moments of reflection, recognition, or, in some cases, reality lessons. As a form of cultural production, contemporary children's literature is highly responsive to social change and political debates, and is crucially implicated in shaping the values, attitudes and behaviours of children and young people.

In this chapter I examine a selection of texts for young people that offer fictional imaginings of ways of being that preserve as well as challenge existing normative conceptions of gender and sexuality. To grasp what these texts propose in terms of the contexts of our present time is to see what adults regard as desirable possibilities or cautionary tales for young people "in the face of a diverse, uncertain, and complex future" (Bindé 2000, 57). The texts I have chosen deal with these contradictory perspectives. I take my title from Judith Butler's book *Undoing Gender* (2004), and, following Butler's lead, I want to interrogate both the doing and undoing of gender with respect to conceptions of a sexual and gendered life, and particularly as it is narrativized in the examples of children's texts. I argue that despite contemporary children's texts' attempts to reflect the changing social and political landscape of the world in which they are produced, a heterosexual matrix is constantly invoked in stories of childhood and adolescence. For Butler, the heterosexual matrix produces sex, gender, and heterosexuality through which the subject is rendered intelligible, and thereby certain "identities" (transgenders, homosexuals, lesbians, even racial minorities) cannot "exist" (Butler 1990, 17). The discussion examines the part played by homophobia, consumerism, coming-out, cross-dressing, and same-sex marriage in challenging or supporting the oppositional logic of heterosexism, a logic based on a gender binary. I begin with a brief framing of the issues that emerge in theorizing conceptions of gender drawing on the work of Judith Butler, before moving on to examine how texts for young people attempt to represent and interrogate identity and social practices that impact gender identity and subjectivity.

Doing and undoing gender

Butler's argument is that "if gender is a kind of a doing, an incessant activity performed, in part, without one's knowing and without one's willing, it is not for that reason automatic or mechanical" (2004, 2). Butler's notion of gender as a performative act has been extensively cited, criticized, and endorsed by scholars across various disciplines. The view that gender is more an activity, a "doing", than a natural attribute is one that is widely accepted within social constructivist frameworks (see for example: Buchbinder 1998; Flanagan 2007). According to Butler, "one is always 'doing' gender with or for another, even if the other is only imaginary" (2004, 1). However, *doing* gender does not mean that we are authors of our own gender, as the terms that constitute our gender are beyond the individual and arise from within a sociality that has no single author. We might enact our own stylized version of a gender, but these are variations on a theme that have been long established before we came into being. These framing narratives about ways of being male or female are what Butler terms "regulatory fictions" as they attempt to regulate and impose limits on what is possible within normative conceptions of gender. For individuals who are transgender, transsexual or intersex, their bodies do not conform to the imposed ideals that a gender binary dictates. However, individuals are not without agency as they can *un*do gender by not living up to normative conceptions of femininity and masculinity. This undoing is not without difficulties as actions are open to assessment, criticism, ridicule, and censure.

*Un*doing gender can result in *becoming undone* in both positive and negative ways. By refusing to comply with the normative conceptions of gender one can undo one's personhood, undermining the capacity to enjoy what Butler terms a "liveable life" (2004, 1). This is especially the case when one is rejected or marginalized because of one's choice. In refusing to be part of a set of norms that are at odds with one's sense/experience of self, it is preferable to choose an alternative version of norms and ideals that enable one to act in a way that offers a life that is more sustaining and more human. In the following discussion, I explore the consequences of "becoming undone" for the fictional characters.

Doing masculinity: new boys on the dock

Adolescence may appear as the site of a free-floating play of desire. However, this utopian idea masks the extent to which heterosexuality is privileged in the narrative and discursive construction of adolescence. The disjuncture between the assimilation of same-sex and opposite-sex desire is one that emerges in the following discussion of David McRobbie's young adult novel *Tyro* (1999). Except in a limited generic field such as the coming-out narrative, discussed subsequently, heterosexuality is already in place as the default sexual orientation. As a framing narrative, heterosexuality sets its own regulatory actions and limits as noted above. One of these regulatory practices is name-calling.

The presumption that some people are more or less human than others is a problem that has plagued civilization for millennia. Nomenclatures such as freaks, poofters, weirdos and lesos, serve to name difference and to separate or ghettoize people who resist normative forms of gender and sexuality. People who do not visibly appear to fit the normative conception of gender and sexuality not only pose a threat to the dominant social order, but are often subjected to acts of violence and harassment. Name-calling and its detrimental effects are an element of children's and young adult fiction and extend to characters who are perceived as different from the dominant group for reasons of gender, sexuality, ethnicity, class, religious belief, or disability. In the case of gay males, the desire to be one of the boys is a significant part of the identification with masculine solidarity, even when the costs of such identification are high. As David Buchbinder (1998) notes, patriarchal power operates through exclusion and marginalization. Same sex desire for females is often treated as a passing phase or a pathology in need of treatment and cure (see Mallan 2004; McInally 2003).

Ways in which enclaves of "them" and "us" are enforced, and the effects of marginalization, supply the dominant theme for exploring homosocial desire and embodied masculinity in *Tyro*. Just as in a heterosexual frame where women are the object of the male gaze, when it is directed on other males, the gaze is a means of both surveillance and voyeurism. In this novel, class intersects with gender and sexuality. The novel provides an example of how the categorical distinction between the two terms of standard binary axis of sexual orientation—heterosexuality and homosexuality—works within and across masculinity and male sub-cultures, defined by class and workplace hierarchies.

The setting is a Scottish shipyard in 1953, a time and place where rigid rules for gender and sexual conformity were enforced. Part of the initiation rites at the dockyard is to strip the new apprentice and grease his genitals. The perpetrators see this transgressive act as a leveller, a way of erasing class and workplace hierarchies and ensuring that the new kid on the dock becomes one of the boys. The new apprentice, Andrew, is marked from the beginning of the story as "a member o' the upper crust" (14) because of his middle-class background and manner of speaking and behaving. He responds to the name-calling and other acts of marginalization by attempting to "fit in" with the perpetrators, Jack Coultree and his lackeys, The Tigers. However, when Andrew is subjected to the humiliating act of genital greasing, he tries to report it to the police, but his complaint falls on deaf ears. He realizes that any whistle blowing will be quickly quashed and so he has to be seen to be going along with the initiating behaviours in order to access the power and privilege associated with shipyard masculine solidarity. When another apprentice, Oliver, is initiated he does not return to the shipyard, too humiliated and shamed that his "small penis" was seen by the bully boys. Only Jimmy Edgar is prepared to separate himself from the group and to name the greasing ritual for what it is, an act of personal violation or what Jimmy terms colloquially, an act of "bastardry" (51). However, Jimmy, too, pays the price for his decision to stand apart from the others, as he is subjected to taunts and name-calling about his perceived homosexuality.

While the homophobic acts and name-calling directed at Jimmy are a way of securing the solidarity of the homosocial group, they are also regulatory acts which attempt to ensure that heterosexuality remains the privileged discourse and that any hint of homosexual desire that could disrupt the sexual taboos of patriarchal masculinity and heteronormativity is literally wiped out. This is an ironic move as the stripping, touching and viewing of the male genitals during the greasing is not regarded by the perpetrators as a sexual violation or an incident of homoerotic play. *Tyro* illustrates most cogently Judith Butler's point that every identification comes at a cost. What this story demonstrates is that for straight males who reject the patriarchal order there is a cost to pay in "undoing" their perceived allegiance to hegemonic masculinity. For gay males, they are already engaging in the risk that comes with refusing to abide by the norms of mainstream gender and sexuality. *Tyro* is not a coming-out story, but it provides readers with subtle lines of thought regarding a subject's ability to live a life according to his own desires, especially when those desires may be seen as disruptive to a heterosexual ontology and epistemology.

Doing femininity: girlie style

A visit to any children's bookshop will reveal shelves of books targeting girl readers aged from eight to twelve years, or "tweens" as they are now categorized. There are numerous series which focus on things that girls of that age range are presumably interested in: friends, having fun, sleep overs, school, dancing, music and so on. Two examples are *Go Girl!* series (published by Hardie James Egmont) and *Totalgirl* series (published by Allen & Unwin). The books come with embossed covers packaged with Manga-style, hip, female caricatures. The caricatures on the *Totalgirl* covers are multiethnic. The stories are formulaic and didactic, resembling instructional manuals on how do to gender, girlie style. Following in the footsteps of the globally popular Idol television shows, Totalgirls—Chloe, Sarah, and Alex—dream of becoming big stars and are quickly accepted into a prestigious dance school. Whereas *Totalgirl* is dedicated to "every girl who's ever dreamt of a life in the spotlight", *Go Girl!* is promoted in the blurb as representing "real life, real girls" and focuses on minor rites of passage such as surviving a sleep over, sibling rivalry, learning to succeed at sports, and so on. The Go Girls are Annabelle, Cassie, Lola, Becky, Charlie, Lucy, and Olivia—all white, middle class girls struggling with the concerns of adolescence: Will anyone come to my pool party? How can I become a surfie girl? Learning the pitfalls of kiss chasey and the worst horror of all–turning up at dance class in the wrong clothes! These books, like others such as the *Go Girl!* graphic novels produced by Dark Horse, provide old-fashioned, puerile plots, catty girls, and superficial values wrapped up in a veneer of postfeminist hype.

Commentating on similar books targeting teenage girls such as *Gossip Girl* written by Cecily von Ziegesar, *A-List* by Zoey Dean, and *The Clique* series by Lisi Harrison, Naomi Wolf (2006) says they represent a new kind of young adult fiction that features a different kind of heroine. In contrast to their tween counterparts, these girls are not suffering girlish identity crises; they are outspoken, in a word EMPOWERED! But as Wolf says, they are empowered to hire party planners, draw up a petition calling for the cafeteria ladies serving their lunches to get manicures, and humiliate the "sluts" in their classes. Wolf calls these "bad girl" books not because of the tacky sex scenes in them but because of the value system they promote: meanness rules, parents "check out", conformity is everything. Stressed-out adult values are presumed to be meaningful to teenagers. The books, like those for younger girls, have a kitsch quality, but whereas the *Go Girl!* series deals with catty girls and harmless plots, these, according to Wolf, package corruption with a cute overlay. There is some truth to what Wolf says, but more important is the fact that despite the proliferation and popularity of girl series such as these, girl readers do not receive many positive messages about their sexuality or positive forms of femininity, which are not based on competition and consumerism. The girls in the *A-List* and *Gossip Girl* series like to shop and the fruits of their labour—the Prada bags, designer clothes and top drawer technological aids—are the means for identification and status in their world. However, the intertextuality extends into the paratext where the clothing featured on the cover is credited to the designer and a website is provided just in case the reader wishes to buy a similar outfit.

In a related way, the Bratz dolls have swept many children and their mothers into a buying frenzy. These ten-inch sexy, party dolls with their marketing slogan—"a passion for fashion"—have enormous amounts of hair, pouty lips, made-up eyes, over-sized heads, and street-chic outfits. Given the targeted age of consumers for Bratz dolls (under eight years generally), it is surprising that the profiling of the Bratz girls includes adult tastes (e.g. Yasmin's "fave food": Mediterranean food; "fave movies": romantic comedies; "fave books": chick lit with happy endings; and "fave music": Black Eyed Peas).

In addition to these examples of girlie-style femininity, other young adult texts attempt a counter narrative which looks at the negative consequences of a commodified femininity, particularly the ideal body and appearance that can come from cosmetic surgery. Melvin Burgess tackles both celebrity culture and the body dysmorphic disorder in *Sara's Face* (2006), a cautionary tale for modern times. While Burgess treats the subject in a journalistic style by an unnamed narrator, he manages to convey caution about cosmetic surgery in today's beauty-obsessed world. At one point the unscrupulous surgeon Dr. Kaye remarks:

> "'young girls dream of operations like this (new boobs, new tummy, new nose). It's like buying new clothes these days… I never met a woman yet who liked her body. Now, for the first time, it's possible to have anything you want'" (197).

Despite their limitations, these cultural artifacts attempt to forge new forms of subjectivity for girls which are located in a new social and economic category that previously had been the reserve of boys. Commodity culture articulates a complex of fiction and fantasy, regulation and persuasion which reinforces gender binary and a femininity that is consumer-oriented, superficial, and individualistic. In short, it positions girls in varying ways in relation to the rise of neoliberalism with its often schizophrenic forces which on the one hand promote a self-determining, do-it-yourself identity, and, on the other, reinforce the risk of failing to secure this idealized go-girl femininity.

The above examples of masculinity and femininity show how heterosexuality is constantly invoked in the subjectivity attached to childhood and adolescence. As noted at the beginning of this chapter, children's literature constructs narratives of personal growth or maturation, stories about relationships between the self and others, and between individuals and society. And in their preoccupation with personal growth, maturation and the development of concepts of selfhood, young adult novels frequently reflect complex ideas about subjectivity—or selfhood— in terms of personal concerns and intersubjective relations. Heterosexuality is privileged in the construction of adolescence in young adult fiction, and narratives of closeted adolescence are set against this default sexual orientation. Michael Cart and Christine Jenkins (2006, 82) note that gay-lesbian-bisexual-transgender-queer (GLBTQ) fiction, like other literature produced for young adults, reflects trends in the larger world of publishing for both teens and adults, and "prevailing cultural, social, economic, and political attitudes". While the 1980s saw an increase in books dealing with GLBTQ issues, including gay/lesbian parents, AIDS, and gay teachers and mentors, the 1990s saw an increase in books that had gay/lesbian central characters. However, as Cart and Jenkins note, the gay character is often a secondary character, which arguably results in a narrative distancing from the gay/lesbian/ queer content.

Coming-out narratives, especially those published in the 1990s, can be seen as following either celebratory or shaming teleologies. The world "is schematised according to gender differences and a presumptive heterosexuality" (Mallan 2009, 125). Eve Kosofsky Sedgwick (1990) claims that "coming-out" is first and foremost a performative act. In the act of coming-out, the person is constituted as a gay or lesbian subject, and thus obliges the observer to recognize the person as such rather than assume heterosexuality. In many young adult texts the coming-out is a moment of epiphany at the end of the story. An example is the Swedish film, *Show Me Love* (aka *Fucking Åmål*) (2000), in which the two young female (lesbian) protagonists literally come-out of the closet when they step outside of the school toilet and triumphantly walk hand-in-hand through the stunned crowd of students and teachers who presumed that one of the girls was in the toilet with a boy. What happens next in many coming-out narratives is outside of the narrative frame.

If adolescence is conceived of as a narrative construction (like the metaphor of coming-out of the closet), then the idea that it is a particular period of life that is structured by transitionality and indeterminacy is brought into question. One could ask: "Is there any time of life which is not characterized by transitionality and indeterminacy?" However, a gay/lesbian person is continually required to "come out" or "undo" normative gender expectations as part of the heternormative culture's requirement that homosexuality always be asked to account for itself. As Edmund White writes: "Since no one is brought up to be gay, the moment he recognizes the difference he must account for it" (1991, ix). A similar situation is called for people who are transgendered or intersexed. In children's fiction, the subject is usually constituted as the effect of an interval or delay between the assumption of (biological) sex and gender, on the one hand, and that of sexual orientation, on the other. A typical delay strategy to mediate gender and sexuality is cross-dressing. In some instances, cross-dressing is used as a transitory space of experimental gender play; in others, it is an indicator of a deeper same-sex desire.

Undoing gender: cross-dressing and homonormativity

Children's fictions such as Anne Fine's *Bill's New Frock* (1989) and *Alias, Madame Doubtfire* (1988), and Louis Sacher's *Marvin Redpost: Is He a Girl?* (1993) employ the trope of cross-dressing as a means to discuss gender inequality and discriminatory social practices. However, the nature of the transgendered subject in these texts is only transitory as the masculine subject has been turned into a feminine subject by a magical trick. This mediation of transgender through comedy has a long lineage which includes Shakespeare's cross-dressing plays, *Twelfth Night* and *As You Like It*. Cross-dressing complicates the heterosexual matrix as it draws attention to the ambiguity of gender, and those identities which cannot "exist". This was given tangible evidence when the "Concerned Women of America" complained about the market-survey questions posed on barbie.com, supposedly directed at four- to-eight-year olds, which asked about their gender, giving three options: "I am a Boy"; "I am a Girl"; and "I Don't Know". The third option was seen as a transgendered category. A Mattel spokesman quickly responded by saying that it was an innocent oversight; it should have read "I don't want to say" (Tapper 2006).

In the Belgian film, *Ma Vie en Rose* (1997), seven-year-old Ludovic Fabre describes himself as a "boygirl" (*garçon-fille*): a neologism that captures the transgendered nature of his identity. When Ludo comes out at a party his family is hosting as a "welcome to our home" gesture to meet and greet their neighbours after their arrival in a middle class neighbourhood, the response from the guests is one of confusion. While his father defuses the situation by explaining to the assembled party-goers that Ludo is a bit of a trickster, his mother explains gently to Ludo, as she washes off his makeup, the inappropriateness of a child of his age (and gender) dressing up like a girl: "You're seven, Ludo. Too old to dress as a girl". Ludo simply looks puzzled by everyone's reactions.

This film demonstrates the painful consequences of undoing gender. The family is almost destroyed by internal conflict and they eventually respond to the ostracism by their neighbours by moving to a more downmarket neighbourhood after the father loses his job. Ludo and his mother become estranged. In one scene the mother coldly cuts Ludo's longish hair into a short boyish style erasing the ambiguity of his androgynous appearance. However, resolution is gained through a dream-like sequence when the Mother falls into a television fantasy space, "Pam's World". Her move out of the real world into the fantasy world and again back into the real world provides her with renewed understanding and tolerance for her son. But the film's closure leaves it to the viewer to imagine what will become of Ludo as he grows older, an open ending that is similar to the coming-out story.

While the appearance of alternative gender and sexual identities in popular culture has become more acceptable in recent years for both child and adult audiences, same-sex couples' rights in the real world remain restrictive and prohibitive. For example gay and lesbian marriage has caused heated debates in many countries as it is invariably seen as threatening marriage and parenting norms. In Australia in 2004, an episode of the children's television programme *Playschool* which featured a same-sex family was publicly criticized by the then Prime Minister, John Howard, who made it clear that the subject matter was not for children. In the report below from an Australian newspaper, *The Age,* it is clear that the strategy of delay is being invoked as a form of protection for children from exposure to an alternative to the heterosexual matrix:

> "Mr Howard would not accept the program's claim that its 'Through The Windows' segment reflected the variety of the contemporary world. 'That doesn't wash with me and I don't think it would wash with most of your viewers,' he said. 'You're talking about a very, very small number and to intrude that into a children's program is just being politically correct and I think is an example of the ABC running an agenda'" (Wroe 2004).

In the same article, another Liberal Party politician, John Anderson, added further endorsement of binary gender and stereotypical gender roles:

> "Gays and lesbians should accept that their choice of lifestyle meant other life options were closed to them....We know that from an incredibly early age children of both sexes look to mum for nurture and warmth, dad for stimulation and play" (Wroe 2004).

A more recent example of censorship occurred in 2009 when the popular Australian television family series *Home and Away* cut a "lesbian kissing" scene after public protest. As reported in *The Australian* newspaper:

> "Some mothers contacted the network to say they didn't want their children exposed to same-sex relationships in a family show. *Home and Away* is screened at 7pm and is rated PG" (Meade 2009).

What these comments reveal is that there is a gap between the reality of many people's lives and the social conditions which both produce and obstruct those realities. Different family configurations are representative of complex societies of late modernity, and same-sex families exist in spite of restrictive governmental agendas and laws. New family configurations are reflected in literature, film, and television sitcoms, thus serving as privileged sites and sights of cultural change. However, it is my contention that despite the diversity of families represented in children's media, there remains, for the most part, a conservative strain which works against the stories' utopian enterprise. For instance, the heterosexual marriage norm remains a highly valued social arrangement, and fictional families remain tied to societal notions of "normality", even when they attempt to subvert them.

Commenting on efforts in various countries to promote lesbian and gay marriage, Judith Butler argues that matters of kinship are invariably tied to family and marriage:

"efforts to establish bonds of kinship that are not based on a marriage tie become nearly illegible and unviable when marriage sets the terms for kinship, and kinship itself is collapsed into 'family'" (2004, 4).

Children's books have attempted to show alternatives to the heterosexual family life. However, these texts are often at pains to point out how same-sex families are different from, but in many ways are just the same as, heterosexual families. This eliding of sexual difference through an accommodating sameness appears in the picture book, *Molly's Family* (2004), by Nancy Garden and Sharon Wooding. The book's utopian impulse can be seen as founded on difference as the phrase "all kinds of families" is repeated throughout the book, and the book's cover blurb states that "even if a family is different from others, it can still be a happy, loving—and *real*—family" (emphasis in original). The story's implicit double bind emerges here in that the wording provides an explicit, sanctioned endorsement of same-sex families as being as legitimate (as real and as loving) as heterosexual families; yet at the same time it dissipates lesbian sexuality's potential for subverting power relations that exist as part of society's ideal—the patriarchal family.

Another picture book, *And Tango Makes Three* (2005), by Justin Richardson and Peter Parnell, tells the true story of how two male chinstrap penguins became a couple and eventually parents to a female chick named Tango. The story begins by introducing readers to the various heterosexual animal families who live at the Central Park Zoo in New York. It then continues with the familiar courting and mating narrative as follows:

"Every year at the very same time, the girl penguins start noticing the boy penguins. And the boy penguins start noticing the girls. When the right girl and the right boy find each other, they become a couple" (2005 unpaged.)

The disruption to the heterosexual romance narrative occurs when two male penguins—Roy and Silo—prefer each other's company to that of the female penguins. Their playful and affectionate behaviour prompts the zoo attendant to think that they "must be in love". After observing the home-making techniques of the other penguins, Roy and Silo build "a nest of stones for themselves", sleeping there together like other penguin couples. However, after their failed attempts to hatch a chick from a rock, they eventually hatch Tango when the zoo keeper places an abandoned egg in the nest. The text explains to the child reader that "Tango was the very first penguin in the zoo to have two daddies". The paratext explains that the story is based on fact as two penguins (Roy and Silo) "discovered each other in 1998 and they have been a couple ever since". However, the book was considered off limits for some parents who objected to its "homosexual undertones" (*Deseret News*, March 2006)[1].

Molly's Family and *And Tango Makes Three* open up ways of thinking about different familial and social alliances which re-imagine kinship. While Tango is raised without a mother, Molly is raised by two mothers. Thus, "mother" becomes a shifting signifier that can be temporarily attached to males or females. Or to put this in queer terms, by denying the category "mother", these texts show how mothering behaviour/performance is not necessarily tied just to the female parent (Mallan 2009, 141). In distinguishing between "kinship" and "marriage", Butler (2004, 102) makes the point that both terms are often confused (at least in the United States, but arguably in other countries too); marriage is often regarded as a sacrosanct heterosexual institution and unless kinship too assumes a recognizable family form it does not qualify for recognition. A further point is the affective and political dimension. Stories of gay couples and gay marriage signal an emotionally satisfying resolution to the dilemma that many gay couples experience: how to be socially conventional while also sexually deviant. This dilemma is not addressed in the texts discussed in this chapter, and rarely is it raised in young adult fiction featuring same-sex families. It would seem that gay marriage in these texts is a fantasy which does not undo normative structures but incorporates these structures into a conventional story of emotional fulfilment, rather than re-envisioning new social relations.

Conclusion

This chapter has raised some issues which texts for young people address with respect to ways to do and undo gender. The examples are representative of the various ways that children's books (and other cultural products) are responding to new gender relations. Some texts confirm existing gender orders and configurations, while others challenge them. Children's literature will not change the world but it does make significant and often undervalued contributions to how its readers see the world and their place in it. All literature, regardless of its implied readership, is a vehicle for carrying, as well as exposing, ideologies about the hierarchical arrangements in society (Culler 1997, 39). By exploring the complex and various relations between individuals and social contexts represented in children's fiction, we can reconsider how the doing and undoing of gender raise questions about the restrictions and regulations of social norms on gendered and sexual identities, and the ethical concerns that arise when individuals are limited in their ability to live a fully human existence.

Note

[1] See Inappropriate Penguins? Children's Book Moved. *Deseret News*, Salt Lake City, 5 March 2006: http://www.deseretnews.com/home

References

Berliner, Alain, dir. 1997. *Ma Vie en Rose.* Canal+.

Bindé, Jérôme. 2000. Towards an Ethics of the Future. *Public Culture* 12(1): 51-72.

Buchbinder, David. 1998. *Performance Anxieties.* St Leonards: Allen & Unwin.

Burgess, Melvin. 2006. *Sara's Face.* London: Andersen Press.

Butler, Judith. 2004. *Undoing Gender.* New York: Routledge.

—. 1990. *Gender Trouble: Feminism and the Subversion of Identity.* New York: Routledge.

Cart, Michael and Christine Jenkins. 2006. *The Heart Has Its Reasons: Young Adult Literature with Gay/Lesbian/Queer Content, 1969–2004.* Lanham, MD: Scarecrow Press.

Culler, Jonathon. 1997. *Literary Theory: A Very Short Introduction.* Oxford: Oxford University Press.

Fine, Anne. 1988. *Alias, Madame Doubtfire.* Boston: Joy Street Books.

—. 1989. *Bill's New Frock.* London: Methuen.

Flanagan, Victoria. 2007. *Into the Closet: Cross-Dressing and the Gendered Body in Children's Literature and Film.* New York: Routledge.

Garden, Nancy and Sharon Wooding. 2004. *Molly's Family.* New York: Farrar Strauss Giroux.

Mallan, Kerry. 2004. (M)other Love: Constructing Queer Families in *Girl Walking Backwards* and *Obsession. Children's Literature Association Quarterly* 29 (4): 345-357.

—. 2009. *Gender Dilemmas in Children's Fiction.* Houndmills: Palgrave Macmillan.

McInally, Kate. 2003. Camphor Laurel: A Re-vision of Desire. *Papers: Explorations into Children's Literature* 13 (2): 27-36.

understandings of childhood which are then perpetuated in "approved" children's literature. As stated above, multiple childhood experiences are in existence at any given time, yet the gatekeepers of children's literature in Western cultures do privilege specific versions, reflecting images of childhood considered normative, or, at worst problematic but with the potential for resolution. The ever-popular author Jacqueline Wilson, for example, writes domestic family novels, which portray challenging but ultimately optimistic narratives that resonate with young people en masse in contemporary Britain. This desire to retain a sense of optimism, to shield young people from the darker recesses of human knowledge or experience can, as Mills and Mills suggest, be understood as a need to protect them but at the same time, a need also to protect ourselves and ultimately, retain the hope of innocence. The consequences of this ideological position lead inevitably to questions about the impact on young people: does protectionism lead to safety, or simply ignorance? Can we accept young people as "knowing" without positioning this as problematic? Is it possible to reconceptualize what I term the "innocence project", that is, our own aspiration to maintain childhood as a time that is pure? What happens to young people who find themselves as "outsiders"? Ultimately, is it productive to think about the experiences of young people through a framework which leaves many isolated?

In relation to children's literature, the version of childhood which has retained an especial, ongoing influence is found in the concept of the "Romantic child", introduced in the writings of Rousseau (1712-78), specifically in his influential 1762 novel, *Emile, or On Education* and recognizable in the works of poets such as William Blake (1757-1827), William Wordsworth (1770-1850) and Lord Byron (1788-1824). Deborah Cogan Thacker and Jean Webb highlight the emphatic position of Romanticism in children's literature:

> "The fascination with childhood and a desire to recapture an innocent apprehension of the world are key features in any definition of Romanticism. It is often claimed that the image of the romantic child has been a key point of reference for the birth of children's literature since the beginning of the nineteenth century" (2002, 13).

However, the natural, unspoilt child discernible in these Romantic imaginings has metamorphosed into a picture of innocence in the sense of "without knowledge" as opposed to "without artifice" and has resulted in the ongoing disputes among authors and academics, as outlined by Tucker. This does not mean, however, that children's literature simply absorbs and reflects the dominant ideological position of the culture in which it is produced, in relation to childhood; otherwise there would be no need of debate about what is acceptable or appropriate.

Children's literature is neither passive nor without innovation, hence the publication of landmark novels such as *Forever* (1975) by Judy Blume, *Doing It* (2003) by Melvin Burgess, and David Levithan's *Boy Meets Boy* (2003). All of these novels portray young people coming to terms with their sexuality and seeking out sexual encounters, which resulted in them being considered controversial at the time of publication due to the high levels of anxiety which surround novels that portray sexual relationships between young adults, especially any that may be considered enjoyable (Seelinger Trites 2000). Levithan's novel has the added significance of presenting a gay relationship as unproblematic which makes it deeply contentious in relation to the "innocence project", a subject to which I will return. All of these novels, in terms of categorization, would be considered as belonging to young adult (YA) fiction which does have a wider mandate in relation to what kinds of subject matter can be published. However, the possibility of a landscape which opens up space for the presentation of more controversial subjects does not necessarily lead to numerous radical or even subversive narratives. Much of the literature which has been developed in this genre in Western cultures has presented challenging subjects within a conservative framework in so much as they portray transgressive youth as victims or misunderstood, creating a sympathetic protagonist while simultaneously shutting down the potential to explore the complexity of ambivalent behaviours. In relation to the innocence project, if childhood is to remain "unpolluted" then the young person involved must be a victim to be saved or redeemed.

Prostitution, already a divisive subject in popular culture, becomes even more emotive when young people are involved and therefore, unsurprisingly, it is not a subject that has received sustained or mainstream attention in YA fiction. Here I discuss three novels which I consider to be for the YA market—Thorn Kief Hillsbery's *What We Do Is Secret* (2005), Alasdair Duncan's *Sushi Central* (2003) and J.T. LeRoy's *Harold's End* (2004)—all of which present teenage male prostitution as part of a risk-taking behaviour pattern among the protagonists, who are portrayed as morally ambiguous. Although other novels have been published which explore this subject, they are either intended for an adult audience, for example, Gary Indiana's *Rent Boy* (1994) and Jason Charles's *Tree Frog* (1998), or present the young male sex worker as a victim, exemplified by Rosie Goodwin's *The Boy from Nowhere* (2009). My research has not uncovered further examples of male teenage prostitution in YA fiction where the protagonists are described as morally ambiguous, but as I suggested earlier, the subject in general has received little attention, also reflected by the fact that there is currently no critical material which analyzes the subject in YA fiction.

The three novels examined here have generally been well received by readers discussing the works on populist websites and in blogs, demonstrated by the comments found on the "Good Reads" website, for example (www.goodreads.com). More formal critiques and academic analysis, however, are lacking. *What We Do Is Secret* was short listed for the Lambda Literary Award, which is presented by the US-based Lambda Literary Foundation to published works which celebrate and explore Lesbian, Gay, Bisexual and Transgender (LGBT) themes. *Harold's End* has achieved more notoriety due to a literary hoax carried out by its author: LeRoy is in fact a fictional teenage persona invented by the author, Laura Albert, which she presented as a young man with a history of drug abuse and prostitution, tuning into the themes of her work. The subsequent unveiling of her alter ego was contentious with "fans" unhappy about the perceived deception. None of the works however can be considered as part of mainstream publishing and marketing: in Britain, this may in part be the result of their origins in the USA and Australia respectively, resulting in limited distribution, but undoubtedly both the subject matter and its presentation have impacted on the availability of the titles as concerns about childhood, discussed earlier, influence publishing and marketing strategies.

In portraying boys as involved in sex work, the landscapes evoked in these novels become more transgressive due to assumptions in popular culture which equate male prostitution with homosexuality, itself a problematic trope in mainstream YA publishing as I suggest above. Further, in relation to prostitution, the body becomes objectified and is viewed as a commodity, undermining normative masculinity discourses which privilege strength, dynamism and action (Connell 1995), both subjects to which I will return in the course of my discussion of the novels.

Sexualized bodies

Thorn Kief Hillsbery's *What We Do Is Secret* portrays the life of Rockets, a young, homeless boy on the fringe of street prostitution and drug addiction. The story is told through Rockets's first person narration and recounts retrospectively twenty-four hours in his life leading up to his birthday. Situated in Los Angeles, the story takes place in the early 1980s in the aftermath of the heroin induced suicide of Darby Crash, lead singer with punk rock band, The Germs, and "mentor" to Rockets. "What We Do

Is Secret" is the title of a Germs song but also indicative of the lives of the young people in the narrative who are homeless and drift on the borders of society, visible only to clients who seek them out or the police with whom they constantly clash.

As young sex workers are largely invisible to society in general, either through a process of erasure or censure, it is ironic that the world they inhabit relies on visual impact, with their appearance determining their ability to survive. As such, their existence can be decided by their abilities to perform, to act out the fantasies of their clients, from the moment of engagement to the sexual transaction itself. Hillsbery represents Rockets as aware that it is his body and the ability to sell it successfully which allows him to buy the food and clothes that sustain him and make it possible for him to carry on with this life, a cruel paradox. He knows where to go and how to "strike a pose" to initiate interest:

> "Broke as usual and even hungrier than. So I walk down the chop chop chopping block to Arthur J's on the corner of Highland and Santa Monica and stand holding up the windowless wall facing Highland, same ways I always stand: one leg knee-bent, Monkey Boot sole planted flush on the sun-heated metal door..." (11).

In a research project carried out with male sex workers in Montreal and Quebec, Michel Dorais found that there were a number of visual factors involved in identifying and engaging with a sex worker on the street, through strategies the workers themselves employed:

> "They are easily identifiable with practice by the way they lope along the sidewalk trying to entice potential clients. 'It's all in the body, the attitude, the posture, especially the look in the eye,' said one youth, and several of his peers concurred. For others, the clothing and what it suggests count for a great deal. Clothes advertise a personality type likely to please certain types of clients—ideally, the largest possible number" (2005, 28).

The body then becomes a site of negotiation which is simultaneously passive and active, a subject which is portrayed in a more nuanced way in the novel *Sushi Central* by Alasdair Duncan, a nihilistic and provocative exploration of the search for oblivion. Unlike Rockets, Calvin, the protagonist of Duncan's narrative, lives in an affluent suburb of Brisbane with his parents which initially suggests to the reader a wealthy and socially successful family unit. However, an atmosphere of ennui and world weariness pervades the narrative despite Calvin being only sixteen years old. The reader first encounters him at school where he radiates a sense of boredom and detachment from what is happening around him:

"Yet another afternoon at school and it's a case of hormones and anxiety running wild, and it's all very teenage and suburban and kind of, you know. Blah. I'm sure you're heard it all before [...] Afternoons like this I really don't know what to do with myself. I don't even feel human. After class I walked around for a while in kind of a daze…" (7).

The environment in which Calvin lives is all about appearance; he also actively surrounds himself with individuals who have an over-riding preoccupation with image and, while it can be argued that it is not unusual for teenagers in particular to be very egocentric and engrossed in their own self-image, Duncan portrays Calvin as obsessed, believing that his physical appearance gives him power and control in the social arena:

"[…] I'm young. That's the ultimate attraction. In this particular world, that's the ultimate power, and you can say whatever you want and make whatever excuses you want, but it's true. Being young and pretty means having power. And it's the kind of power that we have to exploit while we can" (165).

The sense of disengagement is increased by Calvin's use of social networking internet sites; the very nature of online "relationships" allows him to choose who he wants to be, how he wants to present himself in the pseudo cyber community. Calvin is initially involved on the edges of pornography, receiving photos via email of men and boys having sex, and is himself promiscuous, drifting in and out of meaningless sexual liaisons with other boys. Tim Edwards's (2005) research into gay masculinities would suggest that Calvin's behaviour can be interpreted as the stereotypical image of homosexual boys and men, an exaggerated version of male heterosexual sexual practice, which values sex over intimacy. However, while this might have represented a political statement about free will and choice in the 1970s and 1980s, in the environment which Duncan creates it merely adds to a sense of futility, where bodily practices do not complement emotional engagements but simply replace them. Although Duncan offers an explanation for Calvin's behaviour—the death of a younger brother in an accident resulting in his parents' inability to cope and subsequent emotional withdrawal—there remains a sense that Calvin actively "sells" his body, buying into an idea of power through sex, however distorted or distasteful this may appear to the reader. That he finally steps over the line at the end of the narrative, being paid to become actively involved in pornography, leaves the reader in a quandary; should this be understood as a natural progression from the already sexually permissive behaviour which he has chosen, or is it a cry for help, making him a victim of circumstances which have emotionally overwhelmed him? Duncan does not clarify.

Vulnerable bodies

What We Do Is Secret lends itself more readily to a reading of victimization due to the landscape of extreme poverty and the ever present threat of violence. In an ethnographic study of young male prostitutes, Barbara Gibson (1995), while working as a health consultant for the charity Streetwise Youth in London, found that many of the young men had left home to escape abuse or violence and found themselves on the streets looking for alternative communities. Hillsbery's novel presents Rockets and his friends as identifying as punk rockers, forming themselves into such a community to give meaning to their lives and some sense of security, however fleeting. Viewed by mainstream society, they are essentially outcasts, homeless young people living in groups of abandoned buildings. Rockets recounts his experiences of one of his earliest "homes" after running away from a care centre:

> "Then we'd bail for home street home, not exactly the Apartment of Water and Power with both H2O and AC-go juice cut completely, and since none of us could A and Q how to run the hellevators off D for Duracells we climbed the fire stairs past where any street trash squatters ever had the guts or glory for, and just for insurance against any dirtbags or elderqueers who maybe might we built booby traps…" (8).

The socialization of boys into dominant versions of masculinity which privilege characteristics such as strength, control, competitiveness and success, over emotional engagement, empathy and care, still has the expectation that boys will receive nurture and protection as they mature. However, as this "process" takes place, they are expected to absorb normative masculinity scripts which somewhat ironically seek to "hide" many of the positive outcomes of nurture to ensure survival in male landscapes (Connell 2000). The fictional boys in Hillsbery's narrative and in the life stories recounted by Gibson are devoid of nurture which leaves them vulnerable as they seek out "love" in unsafe places. This is demonstrated in Paul's life history as he recounts how he started out looking for love but through experience became disillusioned:

> "When I met this man, I was looking at him as a father, which I wanted more than anything. I thought that sex was love and that he was showing me love. I wanted it and enjoyed it in a way […] Very recently I seen this

guy's face on Crimewatch, I got the shock of my life! He was wanted in connection with a series of rapes" (Gibson 1995, 68-9).

The theme of vulnerability and the dangers inherent in a life on the streets selling sex is evident in J.T. LeRoy's *Harold's End*. The slight appearance of *Harold's End*, in the form of a novella containing a sequence of colour plates, implies a book for younger children. The quality of production suggests a work which has received much time and attention to detail in its development. However, reader expectation is shockingly challenged as the narrative unfolds, revealing a world of young heroin addicts who spend their time selling themselves to make enough money to fund their addictions. The contrast between the appearance of the novella and the implied loveless and hopeless existence of the characters that inhabit it is horrific in its starkness. This is further highlighted when closer examination of the colour portraits of the young people, by Australian illustrator Cherry Hood, reveals faces that encompass despair and defeat.

The "Harold" of the title is actually a snail which is given as a pet to the boy narrator—unnamed in the narrative but his "portrait" suggests that he is called Oliver—by an older man, Larry, who befriends him and then invites him to live in his house. Larry is presented as a wealthy man and initially appears as a benign character but becomes more ambiguous as the narrative progresses:

> "At night, Larry and Harold and I watch movies, my head in Larry's lap while he softly strokes my cheek. Before bed I climb into the pyjamas he got me, even though they're covered in dancing penguins, and I let him watch me do my balloon. And then I talk. I tell him what I tell no one until I fall asleep against him" (46).

The picture which is presented here is at once contradictory and conflicting; LeRoy suggests innocence, symbolized in the pyjamas, and summons up thoughts of a family watching television together. However, contradicting this is the image of the boy feeding his addiction while Larry fulfils his own sinister needs; neither is entirely innocent. Larry's intentions are finally revealed in a shocking scene in which he has the boy carry out a sex act on him and then feels shame and embarrassment. This results in him asking the boy to leave, effectively returning him to his life on the streets. Any security which the boy has built up is dashed and he is reminded of previous experiences, with the expectation that pain will follow:

"I felt an icy slit along my side and remember this is how pain always comes on, from a vague distance before revealing its detailed facts. I lie there and wait to know how bad it will be" (54).

Although the boy is portrayed sympathetically by LeRoy, there is no information or explanation offered as to why he is a drug addict and working as a prostitute; the reader remains uncertain about his innocence. The consequences of his predicament, however, mean that in his relationship with Larry he is positioned as a commodity, something to be bought and used and then disposed of because he lacks power. The landscapes in which the boys in both LeRoy's and Hillsbery's novels come into contact with older men demonstrate their powerlessness because of their age and social status. Reflecting on the interviews she conducted, Gibson points to the disparity between the boys and their clients, suggesting that some of these men are in powerful positions and that it serves their interests to criminalize the boys' activities. Perversely, social censure in response to prostitution ensures a level of protection for clients which is not available to the sex workers.

Teenage male sex workers are further marginalized and disempowered as male prostitution is closely associated with homosexuality, still considered as the ultimate Other in hegemonic masculinity scripts (Edwards 2005). Savin-Williams points to the dangers of marginalization in relation to homosexuality but this is even more pertinent when discussed in relation to male prostitution:

"To the extent that alternatives to heterosexuality are misrepresented, myths flourish, stigma abounds, and those who by their very nature are sexually unconventional are condemned. Few individuals concerned with the well-being of youths would advocate that being thus marginalized, especially during the vulnerable years of childhood and adolescence, is desirable" (2004, 291).

Although the majority of clients seeking their services are male, and while many of the young men identify as gay, this is not uniform. Cultural understandings of prostitution focus initially on the sexual encounter rather than perceiving the act as a financial transaction. In reaction to the findings of her research, Gibson, while not advocating prostitution as a viable career choice, does take a more pragmatic approach, attempting to remove the stigma attached to the damning and usually judgemental, emotional reaction meted out to the young men:

"They had great initiative in finding places to sleep, and they learnt to deal with exploitative people. They had no legal entitlement to money, yet they found money to live [...] They lived in an environment where there was no protection; only hostility and condemnation of their presence. In spite of this they needed to survive, to carry on and make lives for themselves..." (172).

Gibson is not attempting to engender sympathy, merely suggesting that a rational rather than a hysterical approach should be taken when discussing the subject of prostitution. Although she found that many of the young men were victims of circumstance, she does not suggest that they are all therefore innocent, taking no active part in the direction of their lives.

Ambivalent bodies

In none of the novels discussed here do the authors suggest that the boyhoods they portray are solely accounts of victimization. While the dangerous landscapes in which they exist—especially in relation to *What We Do Is Secret* and *Harold's End*—are the result of abuse and neglect, the young male protagonists are active participants in the events which take place and make decisions which impact on their futures. In *What We Do Is Secret*, Hillsbery portrays Blitzer, Rockets's boyfriend, as a con artist, prepared to scam two "out-of-towners" to finance a trip and Rockets is aware of this. There is also a suggestion that Blitzer may have been involved in the death of another street boy, Rory.

Hillsbery's narrative is dense, lyrical and packed with intertextual illusion, challenging the reader to create a meaningful narrative. By imposing this style onto the reader, he illustrates symbolically the chaotic world that his fictional characters inhabit. The result for both parties is a morally ambiguous landscape in which meaning is created but without any certainty as to its truthfulness. The reader eventually learns that the birthday Rockets is celebrating is his thirteenth, but Blitzer is an older teenager; is he then a protector or an abuser, or is either label valid to describe their situation? In structuring the narrative in this way, Hillsbery demands a less obvious, "non-traditional" response to the moral ambiguities his writing discloses. The conclusion to the story leaves the reader uncertain as to Rockets's fate. The question of whether he should stay or go, again, is more ambiguous than it initially appears. It is not a decision about the road trip to Idaho with Blitzer, but whether he should commit suicide, a shocking revelation at the end of the narrative. Instead, however, he takes up a job offer from Phranc, an old friend from "Darby days", who picks him up on his way to the pier where he is contemplating throwing himself into the water:

"She says speaking of checking out, she's up to something way more punk that that. She's planning on making a living hosting Tupperware parties for Westside JAPs, no not Asians, I get it now, Jewish American Princesses, and yes with her flat-top, and yes in her combat boots.
    And how punk is that?
    She says the only thing more punk would be me signing on as her assistant" (339-40).

The random and bizarre nature of this career change for Rockets again highlights the ambiguity inherent in the novel, while also emphasizing the vulnerability of Rockets. In one final irony, Hillsbery reveals bluntly Rockets's blindness, a fact that has been alluded to earlier but without positive confirmation. The boy through whom Hillsbery has taken the reader on a roller-coaster assault on the senses cannot see, but can only imagine the world which he describes, a world in which appearance is imperative for survival.

Sushi Central is an especially ambivalent novel. With no obvious material deprivation to contend with, Calvin's decisions can be interpreted as egocentric, something Duncan does not discourage through his portrayal of Calvin as selfish and vain, and yet there is also a sense of quiet desperation which overtakes Calvin, and through him the reader, at unexpected moments:

"It's late at night. I stare at the television, half interested, spacing out.[…] Suddenly a gaping void opens up before me and I wonder what it would be like to die, if it would be painless, and how I'd do it, but I ignore those thoughts and keep watching the movie instead" (59).

Although the immediate ability to return to the movie somewhat trivializes the episode, the sense of emptiness and misery remains, which makes Calvin's subsequent actions both hedonistic and desperate; to the outside world he presents the image of a rather promiscuous party animal intent on having fun, while simultaneously trying to find oblivion, a way not to feel. The novel ends unsurprisingly on an uncertain and unsettling note; Calvin asks to take part in a pornographic photo shoot and ends up having sex with the anonymous older man who is filming, achieving his goal of nothingness:

"[…] and I try not to feel anything when he's inside me, and after a while I don't, I'm somewhere else. I'm gone" (257).

Duncan offers no resolution, no suggestion of a happy or positive outcome in much the same way that LeRoy and Hillsbery conclude their narratives and in relation to the innocence project this is deeply problematic; all three authors construct their narratives in such a way that suggests both victimization and transgression and therefore the novels cannot be easily classified. As I suggested at the outset, there is a collective will in Western cultures to retain childhood as a safe and precious time, an instinct which stretches back through time and can be traced in the literature written for children since its earliest production. "Taboo" subjects are the obvious target for censors although what is considered unthinkable and therefore unmentionable has changed through time. While infant mortality and original sin preoccupied the eighteenth and early to mid-nineteenth centuries, witnessed in the "lessons" of *The Fairchild Family* (1818, 1842, 1847) written by Mrs. [Mary Martha] Sherwood (1775-1851), the need to repent was an overriding concern. However, taking a child to witness a hanging—an event which takes place in these narratives—would now be considered tantamount to child abuse, a preoccupation of millennium society where child protection is at the centre of all discourses relating to childhood.

While teenage prostitution is not an obvious theme for young adult literature, it exists, and real boys are involved in what is inevitably a dangerous world, as is evident from the life stories recounted by Gibson. What do we do with this knowledge? Should it be hidden from view and if so, what are the consequences for the boys living their lives this way? In considering the question of the "outsider child", Christine Wilkie-Stibbs (2008) suggests that the frame of reference through which such categorizations are formed needs to be challenged. In doing so, she alludes to the power of empathy:

> "It is commonplace that we care for others unequally, in proportion to how much we think we know about them, how easily we can imagine ourselves to be in their plight, or how likely we judge that we should find ourselves in their situation. It is hard to empathize with people who seem Other, and it is hard to sympathize with those we cannot empathize with" (21).

Perhaps here she offers an explanation for our need for a victim when transgressive behaviour is identified; it is difficult to empathize with "badness". Aside from our wish in children's literature to retain innocence in relation to the subject matter that is given to young people, how it is portrayed is also key. The novels which I have discussed here break the rules, not simply because of the subject they address, but the ways in which they do so. I would suggest, however, that the ambivalence they display ultimately allows for complex, multi-dimensional portrayals of boys involved in, and on the borders of, sex work. This challenges the reader to "view" the boys' worlds without the safety of a framework which portrays "innocence corrupted", a version considered more socially acceptable and less confrontational as it induces sympathy and allows us to retain our prized image of childhood; it is, in effect, a barometer of adult sensibility rather than a truthful denouement and therefore dishonest.

In discussing the ways in which teenage boys go about forming their personal masculine identities in relation to the social landscape they inhabit, Judy Chu emphasizes the importance of agency in determining the outcome, which is equally applicable to the wide range of opinions and attitudes that young people develop:

> "As active participants in their identity development, boys are responsive in the sense that they have the capacity to internalize and resist masculine norms and ideals that manifest, for instance, through other people's expectations for and assumptions about them. However, boys are also creative in the sense that they construct their identities, or senses of self, in ways that reflect their individual experiences as well as their cognitive abilities" (2005, 79).

While not advocating teenage prostitution as a discussion subject for young children, I would suggest that, when it is encountered by teenagers, we should not attempt to shield them by automatically projecting a discourse of victimization, but instead, allow young people to consider their own responses. As Rockets remarks, it is important to see the world through your own particular hue:

> "[…] I remember Darby telling me about the purple sky and making it so perfect with words that I could see it just like you and all those jacks and all those jills and even love it from a distance like a surfer or a Spaniard watching morning touch the golden land. And I always thought it was thanks to Darby but really maybe it's thanks to me" (346).

References

Beachy, Stephen. 2005. Who Is the Real J.T. LeRoy?
    http://nymag.com/nymetro/news/people/features/14718. Date accessed 20 June 2011.
Blume, Judy. 1975. *Forever*. Scarsdale, New York: Bradbury Press.
Buckingham, David. 2000. *After the Death of Childhood: Growing Up In the Age of Electronic Media*. Oxford: Polity.
Burgess, Melvin. 2003. *Doing It*. London: Andersen Press.
Charles, Jason. 1998. *Tree Frog*. London: Hamilton.

Chu, Judy Y. 2005. Adolescent Boys' Friendships and Peer Group Culture. *The Experiences of Close Friendships in Adolescence,* eds. Niobe Way and Jill V. Hamm, 7-22. California: Jossey-Bass.

Connell, R.W. 1995. *Masculinities.* California: University of California Press.

—. 2000. *The Men and the Boys.* NSW: Allen & Unwin.

Cunningham, Hugh. 2006. *The Invention of Childhood.* London: BBC Books.

Dorais, Michel. 2005. *Rent Boys: The World of Male Sex Workers.* Montreal: McGill-Queen's University Press.

Duncan, Alasdair. 2003. *Sushi Central.* Queensland: University of Queensland Press.

Edwards, Tim. 2005. Queering the Pitch? Gay Masculinities. *Handbook of Studies on Men and Masculinities,* eds. Michael S. Kimmel, Jeff R. Hearn and R.W. Connell. 51-68. Thousand Oaks and London: Sage.

Gibson, Barbara. 1995. *Male Order: Life Stories From Boys Who Sell Sex.* London: Cassell.

Good Reads website. www.goodreads.com. Date accessed 20 June 2011.

Goodwin, Rosie. 2009. *The Boy From Nowhere.* London: Headline.

Hillsbery, Thorn Kief. 2005. *What We Do Is Secret.* New York: Villard Books.

Indiana, Gary. 1994. *Rent Boy.* New York: High Rise Books.

LeRoy, J.T. 2004. *Harold's End.* California: Last Gasp.

Levithan, David. 2003. *Boy Meets Boy.* London: HarperCollins.

Mills, Jean and Richard Mills. 2000. Eds. *Childhood Studies: A Reader in Perspectives of Childhood.* London and New York: Routledge.

Morrison, Todd G. and Bruce W. Whitehead, eds. 2007. *Male Sex Work: A Business Doing Pleasure.* New York: Haworth Press.

Nayak, Anoop and Mary Jane Kehily. 2008. *Gender, Youth and Culture: Young Masculinities and Femininities.* Basingstoke: Palgrave Macmillan.

Rousseau, Jean Jacques. 2009. *Emile, Or, An Education.* Sudbury, MA: Dartmouth.

Savin-Williams, Ritch. 2004. Boy-on-Boy Sexuality. *Adolescent Boys: Exploring Diverse Cultures of Boyhood,* eds. Niobe Way and Judy Y. Chu, 271-292. New York: New York University Press.

Sherwood, Mary Martha. 2010. *The History of the Fairchild Family, Or, A Child's Manual.* Charleston: Nabu Press.

Thacker, Deborah Cogan and Jean Webb. 2002. *Introducing Children's Literature: From Romanticism to Postmodernism.* London and New York: Routledge.

Trites, Roberta Seelinger. 2000. *Disturbing the Universe: Power and Repression in Adolescent Literature*. Iowa City: University of Iowa Press.

Tucker, Nicholas, ed. 1976. *Suitable for Children? Controversies in Children's Literature*. London: Sussex University Press.

Wilkie-Stibbs, Christine. 2008. *The Outside Child, In and Out of the Book*. London and New York: Routledge.

DOING IT - BUT NOT IN FRONT OF CHILDREN'S LITERATURE

NORMA CLARKE

Peter Pan's cry, "I want always to be a little boy and to have fun", resonates throughout twentieth-century children's literature (Barrie, 99). Peter is the iconic figure of the Victorian cult of childhood. Little boys having fun brought freshness and vitality, a whiff of the outdoors, to what had become in the mid-nineteenth-century a preoccupation with poverty, misery, and death. Boys in late Victorian and Edwardian children's books were energetic, decisive, honourable and reliable (and those who weren't, like Colin in Frances Hodgson Burnett's 1911 *The Secret Garden*, learned in the course of the novel to be so). Like the "lads" who featured in Rudyard Kipling's *Stalky & Co* (1899) or the "boyish" chums Ratty, Mole and Badger in Kenneth Grahame's *The Wind in the Willows* (1908), not to mention that earlier trio Ralph, Jack and Peterkin on R.M. Ballantyne's *The Coral Island* (1857), they relished being boys. Their feelings were for each other. Girls other than sisters seldom came their way, and if they did they needed to have boyish inclinations to be understood. When Tinker Bell and Wendy display a sexual interest in Peter, he is mystified.

J. M. Barrie's *Peter Pan, or, The Boy Who Would Not Grow Up* (1904) is in fact a sardonic and wistful meditation on the impossibility of Peter's wish. As Barrie was aware, puberty and sexual maturation claim the attention of all growing boys. Tinker Bell's boudoir and Wendy's maternal domesticity represent the two poles of masculine desire and fear, neither of which Peter seeks to understand. Although the Victorian sentimentalization of childhood was subjected to ridicule almost as soon as it began, one absolute remained: boys in books for the young could be shown earning their manhood in daring deeds and noble enterprises but they never felt nor tried to understand their own sexual feelings. Geoffrey Trease observed in 1949 that "there could be unlimited bloodshed and sadistic torture but no hint of affection between the sexes", even though Freud's work on infantile sexuality had been available for half a century (1963, 8).

In his own novels Trease tried to present intelligent, resourceful girls with sufficient female charms to make the hint of heterosexual attraction a convincing, if understated, element of the plot. His boys, it can be assumed, will develop into sexually active men as a matter of course. In *Cue for Treason* (1940) Peter foils an assassination plot against Queen Elizabeth I while also regaining common lands enclosed by a rapacious local nobleman. He is helped by Kate, or Kit, who is mostly disguised as a boy as she escapes an arranged marriage. Peter marries Kate in the final paragraph and the final sentence reveals that they have sons, but there has been no romance, only comradeship. Denzil's attraction to Deb in the later *The Popinjay Mystery* (1973) is, by contrast, made explicit in the opening pages and powers the story line. Denzil, a junior lieutenant, has been at sea for months and "scarcely seen a woman, let alone a copper-headed glory like this one" (1993, 11). The action takes place in London where Deb, whose passion for a career in theatre Trease loosely modelled on that of the Restoration dramatist Aphra Behn, has a play performed under the alias Nicholas Arden. Denzil's adventure involves Mr Pepys, the Naval Secretary, who is able to ensure that Denzil rises in his career, thus removing possible obstacles to marriage although no marriage actually happens. The novel ends with all the company going to see Deb's play. Deb and Denzil are presented as equals, though encountering different sorts of problems. They like and respect each other and the author takes seriously the fact that each is committed to career success; sex and marriage loom but are cheerfully put to one side. As Deb's uncle says, "'Deb seems so young, and you have known each other barely a month'" (ibid, 175). The sub-plot is actually a whirlwind romance which remains unwritten.

The tone of children's books in the second half of the twentieth century was set by writers like C. S. Lewis (1898-1963), Arthur Ransome (1884-1967) and Enid Blyton (1897-1968), all of whom involve boys and girls in adventures together. When Susan of *The Lion, the Witch and the Wardrobe* (1950) becomes interested in lipstick she is, famously, banished by her creator from Narnia. Ransome's *Swallows & Amazons* series feature boyish girls mucking about in boats, and Blyton's suburban or seaside tales about being in a gang and solving mysteries present a picture of childhood as a sunny, carefree holiday adventure containing plenty of buns and ginger ale and no awkward sexual stirrings. Meanwhile, the true heir to Peter Pan was William in Richmal Crompton's series of books which began with *Just William* in 1922. Remaining about eleven through almost forty books, William is an extreme egotist, full of imagination and dreams, easily bored, indignant and argumentative. Adult life disgusts him; he isn't remotely interested in it. Whatever he believes and wants he pursues with fearful intensity. He is bitter, ferocious, scowling and uncompromising, like Peter. Like Kenneth Grahame's Toad, he is full of pride in himself, vainglorious. Nobody understands him. If he became an adolescent he would probably be Holden Caulfield from J. D. Salinger's *The Catcher in the Rye* (1951), but William will always be a little boy for whom having fun means avoiding the clutches of tiresome grown-ups and girls.

There was no expectation that boys in children's books would show any sexual interest in girls until the 1990s. When Melvin Burgess published his first children's book *The Cry of the Wolf* in 1989 he made an interesting discovery about the category "children's books". Turning up to do readings in schools, he found himself put in front of eleven and twelve year olds: these were the children who were being given his book. But he was marketed as an author who wrote for teenagers. Why, then, was he not reading to teenagers? The teen category seemed to be a "marketing ploy", a "fiction" (Burgess, What is Teen Fiction? 10 July 2011). Professionals knew that his books were being read by those still officially "children" and that teenagers had left children's literature behind altogether because it did not provide them with what they needed. Burgess observed that teenagers "fed on crumbs dropped from the adult table" (Burgess, Sympathy for the Devil, 10 July 2011). No-one in children's literature was actually writing for them in a way that took seriously the realities of teenage life, which included sexual feelings, adventures with drugs and alcohol, and disillusionment with the adult world. Hence, when his publisher suggested he write a novel dealing with drugs and Burgess agreed, he knew the book "was going to have a rough ride" (Ibid.). *Junk* won the Carnegie Medal in 1997, proving that children's literature specialists were ready for the change it signalled, but it generated much controversy in the press. Some adult purchasers as well as teachers and librarians felt betrayed by the break with what had been understood as shared agreements about boundaries. Children's literature, it was argued, had a job to do in representing the world to young people within certain limits. What Kimberley Reynolds calls the "unwritten agreement" decreed restrictions on language, vocabulary and subject matter on the grounds that books were part of the socializing process and should set good examples (Reynolds 2007, 27). Any book officially classed as "children's literature" was to be a safe space for children to enter in their quest for wholesome diversion.

The perceived problem with *Junk,* for those who found it a problem, was the author's willingness to depict the pleasures of drug-taking and under-age sex through the eyes and in the (often self-deceiving) words of the protagonists. The experiences of the young people were not framed in a way that made conventional adult values obvious—namely that it is wrong for young children to take drugs and have sex. Tar and Gemma are fourteen when Tar decides to run away from his abusive father. He falls in with a group of anarchist squatters, somewhat older, who let him stay with them. Under their roof, in sleeping bags, using a donated condom, Gemma has sex with Tar. On the first occasion the sex is implied rather than written: they are together in the sleeping bag, it is getting "a bit steamy" and then there is a section break, followed by the words, "Later on, Tar said in a little voice, 'I love you'" (Burgess 1997, 67). But soon Gemma's enjoyment is such that they are spending whole mornings "splashing about in bed" (76). Tar is needy and vulnerable, easily influenced; Gemma is excitable, selfish, not in love with Tar, and wanting to have a wild time. Punk music with its noisy violence, "obscene and rude and wonderful" (84), makes her scream with delight. Drinking, smoking dope, eating hash cookies, Tar and Gemma hurtle recklessly along. The anarchists make feeble gestures towards protecting them but, like the protagonists' parents, they are inadequate to the task. When the damaged Lily and Rob, who are heroin addicts, enter the story, Gemma is transfixed. Lily and Rob persuade Tar and Gemma to take heroin. The temptation scene is in a chapter narrated by Tar, who is reluctant at first, but when he joins the others and takes heroin he experiences it as profoundly satisfying—not wonderful he notes, but easeful. Little else in Tar's life has been easy. All the pain goes away. Rob has already told him that what people say about becoming a junkie after just one hit is nonsense, merely stories to scare kids and keep them in their place. Tar's apparently moderate but pleasurable reactions seem to confirm Rob's view. Tar feels he is "just beginning to learn how to live" (130) and there is no authorial voice to point out the ultimate message of the novel, which is that he is just beginning to learn how to die.

Teaching children the skills they needed to live was the avowed aim of children's literature in its earliest formation. Among those skills, learning how to distinguish between good and evil was considered essential. The moral message of early children's books, especially those produced by Evangelical Christians, was unambiguous: the good were rewarded and the bad punished. In this respect, very little had changed in the almost two hundred years since the appearance of such foundational classics as Sarah Trimmer's *The History of the Robins* (1786), or Mary Martha Sherwood's *The History of the Fairchild Family* (1818); indeed, it could be argued that the didactic impulse had strengthened as publishers, schools and libraries worked together in the twentieth century to establish children's literature as a distinct and respectable genre. When Melvin Burgess wrote *Junk*, he pushed the content of a children's book further than any British writer had taken it until then. At the same time he removed the moral clarity, the clear lessons about life that most people understood to be defining elements of realistic children's literature.

The second half of *Junk* depicts a lurid descent into addiction. The story shows unequivocally that heroin can kill you: first of all it deceives and then it destroys. For Gemma and Lily, it leads almost at once to prostitution. For all of the young characters, it leads to moral numbness: when Tar's new friends, Alan and Helen, overdose on extra-strong heroin and die, the others make off with the remaining supplies and do not tell the police about the bodies in the room. Lily has a baby and injects herself whilst breast-feeding. A punter tries to strangle Lily but she will not report the incident, thus putting other women's lives at risk. Life becomes more and more difficult and joyless. Tar and Gemma are so damaged by their experiences that their future can only be imagined as a long convalescence: a narrowed, cautious recovery from childhood. Gemma is eighteen by the end of the book and has a baby. When her mother sees her, she thinks she looks like an old woman; but it is a weeping child who begs her mother to let her come home again.

Implicit in the story is a grim moral message. Like the cautionary tales of the earliest days of children's literature, Burgess heaps melodramatic incident upon incident to show the worst possible consequences. However, what the story also depicts is the thrill, the pleasure of heroin. The lives these children might otherwise have been leading seem dreary by comparison, and there is very little sense in the novel of a social order, of social institutions they might aspire to belong to in their quest for fulfilled adult lives. Tar's inability to resist the pull of addiction is convincingly shown and the ending is ambiguous: he will continue trying to come off but may not succeed. Tar's future cannot be guessed at—what he tells himself is still the same sad mixture of half-truth and hopefulness—and in that sense no comfortable moral can be drawn. By using multiple narrators, Burgess shows all the characters in *Junk* as flawed. Nobody's view can really be trusted and there is nobody of any age competent to provide guidance to the young characters.

Burgess defended *Junk* by arguing that children's entry into adult life was "substantially unsupported by literature" (Burgess, Sympathy for the Devil, 10 July 2011). Reading *Junk* now, in the light of Burgess's later books, is instructive. The energy of the book, and surely the reason for its immense popularity with young readers, has nothing to do with entering adult life and everything to do with the intense sensations of adolescence. The support Burgess offered encompassed validation of pleasurable sensations and sensual gratification. One of the ways growing up was "unsupported by literature" was in adult reluctance to acknowledge youth's anarchic pleasures. "When young people become sexual, we ought to throw them a big party, balloons, fireworks, everything", Burgess has written on his website. "You've got sex—great! You're really going to enjoy this" (Burgess, Sympathy for the Devil, 10 July 2011). Becoming sexual and enjoying sex was an understated theme of *Junk*, secondary to the major theme of drug-taking. It might be argued that as experimentation with drugs is not a *necessary* part of growing up and has obvious dangers, any responsible adult writing a truthful story about fourteen-year-olds and drugs would seek to emphasize the dangers and warn them off. Sex, however, is another matter. Why should young people's pleasure in sex not be endorsed by literature aimed at them? This was Burgess's question and it led him to write a number of books in which young people's experience of sex was the central subject.

Lady, My Life as a Bitch (2001) begins with the great feeling of sexual excitement Sandra Francy registers as she walks down the road with her latest boy. Sandra is promiscuous, a sex enthusiast. But something is also wrong, and when she finds herself turned into a dog she discovers that what was wrong was the guilt attached to human sexuality. As a dog her senses are heightened and guilt ceases to be a factor. She has a licence to live according to her true nature. Being a dog gives her freedom: "If you wanna sniff it, you sniff it. If you wanna lick it, you lick it," and no "stupid human judgement" gets in the way (Burgess 2001a, 43). A dog can do what she wants, Sandra reflects. The novel is a comic answer to the way adults get annoyed with adolescents and pressurize them to change their ways. Everybody seemed to think Sandra had gone off the rails and become "some sort of mad bitch" (77); they wanted her to be someone else, and now she is, literally, a bitch. From her point of view, being turned into a dog is the perfect riposte: part wish fulfilment, part revenge for not being allowed to live the life she wants. And although at first she yearns to be back in the bosom of her family, and tries to make them accept her as she now is, they cannot recognize her and so, in the final scene, she jumps from the window of her bedroom to join Mitch and Fella, two dogs who were also once human.

Throughout *Lady, My Life as a Bitch*, echoes and half-references to *Peter Pan*, that seminal text in which the Darling children have a dog for a nursemaid, invite us to read this story of teenage rebellion in relation to Barrie's tale. Like Peter, Sandra wants to have fun but she also wants to do things defined as grown-up, namely, have sex. "Children with sex! It's all wrong," Burgess has sarcastically observed on his website, going on to recall his own sexual experiences at fourteen (Burgess, Sympathy for the Devil, 10 July 2011). Children's literature "with sex" is equally "wrong". But grown-up life in *Lady, My Life as a Bitch* is depicted as a dull, commonplace affair, and decidedly fun-free: "worry, worry, worry, stress stress stress. Don't do this, do that, think this, how dare you—it's just a long stupid game with more and more stupid rules to take up your precious time," (191) Sandra thinks, and little serves to counter this view. Burgess's treatment of Sandra's parents is naturalistic, unlike Barrie's of Mr and Mrs Darling, but the characterization of adult life as a worrying (and ultimately unrewarding) game of rules is a direct point of comparison. Sandra's final thoughts as she stands at the bedroom window weigh the attractions of an imagined long life of work and struggle and parenthood against a short, intense doggy life: "I want to be quick and fast and happy and then dead. I don't want to grow old. I don't want to go to work. I don't want to be responsible. I want to be a dog!" (199). Being a dog is like remaining a child. It is Peter's cry, with the added value of casual sex.

There has been, predictably, much controversy. In a BBC interview in 2001 Eric Hester, vice president of an organization called Family and Youth Concern, declared *Lady, My Life as a Bitch* to be "quite the nastiest piece of children's literature" that he had ever read (cited in Burgess 2001b, 10 July 2011) and accused adults of failing to look after children and young people properly. In the history of children's literature, the question of adult responsibility towards child readers has been a constant theme. The Evangelicals understood books as instruments for shaping character and saving souls. Victorians created images of children that provided nostalgic comfort and sentimental pleasures. Later generations, looking back, were shocked at the willingness of Evangelicals to punish and frighten children—in Mrs Sherwood's *The Fairchild Family*, quarrelling little children are taken to see a rotting corpse on a gibbet precisely so that they will be scared of their own ill temper and its possible consequences. Similarly, later generations were shocked at what seemed an unhealthy, erotic response to the pre-pubertal child amongst Victorians; Lewis Carroll, who photographed naked children and filled his pockets with safety pins when he went to the seaside so that he could pin up the skirts of little girls, was considered a harmless, kindly gentleman in his own time and sexually suspect in ours. *Lady, My Life as a Bitch* throws down a challenge to the long tradition of children's literature, especially the so-called "golden age" which produced *Peter Pan* and other enduring classics. Nastiness is relative. Like A. S. Byatt in *The Children's Book*, short-listed for the Booker prize in 2009, Burgess casts a cold eye on the "golden age", seeing at its heart a false innocence imposed on children by adults. Among the beneficiaries of this cultural and social deformation were those who had a professional interest in children and childhood, especially children's authors.

If *Junk* was given a rough ride and *Lady, My Life as a Bitch* struck some as nasty, that was as nothing compared to the reaction produced by *Doing It* (2003), the novel Burgess referred to with sly humour as his "knobby" book. "What I wanted to write about," Burgess explained, "was young male sexual culture—not always a pretty sight" (Burgess, *Sympathy for the Devil*, 10 July 2011). Research for the book involved asking friends and acquaintances for memories of their early sexual experiences. A "great stack" of stories emerged, "some crude, some pathetic, some funny, some charming, but all with something to say" (Ibid.). These were the raw materials for *Doing It*, which features Dino, Ben and Jonathan, three seventeen-year-olds being led by Mr Knobby Knobster into a variety of relationships. Unlike the fourteen-year-olds of *Junk*, these boys are not legally under-age (although the readership is likely to be considerably younger). Their minds are filthy and they amuse each other by devising disgusting sexual fantasies. Real life is more complicated. Ben is having an affair with one of the teachers, and what started out as the ultimate fantasy has become a terrible burden from which he seeks to extricate himself but doesn't know how; Jonathan fears that he has penis cancer; Dino chances on his mother in the arms of her lover. The boys are vulnerable, out of their depth, confused and anxious. Characterization is thin: the cocky one, Dino, gets everything wrong and the others think he's a prat; Jonathan is soft-hearted and rather likes fat girls but hardly dares say so; Ben can keep a secret. Not at logger-heads with their families or badly treated like Tar and Gemma in *Junk*, nor fed up with feeling misunderstood like Sandra in *Lady, My Life as a Bitch*, they are well-meaning, generally well-behaved boys whose bodies are telling them to "do it".

Even before it was published, *Doing It* elicited an unusual attack. Anne Fine, then Children's Laureate, condemned the book in an article in *The Guardian* on March 29th 2003 headed "Filth, Whichever Way You Look At It." In the genteel world of children's literature reviewing and criticism, such an attack by one respected author on another was as startling as any boundary-shifting book. Fine's outrage was directed at editors and publishers who were responsible for deciding what was marketed on the children's list. *Doing It*, in her view, was pornography. From this followed a second objection: that it was demeaning for girls and young women to be exposed to "this grubby book" (Fine 2003).

Doing It, as the *Daily Telegraph* observed, is "astonishingly explicit" for a children's book (Picardie 2003). Burgess, almost single-handedly, opened up the teenage element of the children's list by bringing in sexual content and he has been rewarded by a large and enthusiastic following of young adult readers. There can be no doubt that his books engage young readers because they address pressing concerns. Children cope with sexual feelings from a young age but children's literature chose not to acknowledge—or in Burgess's words—"support" them in this. When sexuality was generally hidden it was not remarkable that it was absent in children's literature, but children today live in a culture saturated in adult realities of every kind and especially sexuality. There are no Edwardian nurseries where they can be segregated, like the Darling children in *Peter Pan*. New technologies bring adult news, views and stories into all our lives, whatever our ages, and a child has only to type "view free sex" into Google to be watching internet porn. From this perspective, *Doing It* already looks clumsy and worthy rather than shocking. Burgess's affectionate depiction of his three decent boys is agenda-driven: he wants to inform and help. Like the early didactic writers for children, he is an evangelist for a cause. In literary and aesthetic terms his work suffers, as did theirs, from an over-emphasis on its message. Dialogue is often too explanatory, situations contrived, psychology unconvincing. However, in pioneering a more open attitude towards sexuality in children's literature, he refused to accept the artificial conventions that survived from the Victorian era, and the fiction about childhood in children's books that insisted on its asexuality. Other writers, too, have challenged these conventions, in particular Aidan Chambers, Robert Cormier and, most recently, William Nicholson. In *Rich and Mad* (2010), Nicholson includes a scene where two girls do indeed type "view free sex" into their laptop and log on to a pornographic site.

Rich and Mad carries a warning on the back: "some explicit content". The main characters are seventeen and virgins, with older siblings of twenty or so who are sexually active. There's a parent generation having relationship trouble and a much-loved Granny who dies. The central narrative is about Maddy and Richard, neither of whom is extraordinary in any way, falling in love and having sex for the first time. What they discover is that love makes them feel extraordinary. Both are kind, intelligent, likeable individuals inclined to passivity and self-blame. Rich reads poetry and thinks a lot and is attentive to his younger sister and

Gran. Maddy's family is more troubled and less available—although she's the youngest, she doesn't appear to get much help. The point of view moves between Maddy and Rich as they stumble towards each other through a convincing sequence of misapprehension and discovery. Their innocence is highlighted by a plot complication involving one of their friends, Grace, and two older siblings of the group, Maddy's sister Imo and the disturbed and violent Leo. Maddy's sexual awakening brings with it a willingness to act on the anger aroused in her by Leo's abusive behaviour towards Grace and Imo. In a melodramatic and rather unlikely scene in a pub she throws beer in his face and then hits him hard on the head with the empty beer mug. No bad consequences follow: indeed, the bang on the head galvanizes Leo's family to seek psychiatric help for him. Leo's problem, it appears, has been that he can only get an erection if he hurts women. In contrast, Rich and Maddy, who talk openly about what they want in sex and are gentle and patient with each other, move easily from ignorant innocence to satisfactory consummation in the final chapter. The sex scenes are frankly but delicately written. They celebrate the joys of sex without prurience. The authorial tone is tender while the content provides a model for how a young couple might best please each other and so please themselves. It is didactic and idealized, but at the same time unstrained. Nicholson is careful to make sure that Maddy takes some of the initiative in these encounters, and also realistic in assuming that the boy, having his first experience of full penetration, will climax too quickly for the girl to orgasm.

The context for thinking about Nicholson's tone and content in the final sex scene is not some abstract notion of suitability of material for particular age groups which the warning of "explicit" on the back might suggest, but ease of access to pornography. Nicholson's stated intention is to take sex away from the pornographers. *Rich and Mad* was his attempt to "tell girls what boys are feeling, and to tell boys what girls are feeling–boys like the boy I once was. It's my attempt to be truthful about sexual fears and longings" (Nicholson 2010). When Maddy and her best friend Cath decide to look at porn on Maddy's laptop and the "big erect cock" makes them giggle, Cath admits she quite liked seeing it, but both agree that porn is clearly for boys, and what they see is less a turn-on than an annoyance. They do indeed find it demeaning. Maddy says, "'It was like a little god wanting to be worshipped. On and on with the worshipping, bowing before it, kissing it, on and on'" (80). However, Cath thinks she wouldn't mind if she had a boyfriend who liked that kind of thing and Maddy is also more stimulated than she wants to admit. Afterwards she lies on her bed looking at the moon and feeling "a nameless excitement that streamed out of her to touch everything she saw" (82).

In this wise, genial, and respectful book, the young protagonists learn useful knowledge. The title humorously challenges expectations: Rich is not rich, he is no Byronic hero, nor is he Mr Darcy, and Mad is eminently sane and commonsensical. *Rich and Mad* is a romance with its feet on the ground. Like Melvin Burgess's novels it speaks to young people today about matters that concern them in much the same warm, responsible tone that can be found in early didactic literature for children. Nicholson's didacticism is unobtrusive but his aim is to teach. He offers models of ideal behaviour for readers who, if they emulate Rich and Maddy's openness and patience with each other, might also move from ignorance to satisfaction.

Responding to the furore over *Doing It*, and specifically to Anne Fine's comments, Burgess offered the observation that many people seemed not to like young boys very much. He discerned in the article "that same nasty sneer" he remembered from childhood, summed up by hearing the words, "How revolting. Aren't you a dirty little boy?" (Burgess, Sympathy for the Devil, 10 July 2011). It was this attitude that made him want to write his book in the first place, on behalf of "dirty" little boys such as he and his friends had been, and to affirm them in that tendency rather than to reprove or correct. "With *Junk*, I was writing a book not for those who say no to drugs, but for those who say yes; with *Lady*, I was writing a book to those who say yes to sex." (Ibid.). And with *Doing It* he was writing for those who relished the filth but were also open to the tenderness and awkwardness involved in the exploration of sexuality.

Early Evangelicals and other moral writers urged boys to say no to such temptations as idleness and gambling, and made use of "dirty" or badly behaved boys to dramatize the message that boys could learn to recognize and overcome evil. But mostly their impulse in characterizing boys was idealizing rather than denigratory. British boys represented the future of a great imperial nation, hence the keynotes in Victorian representations, from Thomas Hughes's *Tom Brown's Schooldays* (1857) and Ballantyne's *The Coral Island* (1857) to G. A. Henty's tales and beyond, tended towards optimism and uplift. With one or two striking exceptions sex was not addressed—Thomas Hughes fulminated quite explicitly about the wrongness of older boys "petting" younger ones in *Tom Brown's Schooldays*, Charles Kingsley gives Tom a girl to desire in *The Water Babies* (1863)—but mostly being a boy was about excitement and love of adventure. The shared belief that a boy's life mattered and that the values he adopted, such as honour, bravery, fairness, self-command, self-reliance and so on, had a universal significance, beats through the Victorian adventure tale. The emotional tone adopted is affectionate and affirmative, the antithesis of the attitude Burgess describes in recalling the "nasty sneer" and dismissive overheard phrase, "a dirty little boy". Writers like Henty and Kipling are deeply unfashionable nowadays and Burgess probably wouldn't welcome being connected to them, but in his determination to like boys and say yes to their growing selves, he reaches back to this tradition. In his didacticism and desire to offer useful knowledge he reaches further back, to the Evangelicals and the earliest days of children's literature. What he mostly bypasses is the influential Victorian cult of childhood which gave birth to so many classic texts and achieved its iconic expression in *Peter Pan*.

"Golden-age" values and myths of childhood provided much of the energy in children's literature as it grew and developed in the twentieth century. The cult of childhood innocence, the notion of boyhood as the quintessential time of fun, the longing and nostalgia, all contributed to a rich tradition. But writers like Burgess and Nicholson share the disquiet expressed in A. S. Byatt's *The Children's Book*, which critiques the commodification of innocence that accompanied this development and questions adult motivations. In their determination to make room for sexual knowledge in children's literature, Burgess and Nicholson challenge generic definitions. In refusing to accept that children's literature should be an asexual space, they expose the cult of innocence in the genre itself. *Doing It, Lady, My Life as a Bitch*, and *Rich and Mad* are contemporary tales in dialogue with the tradition. Their message is that children's literature needs to grow up.

References

Ballantyne, R.M. 1990. *The Coral Island: A Tale of the Pacific Ocean.* Oxford: Oxford University Press.

Barrie, J. M. 1995. *Peter Pan and Other Plays,* ed. Peter Hollindale. Oxford: Oxford World's Classics.

Burgess, Melvin. 1990. *Cry of the Wolf.* Toronto: Andersen Press.

—. 1997. *Junk.* London: Penguin.

—. 2001a. *Lady, My Life as a Bitch.* London: Andersen Press.

—. 2001b. Row over Teen Novel. www.melvinburgess.net/Lady.htm. Date accessed 10 July 2011.

—. 2004. *Doing It.* London: Penguin.

—. No date. Sympathy for the Devil. www.melvinburgess.net/articles. Date accessed 10 July 2011.

—. No date. What is Teenage Fiction? www.melvinburgess.net/articles. Date accessed 10 July 2011.

Burnett, Frances Hodgson. 2011. *The Secret Garden.* Oxford: Oxford University Press.

Byatt, A. S. 2009. *The Children's Book.* London: Chatto & Windus.

Crompton, Richmal. 2010. *Just William.* London: Pan Children's Books.

Fine, Anne. 2003. Filth, Whichever Way You Look At It. *The Guardian*, March 2. http://www.guardian.co.uk/books/2003/mar/29/featuresreviews.guardianreview24. Date accessed 10 July 2011.

Grahame, Kenneth. 1999. *The Wind in the Willows.* Oxford: Oxford University Press.

Hughes, Thomas. 2008. *Tom Brown's Schooldays.* Oxford: Oxford University Press.

Kingsley, Charles. 1995. *The Water Babies.* Oxford: Oxford University Press.

Kipling, Rudyard. 2009. *The Complete Stalky and Co.* Oxford: Oxford University Press.

Lewis, C.S. 1994. *The Lion, The Witch and The Wardrobe.* London: HarperCollins.

Nicholson, William. 2010. *Rich and Mad.* London: Egmont Books.

—. 2010. Rich and Mad. www.williamnicholson.com. Date accessed 10 July 2011.

Picardie, Justine. 2003. Boys' Own Stories. *Daily Telegraph*, April 13. http://www.telegraph.co.uk/culture/books/3592659/Boys-own-stories.html. Date accessed 10 July 2011.

Ransome, Arthur. 2010. *Swallows and Amazons.* Boston: David R. Godine.

Reynolds, Kimberley. 2007. *Radical Children's Literature: Future Visions and Aesthetic Transformations in Juvenile Fiction.* Basingstoke: Palgrave Macmillan.

Salinger, J.D. 2001. *The Catcher in the Rye.* Boston: Back Bay Books.

—. 2011. *Children's Literature: A Very Short Introduction.* Oxford: Oxford University Press.

Sherwood, Mary Martha. 2010. *The History of the Fairchild Family, Or, A Child's Manual.* Charleston: Nabu Press.

Trease, Geoffrey. 1940. *Cue For Treason.* London: Macmillan.

—. 1993. *The Popinjay Mystery.* London: Pan Macmillan.

—. 1949. *Tales Out of School, A Survey of Children's Fiction.* London: New Educational Book Club.

Trimmer, Sarah. 2009. *The History of the Robins.* Kila, MT: Kessinger Publishing.

PART II

WHAT DO WE TELL THE CHILDREN ABOUT DEATH AND TRAUMA?

"What Bruno Knew": Childhood Innocence and Models of Morality in John Boyne's *The Boy in the Striped Pyjamas* (2006)

Nora Maguire

This chapter reads John Boyne's *The Boy in the Striped Pyjamas* (2006) as a text of childhood and as a piece of Holocaust literature. It argues that the central task of Boyne's narrative is not to educate a child reader about the Holocaust but to reiterate and reinforce the myth of childhood innocence by locating it in a setting that is widely understood as metonymic for total corruption and for the fall from grace of Western culture or civilization. My reading of the text is thus closely concerned not just with the text's address to a child reader, but also with its evidently significant appeal to adult and young adult audiences, and with the adult desires and anxieties about innocence that the narrative invokes and plays upon. I suggest that the commercial success of *The Boy in the Striped Pyjamas*, and particularly its widespread use in primary and post-primary classrooms in Ireland and the United Kingdom, may owe more to the nostalgia for innocence that the text invokes and performs than to the nature of its negotiation of the fraught territory of Holocaust literature. Tied to this nostalgia for innocence is, as I will argue, a model of conservative morality that further complicates the text's address to its child readers. I will begin by situating the novel in the context of Holocaust representation and its dilemmas, and by revisiting the issues raised by the text's historical inaccuracies. I will then examine the construction of innocence and morality present in the text to explore what *The Boy in the Striped Pyjamas* actually does tell its readers about childhood, evildoing and retribution.

It hardly needs to be stated that a peculiar set of ethical and moral demands accrue to artistic representations of and engagements with the Holocaust, regardless of the age of their intended audience. The problem, articulated by Theodor W. Adorno in his essays "Cultural Criticism and

Society" (1981) and "Commitment" (1992), is aestheticizing, and thus deriving artistic beauty or pleasure from, events of incomprehensible cruelty, from innumerable acts of dehumanization and abjection. As Adrienne Kertzer phrases it, there is "the risk of understanding," meaning the ethical dubiousness of seeking to explain, understand and thus affect a sense of closure on matters that ought by rights to remain open, unresolved and present (1999, 249). There is, also, the danger of fetishizing the concept of urepresentability, so that words such as "incomprehensible," "innumerable" or "unimaginable" become a way of avoiding engagement, however incomplete and inadequate such engagement may necessarily be, with the experiences of those who were persecuted. For Ruth Klüger, this assumption of unrepresentability amounts in itself to a form of kitsch (2006, 55). Alongside these issues lie the ethical difficulties of representing the experiences of the dead, which carries the risk of inappropriate identification with or projection onto the figures of Holocaust victims, whereby the contemporary subject may, in Dominick LaCapra's terms, "arrogate to [him]self" the identity or position of the victim, and thus fail to acknowledge the incommensurability of his or her experience (1998, 182).

Besides these complex dilemmas and negotiations, the need for a high degree of historical accuracy in literary approaches to the Holocaust seems reasonably self-evident, particularly given the sadly perennial presence of neo-Nazi subculture and Holocaust denial. This requirement is even more important in the field of children's literature, where the young reader cannot be assumed to have extensive prior knowledge of historical contexts, as Lydia Kokkola has argued (2003, 3). Yet recent years have seen films and texts enjoy widespread popularity that engage with the Holocaust and the Second World War in ahistorical or historically inaccurate or improbable fashion, often invoking fabular or fairytale tropes as well as notions of childhood in the process.[1] Gary Weissman's appraisal of the place of the Holocaust in the contemporary North American popular imagination is illuminating in this regard:

> "Public awareness stops the Holocaust from receding into the distant past, but with no guarantee that the Holocaust we 'remember' is faithful to past reality. Scholars and survivors frequently speak of the unimaginable, unrepresentable nature of that reality, but in practice what can be represented of the Holocaust is often determined through a practical consideration of what is most suitable for a target audience, given a specific set of objectives" (2004, 10).

In other words, contemporary representations of the Holocaust in literary or filmic narratives are shaped by the ideologies and conventions of contemporary culture as well as, if not more than, the conditions of historical truthfulness. In her consideration of artistic engagements with the Holocaust at the end of the twentieth century, Marianne Hirsch (1997), by contrast, emphasizes the centrality of private, emotional and imaginative engagement with events not witnessed at first hand but learned through the recollection of older family members who are Holocaust survivors. Although Hirsch is primarily concerned with the children and grandchildren of Holocaust survivors in her working-out of the concept of "postmemory," it is a concept which has since been applied to post-war generations in a much broader sense, as Weissman points out (2004, 17-18). Hirsch's and Weissman's contrasting approaches to contemporary Holocaust remembrance, Hirsch emphasising the private and subjective through the concept of "postmemory" and Weissman emphasizing cultural memory's ideological contingency through the concept of the "nonwitness," provide a useful framework for my reading of *The Boy in the Striped Pyjamas*. I argue that, within the novel and in statements he has made about it, Boyne assumes, and offers his readers, a "postmemorial" stance towards the Holocaust which privileges imaginative investment and the notion of emotional truth. However, behind this veneer of archaeological and empathic truth-seeking, the melodramatic nexus of childhood innocence and death is at work in the text, producing a highly moralistic narrative that speaks neither about the Holocaust nor to a child reader in its lesson that the sins of parents are visited upon children.

Boyne can clearly be seen to be taking up a postmemorial position in relation to the Holocaust when he states that the choice of subject matter required a naïve narrator:

> "For me, a 34-year-old Irish writer, it seemed that the only respectful way to deal with such a subject was through innocence, using the point of view of a rather naïve child who couldn't possibly understand the horrors of what he was caught up in. After all, that naïveté is as close as someone of my generation can get to the dreadfulness of that time and place. (…) [I]t is the responsibility of any writer who chooses to base a narrative in those places to uncover as much emotional truth within that desperate landscape as he possibly can" (2006).

This statement reveals that the conjunction of the ideology of childhood and the troubles of postmemorial or, in Weissman's terms, nonwitness engagement with the Holocaust is central to Boyne's narrative project in this, his first children's book. The statement ultimately suggests that the text's protagonist, Bruno, is best understood not as a figure to whom any historical authenticity or factual reliability attaches, but rather as a kind of time-travelling avatar for the contemporary reading or writing subject. Boyne's emphasis on the nebulous concept of "emotional truth" is further indicative of the primacy in contemporary cultural memory of imaginative and emotional engagement with and investment in the past. Of course, this engagement need not always be as detached from historicity as Boyne's novel is. As Eaglestone (2007, 23) suggests, there are real "emotional truths" of the Holocaust that might well be broached through imaginative work; they are simply absent from the text of *The Boy in the Striped Pyjamas*.

The ideology of childhood, particularly innocence, as a socio-cultural construct interacts with Boyne's postmemorial position in two ways. The figure of the innocent child is invoked as a legitimization of the author's aesthetic choices in writing about the Holocaust in the first place, and in shaping and directing his narrative as he does. Childhood innocence is thus posited as something which can facilitate a literary engagement with the Holocaust that is both ethical ("respectful") and authentic ("emotional truth"). Implicit here, too, is a legitimization of the text's substantial lack of historical accuracy or probability by way of this stance of child-like innocence. In this sense, the myth of childhood innocence is called upon to establish and to justify what has been identified as a deeply problematic narrative strategy relating to the Holocaust.

If the myth of innocence can be identified as a legitimizing factor with respect to Boyne's Holocaust narrative, the novel's setting might also be said to act as a means of upholding and reinforcing the myth of childhood innocence. Boyne has stated that the germ of the novel was a mental image of two boys sitting by a fence, with the Holocaust setting developing at a subsequent stage in the creative process.[2] This opens up the possibility of reading *The Boy in the Striped Pyjamas* as first and foremost a tale propounding the notion of childhood innocence as a force that can transcend ideology and prejudice, with the boundary fence of Auschwitz (euphemistically termed "Out-With" in the text) standing in metonymically for any or all adult-created social divisions. This reading would exemplify Weissman's suggestion that what is told about the Holocaust generally suits contemporary ideological and, in the case of children's literature, pedagogical currents and preferences. There is, of course, nothing inherently unusual about this aspect of Boyne's novel; what marks it out is hardly its espousal of friendship and solidarity in the face of violence and hatred, but rather its ahistorical handling of its historical setting. There is, however, one other aspect to the role played by innocence in the text which is somewhat more unusual, and that is its connection with death. While the death of the children at the end of the text might be read as a final concession on Boyne's part to the laws of historical probability, it can also be understood—and I would suggest that this is its true function within the movement of narrative and plot—as a melodramatic turn which consolidates the myth of childhood innocence as something that appeals fundamentally to adult, rather than child, readers.

By highlighting the role of nostalgia, melodrama and the myth of innocence in the novel, new light may be cast on the widespread selection of Boyne's novel by adult mediators as a suitable text for children and young people learning about the Holocaust, as well as on the messages about childhood, innocence and retribution that the novel may impart to its child readers. Existing scholarship provides a starting point for this discussion. Ruth Gilbert, comparing the novel with Morris Gleitzman's Holocaust novels, *Once* (2006) and *Then* (2009), argues that Boyne's narrative, particularly through its use of the "fable" conceit, tends to shut down gaps and spaces for a child reader to ask questions, thus failing to carry out what Kokkola has termed a "dialogue with silence" (2010, 25). Siobhán Parkinson has carried out a close narratological examination of the novel, critiquing Boyne's techniques of focalization and narration and raising questions about the role of irony and knowingness in the text's address to its inscribed reader.[3] Although, as Parkinson points out, Boyne's structures of narration and focalization are inconsistent at times, the text's central dynamic, playing off the naïve perspective of the child against a more knowing inscribed reader by way of an extradiegetic narrator, is a well-established one. It is employed, for example, by Henry James in *What Maisie Knew* (1897) where, as in Boyne's novel, a child protagonist negotiates a complex and dangerous adult world of which she is at the mercy. In contrast to James's text of childhood, Boyne's narrator frequently moves away from the focalizing perspective of Bruno in a manner conducive to a more obviously ironic and moralistic narrative tone. Alice Curry's evaluation of *The Boy in the Striped Pyjamas* makes use of intercultural and film theory without, however, engaging to any great depth with the numerous dilemmas of representation and remembrance that are particular to Holocaust literature. Curry's contention that Bruno, a child of the perpetrator collective, is able, by transgressing cultural boundaries and transcending prejudicial constructions of the Other, to "restore visibility and voice" to the figure of the Jewish child Holocaust victim, fails to acknowledge the dangers of projection, false identification and usurpation that inhere in the notion of imaginatively giving or restoring a voice to Holocaust victims (2010, 62). The fact that

The Boy in the Striped Pyjamas lends itself readily to such a reading, however, is indicative of the extent to which it may not primarily be a Holocaust text, but rather a tale whose central myth of transcendent innocence fits numerous contemporary didactic agendas.

It is useful to deal briefly at this point with the historically inaccurate features of the text. These problematic aspects of the narrative have been the subject of a good deal of censure and debate, particularly around the time of the novel's publication. Many of Boyne's public statements about the novel have also addressed this controversy, and the decision to add the subtitle "a fable" to the novel after publication of the first edition was no doubt a response to these criticisms.

On the most fundamental factual level, Boyne's novel sees the two boys meet on either side of a non-electrified wire fence, an error which, as Eaglestone (2007) points out, cannot be put down to the naïve perspective of the protagonist: the perimeter fence at Auschwitz was heavily electrified. According to Eaglestone, other factual errors are evident in Boyne's description of the layout of the camp and location of the Commandant's house. As well as basic factual inaccuracies, the text has a central premise based on a scenario whose historical improbability verges on the impossible: the concept of a pre-adolescent child surviving for a substantial period of time as a prisoner in Auschwitz. The dehumanizing logic of the Nazi genocide was aimed at the complete annihilation of a people. Those deemed "useful" either as labourers or as subjects for pseudo-medical or pseudo-scientific experimentation were not sent to the gas chambers. Others, including children too small for physical labour, were usually murdered very quickly on arrival at the camp (Dwork 2010). The notion of there being a child of Schmuel's age and size alive for a substantial period of time in Auschwitz is more or less impossible. As the perimeter fence of the camp was not only electrified but also under constant, armed surveillance, the notion of such a child being able to sit alone and unobserved at some neglected point of the fence is also highly improbable, to say the least.

Boyne is, however, not the first author to construct an improbable scenario of child survival in a concentration camp. Roberto Benigni's 1997 film *La Vita É Bella* (*Life Is Beautiful*) tells the story of a child who survives the camp because his father protects him by pretending that the experience is a game. Another story, this time rooted in historical fact, is that of Stefan Jerzy Zweig, who survived Buchenwald concentration camp as a young child, and whose story became a staple part of East German cultural memory of the Holocaust, primarily through Bruno Apitz's 1958 novel *Nackt Unter Wölfen* (*Naked Among Wolves*) and its subsequent 1963

DEFA film adaptation (directed by Frank Beyer). As Bill Niven's 2007 study of this East German cultural phenomenon has shown, the popular GDR story of the child rescued and protected by Communist prisoners at the camp has been deconstructed since German reunification, in a manner which has cast more accurate historical light on events, but which has also fed into a post-1989 cultural backlash against the former GDR. The young Zweig, a Jewish child born in 1941, was, in fact, protected at Buchenwald by Communist prisoners, to the knowledge of at least some of the camp's SS guards. During this process, however, he was alienated to some extent from his father, who was also a prisoner, and there is evidence that his name was at one stage removed from a deportation list of 200 children, and replaced by the name of another, gypsy child. Niven's study thus points very precisely to an intersection between cultural memory, political ideology and myths and ideals of childhood. Boyne's tale of children "naked among wolves" belongs to a similar nexus, albeit in a very different cultural context.

In her study of children's literature and the Holocaust, Lydia Kokkola distinguishes between a number of forms of historical inaccuracy that may occur in a text. As well as factual inaccuracy, she discusses the presence of cultural anachronism (2003, 80). Anachronisms such as avoiding representing anti-Semitic attitudes in a prominent character can allow an author to tell the child reader about National Socialism and the Holocaust without risking reproducing, or even inadvertently propagating, the racist ideology and rhetoric of the time. Again, many children's authors prior to Boyne have used this form of cultural anachronism and, as Kokkola implies, it may well be a necessary form of inaccuracy. In Hans Peter Richter's 1972 novel, *Wir Waren Dabei* (*I Was There*), for instance, the nameless protagonist goes through Hitler Youth training and the NS school curriculum, and even participates in the so-called "Kristallnacht" pogroms, without ever actually voicing or seeming to harbour anti-Semitic sentiments. Liesel Meminger, the protagonist of Markus Zusak's 2006 *The Book Thief,* attends BDM classes (as she would have been obliged to do) and knows who to address in the town with a Hitler salute, but nonetheless retains her spirit of resistance and sense of solidarity with the persecuted. Boyne's construction of his perpetrator-collective protagonist is therefore unusual only in the degree of Bruno's apparent isolation from mainstream NS sentiment, pedagogy and culture. Bruno's ignorance as to what the word "Jew" signifies and who Hitler is, coupled with the novel's setting at the perimeter of an inaccurately portrayed concentration camp rather than within the unpleasant social and political intricacies of a German town of the period, means that the narrative provides very little acknowledgement of the ideological indoctrination of children that was central to NS education and youth policy, or to the ubiquity of anti-Semitism in German society under the Nazis.[4]

Although these issues of historical inaccuracy certainly raise significant questions as to the ethics of narration of this particular text regarding its address to both child and adult readers, this discussion is not primarily concerned with taking up a prescriptive or censorious position in relation to the text. Given that the actual content of the novel does not include an accurate or historically faithful engagement with the Holocaust and National Socialism, it may be more productive to explore in further depth what the narrative does contain that has, presumably, contributed to its widespread success. I believe that the myth of childhood innocence lies very close to the heart of the adult desires and ideological demands that are met by *The Boy in the Striped Pyjamas*.

While the concept of childhood innocence has a long history in Western culture [Aleida Assmann (1978) has found evidence of it, for example, in Classical Antiquity], mythologizing childhood and innocence as secular ideals has been traced back to the late Enlightenment period, with Hans-Heino Ewers (1989) identifying the late eighteenth-century "Sturm und Drang" anthropology of Herder, along with Rousseau's *Émile* (1762), as seminal points of development. It can thus be said that childhood innocence is a myth of Western modernity that has served crucial social and cultural purposes since the late eighteenth century, from the regulation of sexuality and the perpetuation of heterosexual normativity in society to the mourning of lost, pre-industrial idylls, and from the promising of pristine origins and unceasing progress to the voicing of caustic social critique and outrage.[5] Because this ideal is deeply embedded in the Western cultural imagination and since the Holocaust can be understood as a traumatic event that undermines, in LaCapra's words, "the image of Western civilization itself as the bastion of elevated values" (1998, 9), the inscription of tropes of childhood innocence into a literary portrayal of the Holocaust marks a conjunction that demands close examination and questioning.

As previously suggested, Boyne's text is by no means unique in carrying out such an inscription. What marks out *The Boy in the Striped Pyjamas* is, rather, its radical refusal to adapt or tailor its construction of innocence to the complex demands of historical accuracy or authenticity. In this sense, the innocent perspective of the child does not function primarily as a vehicle for revealing and critiquing a fascist society saturated in a racist and xenophobic ideology. Rather, the children's innocence, and more particularly their innocent deaths, function as the vehicle for the narrative's indictment and punishment of a corrupt adult world, which is figured much more strongly as one of sexual duplicity and petit-bourgeois, patriarchal conventionalism than one of quasi-religious, fanatical political and racial ideology. That is to say that the death of the children, rather than their agency as fictional subjects, is what is central to the novel's narrative structure and effect, while the agent punished by their deaths (or, more precisely, by Bruno's death) is best understood as bourgeois patriarchy rather than National Socialism. In other words, *The Boy in the Striped Pyjamas* might be said to use its Holocaust setting as an allegory of bourgeois patriarchy, and, in somewhat Old Testament fashion, enacts the punishment of its object rather than earnest critique or self-conscious deconstruction. The lack of agency and ultimate death of the innocent child are central to this narrative project of punishment.

The next part of this discussion closely examines Boyne's construction of Bruno's innocence in the text, arguing that tropes of bourgeois decadence provide the main foil by which it is established, while the text's two Jewish figures serve as accessories to the protagonist's innocence, as well as providing the narrative with a degree of historical contextualization. Narrative acts of ironic framing further emphasize this innocence, and do so in a manner that assumes a knowing reader, so that the inscribed reader of the text is held in a relationship to the protagonist that is often marked by distance rather than identification. Finally, the centrality of death to Boyne's construction of innocence, and the model of retribution espoused in the text will be addressed.

Bruno's world is constructed far more markedly as bourgeois and patriarchal than as German and National Socialist.[6] Despite occasional allusions to bombings, euphemistic references to "Out-With" and "the Fury," and one instance in which the German-language phrase "Heil Hitler" is reproduced on the page (Boyne 2006, 54), there is little detailed information which would locate Bruno with any specificity in this context. The text's single description of a Berlin street scene depicts vegetable stalls (anachronistically plentiful for the wartime setting) and people sitting at café tables, without mention of place names or any other attempt at localization or historicization (2006, 12-13). Similarly, when Bruno finally strikes out to explore the territory around his new home, just prior to his first meeting with Schmuel, the narrative is at pains to remove him from the objects and images that would specify the historical and political contexts that the novel appears to invoke:

> "He walked and walked, and when he looked back the house that he was living in became smaller and smaller until it vanished from sight altogether. During all this time he never saw anyone anywhere close to the

fence.... In fact although the fence continued on as far as the eye could see, the huts and buildings and smoke stacks were disappearing in the distance behind him and the fence seemed to be separating him from nothing but open space" (2006, 104).

In contrast to the novel's minimal evocation of its specific political, topographical and historical contexts, the class structures of Bruno's world are drawn in detail and carry considerable weight in the narrative's construction of his innocence. His developing friendship with Maria, the family servant, indicates his instinctive rejection of hierarchical class structures, constructing his innocence not just as naivety but also as a positive moral force. Indeed it is this feature of the text—its portrayal of the child's transgression of prejudicial and limiting social boundaries— that Alice Curry praises in her discussion of the novel (2010, 72). This aspect of Bruno's innocence, established by means of frequent reference to Maria over the first hundred or so pages of the novel, is extended to include the Jewish figure of Pavel, with whom not only Bruno but also Maria appears to be in sympathy (Boyne 2006, 136-7). The text's other Jewish figure, Schmuel, is also drawn into this master-servant scheme when he is brought into the house to polish glasses in preparation for a party (166-7). This allows the narrative to side-step the matter of anti-Semitism to some extent; it is Pavel's servant-status rather than his Jewishness that is emphasized. Of course, as I discuss below, this representation is framed by ironic knowing, as the inscribed reader is expected to be more keenly aware of Pavel's Jewishness and prisoner status than Bruno is. However, this element of narrative irony does not undo, but rather merely overlays the equivalence the text sets up between bourgeois class hierarchy and Nazi anti-Semitism. Not only does this narrative strategy elide the singular aspects of National Socialist society and the Nazi genocide but also it creates a false equivalence between Jewish figures and other figures of reduced status or agency within the hierarchy, such as Maria and Pavel, Bruno and Pavel, and finally Bruno and Schmuel. Furthermore, it risks suggesting that agency and responsibility for the Holocaust lie only with the male elite of the NS apparatus—an exculpatory claim long rejected in most historical and literary discourse.

As well as being portrayed as oppressively patriarchal, through constant reference to the father's rules and authority, and as rigidly hierarchical, the adult world surrounding Bruno is configured as decadently bourgeois by means of the leitmotifs of alcohol and sexual intrigue. Bruno's naivety as regards alcohol and drunkenness is invoked at regular intervals in the text, beginning with his observation of people drinking at street cafés in Berlin (13) and subsequently linked to his grandmother's and mother's behaviour as well as to that of soldiers who come to dinner. The conceit of a nine-year-old German boy growing up under Hitler and not recognizing beer when he sees it (Boyne repeatedly uses the euphemism "frothy drinks" e.g. 13, 101) is arguably almost as improbable as his never having heard the word "Jew." Bruno does, however, recognize wine and sherry, suggesting perhaps that his innocence of beer represents another demarcation of social class in the novel. The grandmother's drunkenness also invokes a stereotype of Irishness, in what can only be understood as an attempt by Boyne to inscribe his own nationality into the text in some way. A few pages before Bruno notes her "surprisingly slurred" voice, we are told that the red-haired, green-eyed grandmother claims to have "Irish blood" (87, 93). The grandmother's drunkenness, together with the mother's growing alcoholism, serve a wider narrative purpose than this inscription of Irishness, however. The female figures' drinking indicates their unhappiness and lack of agency in a situation engineered, again, by figures of male power. The grandmother's drunkenness is thus linked with her criticisms of her son and husband, while the mother's "medicinal sherries" indicate her increasing unhappiness in her role as the Camp Commandant's wife (167, 78, 87, 88).

Boyne's employment of the trope of alcohol thus performs a complex function in the narrative. Again, it deposits agency and responsibility firmly at the feet of male figures of authority, emphasizing the patriarchal nature of the novel's social world. It suggests that the female figures are at least uncomfortable with, and even resistant to National Socialist ideology, but at the same time allows the text to avoid having to explain this discomfort and resistance in an explicit, informative or reasoned manner; because the women are portrayed as drunk, they need not be portrayed as articulate. In this manner, Boyne is able to prevent specific historical information from impinging upon his narrative. Finally, Bruno's highly improbable naivety with respect to alcohol and drunkenness further serves to exaggerate his innocence, purity and indeed vulnerability against a backdrop of adult insobriety and desperation.

Here again, then, Bruno's innocence is established by means of contrast with an adult world that is specifically patriarchal and bourgeois, and in which National Socialism is only vaguely indicated. The motif of alcohol is linked to the text's Jewish figures too, in a manner more redolent with symbolism than we have seen thus far. Schmuel is brought into the house to polish wine glasses in preparation for the Commandant's birthday party (166-7)—here again the mother's "medicinal sherries" are referenced—and Pavel is savagely beaten and, the reader may infer, killed, after he drops a bottle of wine whilst serving the family at dinner in a chapter entitled "The Bottle of Wine" (148-9). Once again, the National Socialist persecution of the Jews is contextualized as a relationship between unjust masters and powerless servants. The motif of alcohol becomes, perhaps somewhat absurdly, a symbol of anti-Semitic violence. A rather puritanical message about alcohol, power and oppression is thus conveyed in a manner that allows the text to avoid confronting the ideology of Nazi anti-Semitism in a historically informed manner.

Significantly the figure of Lieutenant Kotler, rather than Bruno's father, is the agent of violence in both these alcohol-related scenes of persecution. Like the novel's Jewish characters, Kotler is drawn directly from stereotype: a blonde, perfectly formed, highly perfumed and obviously threatening Aryan youth. A near-identical, highly perfumed, sexually threatening figure is created by Hans Peter Richter in the form of a Hitler Youth leader in his 1978 autobiographical novel *I Was There*.[7] Lydia Kokkola identifies such figures as eroticized bogeymen, although she finds that they register only a faint presence in children's literature in contrast to texts addressed to adult readers (2003, 144). Boyne's figure of Kotler certainly conforms to Kokkola's model, both in the faint eroticization of the figure and in the manner of his eventual exorcism from the text:

> "On most days the young lieutenant looked very smart, striding around in a uniform that appeared to have been ironed while he was wearing it. His black boots always sparkled with polish and his yellow-blond hair was parted at the side and held perfectly in place with something that made all the comb marks stand out in it, like a field that had just been tilled. Also he wore so much cologne that you could smell him coming from quite a distance....On this particular day, however, since it was a Saturday morning and was so sunny, he was not so perfectly groomed. Instead he was wearing a white vest over his trousers and his hair flopped down over his forehead in exhaustion. His arms were surprisingly tanned and he had the kind of muscles that Bruno wished he had himself" (71).

The figure of Kotler is, in fact, the main vehicle for the narrative's not inconsiderable erotic subtext, as it is heavily implied that he is engaged in a flirtation with Bruno's twelve-year-old sister, and is having an affair with the children's mother to boot. Echoing Henry James's rendering of the child's perspective in *What Maisie Knew*, this erotic subtext of sexual intrigue and adultery is relayed to the reader through the sexually innocent perspective of Bruno who, unlike Maisie, is instinctively suspicious of Kotler and worried about his interactions with his sister and mother.

Bruno's naivety is thus linked again with intuitive morality, a morality which is defeated only by the child's fear of the bogeyman, Kotler.[8] The novel's erotic subplot thus serves to emphasize Bruno's innocence, this time in sexual as well as moral terms, and to further construct the adult world of the text in accordance with a moralistic scheme that nonetheless avoids historically informed or detailed engagement with the real evils of National Socialism, portraying instead a corrupt and decadent bourgeois world of alcoholism, sexual intrigue and adultery.

As stated above, these tropes of bourgeois moral corruption and patriarchal oppression do not simply establish the young protagonist's innocence, but also position the inscribed reader in relation to it. In contrast to Morris Gleitzman's novels *Once* and *Then*, *The Boy in the Striped Pyjamas* does not have its implied child reader move with the protagonist from a position of innocence into a more knowing one, as Ruth Gilbert (2010) has convincingly argued. The trajectory of Boyne's protagonist moves not from naivety to knowledge, but from life to death. In this sense, the text produces narrative closure in a more profound manner than Gilbert's discussion of Boyne's use of the "fable" conceit suggests. Most, if not all, of Boyne's narrative gaps and silences work on the principle of a knowing reader who can fill in the blanks in Bruno's perception. Gleitzman's texts, by contrast, use moments of conscious self-reflexivity to suggest the limitations of narrative itself rather than of child protagonist's consciousness, as Gilbert demonstrates. Boyne's text's euphemistic references to beer, Hitler and Auschwitz, and its coy nods at sex and drunkenness, assume a reader more knowing than the child protagonist, as Parkinson (2008) has pointed out. The novel brings this knowing reader on a journey not from limited to increased knowledge, but rather from a position of mildly comic ironic distance from the protagonist to one of melodramatically tragic irony, as we watch the innocent children unwittingly enter the gas chamber.

Although this ironic, knowing position in relation to innocence, by turns comedic and mournful, may well appeal to child and teenage readers who encounter Boyne's novel in the classroom or in their own, private reading, I would argue that this picture of innocence is one which caters primarily to adult sensibilities, particularly adult desire, nostalgia and mourning in relation to childhood. As Jacqueline Rose (1994) and James Kincaid (1992) among others have shown, death is of central structural importance to this nostalgic production of innocence as a "portion of adult desire" (Rose 1994, xii). The deaths of Bruno and Schmuel preserve their innocence and naivety, so that the text never has to cope with the child's comprehension of violence and terror, something authors such as

Gleitzman and Sharon Dogar, in her 2010 novel *Annexed,* do attempt to negotiate. In this sense, and in contrast to Gilbert, I would argue that the death of the protagonist and of his "shadow," Schmuel, at the close of Boyne's novel is not primarily a concession on the author's part to the laws of historical probability as regards children in concentration camps (2010, 363). Rather, it is an essential structural element in a narrative which constructs childhood innocence as an elegiac myth, allowing innocence to remain static and frozen and cementing the boundaries between childhood and adulthood.

Death plays another, related, structurally crucial role in Boyne's narrative, in that it is the vehicle for the text's punishment of its adult and adolescent protagonists, namely Bruno's parents and sister. The novel's central tragic figure in this sense is Bruno, not Schmuel, and a further irony attaching to this figure is that he is killed as a result of his father's actions within the murderous regime. The suffering of father, mother and sister following Bruno's death is thus cast as a kind of punishment for their complicity with National Socialism. This plot structure carries a great deal of emotive and ironic appeal. The fact that the father's murderous actions bring about his own son's death also creates a kind of tragic full circle in the narrative that readers may experience as aesthetically satisfying to some degree, as it produces a strong sense of closure. This sense of closure, however, together with the ironic plot element of the "wrong" child being murdered, does not leave much room for acknowledgement for the real, intended victims of the Nazi genocide, whose fates, condensed into the figures of Pavel and Schmuel, function as accessories to the demise of Bruno in Boyne's text. As Kertzer argues, children's literature about the Holocaust often offers closure and explanation in a problematic manner, "function[ing] primarily to explain what adult texts often claim is ultimately inexplicable" (1999, 239-40). In this sense, *The Boy in the Striped Pyjamas* is not unusual in its offering of closure to the reader; the nature of this closure however, which centres on innocence, death and punishment, is somewhat unusual. Weissman's suggestion that remembrance of the Holocaust usually reflects contemporary socio-cultural aspirations and ideologies, coupled with Kertzer's awareness of the didactic goals of children's literature dealing with this event (2002), thus casts an ambivalent light on Boyne's novel. While on one level the text has a clear didactic and moral intent in encouraging its readers to overcome and transgress prejudicial boundaries, it also suggests that the wrongdoings of parents are visited upon their children in a potentially frightening echo of the Old Testament: "Thou shalt not bow down thyself unto them, nor serve them: for I the LORD thy God [am] a jealous God, visiting the iniquity of the fathers upon the children (…) of them that hate me" (Deuteronomy 5:9, King James Bible).

In conjunction with Boyne's use of alcohol, sexual intrigue and adultery as leitmotifs in his construction of the corrupt adult world that surrounds and offsets Bruno's innocence, I would argue that this biblical echo suggests that *The Boy in the Striped Pyjamas* espouses a more old-fashioned, conservative morality than the "multicultural" agenda celebrated by Alice Curry (2010). This somewhat puritanical vein within the narrative, together with its idealizing, death-oriented construction of childhood innocence, may well be transmitting a troubling message to child readers as regards their own putative innocence as children, the degree of their agency within the adult-driven social world, and their culpability for the misdeeds of others. Furthermore, the novel's gross historical inaccuracy and highly problematic, stereotyped-based representation and sidelining of its Jewish figures mean that it is of limited educational value, to adult or child readers, as a text of the Holocaust. Rather, the text invokes the Holocaust as a highly-charged backdrop to its mythologizing of childhood innocence, its roughly-hewn critique of bourgeois patriarchy, and its moralistic fable of Old Testament retribution. Whether *The Boy in the Striped Pyjamas* contradicts Weissman's hypothesis that contemporary culture narrativizes the Holocaust according to its own ideological requirements, or alternately confirms it in signalling a new emergence of Christian-type conservatism in Anglophone literary production, remains to be seen. The novel certainly demonstrates the fact that Holocaust literature for children is far from being an ideologically "innocent" space, whilst this article has found its post-memorial stance of imaginative investment and "emotional truth" to conceal peculiar undercurrents of nostalgic desire and archly conservative, biblical morality.

Notes

[1] See, for example, Roberto Innocenti's 1985 picture book *Rose Blanche* (original French-language text by Cristophe Gallaz, Lausanne: Editions 24 Heures). See also Emer O'Sullivan's 2005 essay, Rose Blanche, Rosa Weiss, Rosa Blanca: A Comparative View of a Controversial Picture Book. *The Lion and the Unicorn* 29 (2): 152-70.

[2] See, for example, John Boyne's transcript of a talk given at Dublin City Libraries (Dublin City Libraries website: 10/11/2010).

[3] Siobhán Parkinson. Narrative Strategies in Two Recent Holocaust Novels in English. Unpublished paper presented at The Irish Society for the Study of Children's Literature conference: *What Do We Tell the Children,* Coláiste Mhuire,

Marino Institute of Education, Dublin: 8 and 9 February 2008. I am grateful to Siobhán for her permission to cite this paper here.

[4] For a historical study of childhood during the Third Reich, see Nicholas Stargardt's 2005 book, *Witnesses of War: Children's Lives Under the Nazis*. London: Jonathan Cape. See also Debbie Pinfold's 2001 analysis of the child's perspective in post-war German literature for adults, *The Child's View of the Third Reich in German Literature: The Eye among the Blind*. Oxford: Open University Press.

[5] See, for example, Hugh Cunningham. 2005. *Children and Childhood in Western Society Since 1500*, 2nd ed. Harlow: Pearson Longman; Hans-Heino Ewers. 1989. *Kindheit als poetische Daseinsform. Munich: W. Fink.;* James R. Kincaid. 1992. *Child-Loving: The Erotic Child and Victorian Culture.* New York; London: Routledge; Kevin Ohi. 2005. *Innocence and Rapture: The Erotic Child in Pater, Wilde, James, and Nabokov.* New York; Basingstoke: Palgrave Macmillan; Jacqueline Rose. 1994. *The Case of Peter Pan, Or, the Impossibility of Children's Fiction*, 2nd, revised ed. London: Macmillan.

[6] National Socialist culture is, of course, frequently represented through tropes of bourgeois decadence and patriarchal oppression. My point is that Boyne draws almost exclusively from this less historically specific mode of representation, at the expense of the text's historical reliability and accuracy.

[7] From Richter's 1978 novel, *I Was There*, 98: "A gorgeous fragrance wafted into the room….A blond platoon leader in Hitler Youth uniform minced in behind it. Cologne filled the room to the last corner. There wasn't a hair out of place, or a speck of dust on his uniform. His shoes were polished to a hard shine….A smile on his face, the sweet-smelling platoon leader looked us over….When he came to Otto, he chucked him under the chin and raised his head, forced him to meet his gaze. 'We will be friends,' he said in a velvety voice."

[8] Boyne, *The Boy in the Striped Pyjamas*, 172. The obvious biblical overtones of this scene, in which Bruno betrays Schmuel by denying that he knows him, are remarked upon by Siobhan Parkinson in her essay, Narrative Strategies in Two Recent Holocaust Novels in English.

References

Adorno, Theodor W. 1992. Commitment. *Notes to Literature*, eds. Theodor W. Adorno and Rolf Tiedmann, 76-94. New York: Columbia University Press.

—. 1958. Cultural Criticism and Society. *Prisms*, 17-34. Cambridge, MA: MIT Press.

Apitz, Bruno. 1958. *Nackt unter Wölfen*. Halle: Mitteldeutscher Verlag.

Assmann, Aleida. 1978."Werden was wir waren." Anmerkungen zur Geschichte der Kindheitsidee. *Antike und Abendland* XXIV: 98-124.

Benigni, Roberto. 1997. *La Vita É Bella (Life Is Beautiful)*. Cecchi Gori Group. 116 mins. Italy.

Beyer, Frank. 1963. *Nackt unter Wölfen (Naked among Wolves)*. Deutsche Film.116 mins. East Germany.

Boyne, John. 2006. *The Boy in the Striped Pyjamas*. Oxford: David Fickling.

—. Through the Eyes of Suffering Children. *The Times*, 21 June 2006. http://www.johnboyne.com/articles/Through%20The%20Eyes%20of%20Suffering%20Children.jpg. Date accessed 16 June 2011.

—. Transcript of Talk Given at Dublin City Libraries, 10 November 2010. Dublin City Libraries website, http://www.dublincitypubliclibraries.com/john-boyne-transcript. Date accessed 16 June 2011.

Cunningham, Hugh. 2005. *Children and Childhood in Western Society Since 1500*. 2nd ed. Harlow: Pearson Longman.

Curry, Alice. 2010. The "Blind Space" That Lies Beyond the Frame: Anne Provoost's *Falling* (1997) and John Boyne's *The Boy in the Striped Pyjamas* (2006). *International Research in Children's Literature* 31: 61-74.

Dogar, Sharon. 2010. *Annexed*. New York: Houghton Mifflin.

Dwork, Debórah. 1991. *Children With a Star: Jewish Youth in Nazi Europe*. New Haven, Connecticut and London: Yale University Press.

Eaglestone, Robert. 2007. Boyne's Dangerous Tale. *The Jewish Chronicle*, 22 March 2007: 23.

Ewers, Hans-Heino. 1989. *Kindheit Als Poetische Daseinsform: Studien zur Entstehung der Romantischen Kindheitsutopie im 18. Jahrhundert: Herder, Jean Paul, Novalis und Tieck*. Munich: W. Fink.

Gilbert, Ruth. 2010. Grasping the Unimaginable: Recent Holocaust Novels for Children by Morris Gleitzman and John Boyne. *Children's Literature in Education* 41(4): 355-66.

Gleitzman, Morris. 2006. *Once*. London: Penguin.

—. 2009. *Then*. London: Penguin.

Hirsch, Marianne. 1997. *Family Frames: Photography, Narrative, and Postmemory*. Cambridge, Massachusetts; London: Harvard University Press.

Innocenti, Roberto and Cristophe Gallaz. 1985. *Rose Blanche*. Lausanne: Editions 24 Heures.

James, Henry. 1985. *What Maisie Knew*. London: Penguin Classics.

Kertzer, Adrienne. 1999. "Do You Know What 'Auschwitz' Means?" Children's Literature and the Holocaust. *The Lion and the Unicorn* 23 (2): 238-56.

—. 2002. *My Mother's Voice: Children, Literature and the Holocaust*. Ontario and New York: Broadview Press.

Kincaid, James R. 1992. *Child-Loving: The Erotic Child and Victorian Culture*. New York and London: Routledge.

Klüger, Ruth. 2006. *Gelesene Wirklichkeit: Fakten und Fiktionen in der Literatur*. Göttingen: Wallstein.

Kokkola, Lydia. 2003. *Representing the Holocaust in Children's Literature*. New York and London: Routledge.

LaCapra, Dominick. 1998. *History and Memory After Auschwitz*. Ithaca and London: Cornell University Press.

Niven, Bill. 2007. *The Buchenwald Child: Truth, Fiction and Propaganda*. Rochester and New York: Camden House.

Ohi, Kevin. 2005. *Innocence and Rapture: The Erotic Child in Pater, Wilde, James, and Nabokov*. New York; Basingstoke: Palgrave Macmillan.

O'Sullivan, Emer. 2005. Rose Blanche, Rosa Weiss, Rosa Blanca: A Comparative View of a Controversial Picture Book. *The Lion and the Unicorn* 29 (2): 152-70.

Parkinson, Siobhán. 2008. Narrative Strategies in Two Recent Holocaust Novels in English. Presented at The Irish Society for the Study of Children's Literature conference: "What Do We Tell the Children". Coláiste Mhuire, Marino Institute of Education, Dublin, 8 and 9 February 2008.

Pinfold, Debbie. 2001. *The Child's View of the Third Reich in German Literature: The Eye Among the Blind*. Oxford: Open University Press.

Richter, Hans Peter. 1972. *I Was There*, trans. Edite Kroll. New York: Puffin.

Rose, Jacqueline. 1994. *The Case of Peter Pan, Or, The Impossibility of Children's Fiction*. 2nd, revised ed. London: Macmillan.

Stargardt, Nicholas. 2005. *Witnesses of War: Children's Lives Under the Nazis*. London: Jonathan Cape.

Weissman, Gary. 2004. *Fantasies of Witnessing: Postwar Efforts to Experience the Holocaust*. Ithaca and London: Cornell University Press.

Zusak, Markus. 2006. *The Book Thief*. New York: Random House.

DEATH AND THE LANDSCAPE
IN *THE DARK IS RISING* AND ITS ADAPTATIONS

JANE SUZANNE CARROLL

Death is an uncomfortable subject. Though it can raise complicated moral, social and spiritual questions, it is often treated as "taboo" (Wells 1988, 3). In Western cultures where old age is deferred through cosmetics and surgery, and illness is treated as unnatural, death has become "a forbidden subject, an embarrassment one would like to silence" (Bronfen and Goodwin 1993, 3). This silence may amount to a refusal to discuss death with children even though "youngsters need to learn not only about where babies come from, but also about this other very basic 'fact of life'" (Gibson and Zaidman 1991, 232). Knowledge of death and the acceptance of one's own mortality are an essential part of growing up. Of course, literature cannot prevent death or shield a reader from the grief it brings, but it can help a reader to deal with it. By allowing characters to "confront many of the same dilemmas faced by the children in our society [...] children's literature becomes a powerful tool for helping youngsters develop strategies for coping with their own struggles" (Nicholson and Pearson 2003, 6). By presenting death within a controlled environment, by providing a forum for both metaphorical and physical deaths, literature can offer a space within which the fears and questions death prompts can be explored.

This chapter will show how the landscape can provide a medium in which death can be treated in a mature, complex and articulate manner and will examine how Susan Cooper uses landscape in this way in her 1973 novel *The Dark Is Rising*. I will explore the representations of death in Cooper's text and in its two multimedia adaptations, the 1997 BBC4 radio play by David Calcutt and the 2007 film *The Seeker: The Dark Is Rising*, directed by David L. Cunningham and scripted by John Hodge. In both adaptations the significance of landscape is much reduced and, as a result, neither of these texts can draw upon the wealth of connotations and suggestions that Cooper builds in to her fictional world. While the world of the Old Ones is divided into forces of absolute good, spearheaded by

Merriman and the Lady, and forces of absolute evil, represented by Mitothin, also known as the Rider, it would be overly simplistic to read Light and Dark as analogous to Life and Death. For Cooper, life and death are not opposing forces but two elements of a continuous cycle which is evidenced in and supported by the natural world. Through landscape imagery Cooper's text articulates a complex relationship with death, and, through green spaces, integrates death within a cycle of life, decay and renewal which is ultimately positive. Calcutt's radio play, divorced from the visual qualities which are so essential to our traditional understanding of landscape (Johnson 2007, 22), is unable to present these cycles of death and renewal so convincingly and so removes many of the references to death from the text. On the other hand, Hodge's screenplay completely shies away from representing death and refuses to engage with it as anything other than destructive. I will argue that it is the absence of any meaningful relationship with landscape, rather than any particularly censorial impulse, which has led to the omission of death in these texts.

Literary landscapes may be read as an integrated mesh of topoi, each with its own unique physical features and symbolic functions. One of the most prominent—perhaps even dominant—topoi of Western literature is the green topos. Manifested as gardens, farms, pleasances and forests, the green topos, from its earliest inception in English literature, is expressly associated with the cycle of life, death and renewal (Wilhelm 1965). Although it may be "perverse to see only [...] decay and death [in green spaces]" (Robinson 2007, 153), it is impossible to overlook the continuity between the vital and lifeless aspects of the topos. Able to renew themselves, plants are emblems of immortality, but among them humanity is faced with its inevitable mortality. The green topos therefore, is both an expression and a symbol of the intricate relationship between linear and cyclical time in the landscape.

Through her effective use of green spaces, Cooper draws upon these associations and so, though death is omnipresent in *The Dark Is Rising*, it is always tempered by the promise of renewal. The novel opens on the day before Midwinter, and there are many signs of death—skeletal trees and carrion birds—but there are also signs of life and growth. These signs are integrated through an image of a green space: the Stantons' garden. Will looks out the window at the "wide grey sweep" of the lawn "with the straggling trees of the orchard still dark beyond [and] the old barn, the rabbit hutches, the chicken coops" (11). The orchard with its promise of fruit is "dark" and the connotations of harvest and plenty promised by the barn are undermined by the adjective "old". A little later, the interconnectedness of life and death is made abundantly clear when Will and his brother James visit a neighbouring farm, another manifestation of the green topos, in order to collect food for their pet rabbits. Farmer Dawson gives Will a message:

> "'Tell your mum I'll have ten birds off her tomorrow. And four rabbits. Don't look like that, young Will. If it's not their happy Christmas, it's one for the folks as'll have them'" (15).

This is the first direct reference in the text to death. Although Will is sad that his pets will be killed and eaten, Farmer Dawson makes it clear that such an attitude is unacceptable and reminds Will that the animals exist as part of a food chain, a natural, ecological cycle. He insists that we should not consider their feelings, but rather the feelings of the people who will enjoy eating them, who will have a happy Christmas. Here, on the farm, the deaths of some organisms prolong and support the lives of others.

Other references to the green topos and to the integration of death and regeneration include the greenery of the Christmas tree and the holly Will hangs over the doors and windows of his home both of which serve as a reminder that even in the bleakest winter there are green things: there is still the hope and the possibility of life. Cooper states that part of the Yule Log which the Stantons burn on Christmas Eve will be "saved as kindling for its successor" the following year (90). Thus, there is a direct continuity between the dying of one fire and the lighting of another. Though the individual log is used up, the values it represents continue indefinitely. The pattern of individual mortality and universal immortality is echoed through the hunting of the wren. In this St. Stephen's Day ritual the wren, the "king of the birds", is slain and buried (Lawrence 1997, 23). The hunting of the wren may be a version of the ancient and apparently universal fertility ritual identified by James Frazer. He suggests that the death of any green king—as the wild, hedge-dwelling bird must be regarded—is expressly linked to renewal (Frazer 1994, 273-99). The wren's death, like that of the rabbits and the hens, is a kind of sacrifice which ensures the continuity of life. Thus, the ritual of the Wren Boys is not just a quaint country custom Cooper refers to for a sense of rustic authenticity; it serves as a sure reminder that the wren, like all kings, is to be buried and its successor appointed and, as the ritual takes place within the forest, it reinforces the symbolic meaning of the green topos.

Closely linked to the hunting of the wren and to the midwinter fertility rituals is the figure of the Lady of the Light. At one level, she may be read as a version of Robert Graves's White Goddess, or as a positive, if somewhat distant, maternal figure, such as those identified by Naomi Wood (2004). These female figures are powerful symbols of fertility and, if the Lady is treated as part of this tradition, she may be seen to embody and internalize the cycles of death and renewal which were implicit in the green spaces of the text. Her disappearance from the great Hall of the Light comes as a devastating blow for Will, but she is symbolically resurrected during the hunting of the wren. Like the green king, the Lady's death is shown to be necessary, redemptive, purifying and one which carries the promise of renewal, both of the landscape and of life within that landscape.

These topological cycles of decay and renewal are once again embodied in the figure of Herne the Hunter. The power of the green space—the Wild Magic—is manifested in Herne. He is at once a symbol of growth and vitality and a symbol of death, related to Cerrunnos, a Celtic horned deity (Pennick 1996, 170), and to Arawn, the lord of the underworld who appears in the *Mabinogion* (Davies 2007, 3). While Cerrunnos and Arawn provide indigenous intertextual sources for Cooper's character, the story of a ghostly hunter and the wild hunt is "one of the most widely disseminated in Europe" (Bechmann 1990, 285). Though Herne is situated in Windsor Park he is also a universal figure, a manifestation of the awesome power of the green space. Appearing as a man with a stag's antlers and owlish eyes, he is at once predator and prey, a self-consuming figure which epitomizes the cycles of death and renewal inherent in the green topos (Bramwell 2009, 45). The Wild Hunt he leads brings violence and destruction, but also heralds the end of the winter and the beginning of the New Year.

However, while Herne and the Lady offer a means by which death may be celebrated, Cooper includes other deaths in her text which are more problematic. The deaths of Tom Stanton and Hawkin are precisely the kinds of human deaths which Gibson and Zaidman suggest have become "taboo" in modern children's literature (1991, 232). Tom's death, which takes place many years before the events of the novel, offers the reader a glimpse of the reality and hardship of human death. Significantly though, Tom's death is still linked to, and contextualized by, the green space because Will finds out about it while decorating the Christmas tree. While unpacking the decorations, Will finds a box of wooden ornaments that he does not remember seeing before. The ornaments are shaped like a set of initials, one for each member of the family. But there is an extra letter, a "T" which, as Mrs. Stanton explains, belonged to Tom, her first-born who died as an infant:

> "'That was Tom,' his mother said. 'I don't really know why I've never spoken to you younger ones about Tom. It was just so long ago…Tom was your little brother who died. He had something wrong with his lungs, a

disease some new babies get, and he only lived for three days after he was
born.' [...] Her voice sounded slightly muffled, and Will suddenly
regretted finding the letters" (93).

Here, the child's death is untimely and seems to jar against the ordered
cycles of death and regeneration posited throughout the novel through
references to the green topos. Will certainly feels this, and the box of
letters makes him uneasy. Nevertheless, Mrs. Stanton's words echo those
of Farmer Dawson. Death is something that happens, a natural and
intrinsic part of life and she remains pragmatic, assuring Will that she has
accepted Tom's death:

> "'Oh, gracious,' said Mrs. Stanton briskly, 'I'm not sad, love. It was a very
> long while ago [...] and, after all'—she gave a comical look around the
> room, cluttered with people and boxes—'a brood of nine should be enough
> for any woman'" (93).

Although her laughter seems to inadequately mask her emotions, Mrs.
Stanton does not try to shield her youngest son from the reality of Tom's
death, but she assures Will that the pain of death has been softened by time
and that life goes on. Her language is straightforward, practical. Although
Tom died as an infant, he died as a result of a disease. Thus, she provides
Will with causes and consequences and facts, avoiding euphemism and
analogy. Implicit in their conversation is her awareness that Will is now
old enough to discuss death and to be made aware of the facts of life. Mrs.
Stanton impresses upon Will the fact that there is logic and order to the
world and part of that order may include the deaths of children through
illness or accident. She also reminds her son that, though Tom's untimely
death was terrible and upsetting, her grief has blunted a little by the
passage of time. Furthermore, she hints at the need to keep living rather
than dwelling on the past. The death of an individual does not mean an end
to all life. Throughout the scene, the Christmas tree acts as a synecdoche
for the green topos, reinforcing the message that death leads, in time, to
growth and new life. For the topoanalytically attuned reader, the greenery
serves as a reassuring reminder that Tom's death is part of a natural cycle.

Cooper's awareness of the symbolism embedded in landscape topoi
allows her, not only to engage with, but also to subvert the expected tropes
and to present deaths which the topologically aware reader will understand
as problematic. Having witnessed a variety of real and metaphorical green
deaths which are ultimately positive, the young reader is presented at the
very end of *The Dark Is Rising* with a death which is traumatic, subversive
and unsettling.

Through her depiction of Hawkin's death, Cooper challenges the role of the Light and complicates the simple binaries of positive and negative which are so often, erroneously, attributed to the Light and the Dark. Though Hawkin appears as an old man, he is "a child of the thirteenth century" (112) and, in many ways, his childhood has been unnaturally extended. Hawkin is cursed with longevity as a punishment for betraying the Light and, though he longs for death, the event of his death and its implications within the text are hugely problematic. While adult deaths, and particularly parent deaths, often figure "as a plot device designed to place children in new, often precarious, situations—or to free them for adventures" (Gibson and Zaidman 1991, 232) and generally occur at, or just before, the start of the text, Hawkin's death in *The Dark Is Rising* is a graphic part of the narrative. He is thrown from his horse by Mitothin when the Wild Hunt arrives to chase the forces of the Dark from the Thames Valley. Although images of decay and mortality are omnipresent in the novel, this is the first and only death that Cooper forces us to witness:

> "Will peered closer, and saw with a shock that the dark heap was not a cloak, but a man. The figure lay face upward, twisted at a terrible angle. It was the Walker; it was Hawkin" (249).

The details of his agony are disturbing. Unlike the other deaths in the text, this death is ugly and undignified, full of physical and psychological pain:

> "He gasped with pain as he tried to move his head; then panic came into his eyes. 'Only my head...I feel my head, because of the pain. But my arms, my legs, they are...not there....'
> There was a dreadful, desolate hopelessness in the lined face now. Hawkin looked full at Merriman. 'I am lost,' he said, 'I know it. Will you make me live on, the worst suffering of all now come? The last right of a man is to die. You have prevented it all this time; you have made me live on through centuries when often I longed for death [...]' The grief and longing in his voice were intolerable; Will turned his head away" (250).

This scene forces a complex range of emotions upon the reader. We are torn between pity and horror but Will Stanton cannot even bear to witness Hawkin's final moments. Cooper does not shy away from the horror of Hawkin's suffering, but lays the facts of human mortality bare.

Hawkin's death is topoanalytically distinct from all others in the novel. At first glance, his death appears closely connected with the green topos. He dies on a little island in the centre of the swollen river Thames which Cooper deftly connects to the green topos by mentioning a gentle breeze, the trees, the shade and the moving water which are characteristic of the *locus amoenus,* the "lovely place" of classical literature (Cuirtius 1953, 186). Though Cooper seems to preserve the basic elements of the topos, the astute reader will note that something is very wrong with this *locus amoenus.* The regenerating water is dark and freezing cold, the breeze is chill and the trees are gnarled and bare. Close attention to landscape—to the subtle signals which are encoded within the imagery— enables the reader to see that Cooper is doing something different here. Once we are aware the landscape is not quite right, we can understand that the death framed by this space is also at odds with the natural cycles of decay and regeneration posited by the green topos.

While the other green deaths are shown to be of practical use or even as something positive, Hawkin's prompts the reader—and Will—to question the Light and what it stands for. It does not free Will for adventures but rather problematizes the adventures he has already had. Readers of the *The Dark Is Rising* sequence will know that the Old Ones have the power to alleviate suffering, but Merriman does not attempt to ease Hawkin's pain, despite claiming to love him "as if he were a son" (133). Merriman's decision to put his servant's life in danger in the past is cruelly parodied in his decision not to help Hawkin die in the present. In this moment, Merriman is revealed by Cooper to be just as capable of selfishness and cruelty as any of the Lords of the Dark. In an interview, Cooper observes that "the sinister side of Merriman Lyon, and indeed all the Old Ones, is that absolute good, like absolute evil is fanatical" (Cooper 1996, 193). Merriman's decision to put Hawkin's life in danger is the first hint of this fanaticism, but all through Cooper's novel there are hints that Merriman may not be as good or as moral as he initially appears. He is continually described in terms of the fierceness of his face and the coldness of his demeanour. Unlike the warm, friendly Light in John Hodge's screenplay, the Light of Susan Cooper's novel is fierce, blinding, and absolute. Merriman cares only for his cause; he does not really value the friendship and love of the mortal Hawkin and so does not move to relieve his suffering. In this moment it becomes clear that Merriman regards each human life as being like the Yule Log, individually expendable so long as a greater chain of life may continue.

Hawkin's death also complicates Will's status as an Old One. In his final moments, Hawkin confesses that death is something he has "longed for" and wanted desperately. For Hawkin, death is the essence of mortality and, thus, the essence of what is human. As an Old One, Will is "outside time" (112) and cannot die. In this moment, in this subverted green space, the reader suddenly understands that his immortality is as much a curse as a blessing. His unnaturally long life will bring him untold pain as he has to watch all of his family and all of the things he has loved as a mortal child pass away. When he turns away from Hawkin, he symbolically turns away from mortality and becomes closer to the fanatical Light that Merriman represents. Indeed, as the *The Dark Is Rising* series progresses, we see Will transform into a version of his master. Towards the end of *The Grey King* (1975), Will tries to justify the "cold absolute good" of the Light, arguing that "'in this sort of a war, it is not possible to pause, to smooth the way for one human being, because even that one small thing could mean an end of the world for all the rest'" (Cooper 1975, 136). At this point it is clear that Will has grown to be like Merriman, willing to expend human life for what he believes to be a greater cause. In doing this, Cooper makes Hawkin's death far more than a simple event, using the episode to open a discourse on the true priorities and values within her text. Thus, Cooper positions her text in relation to what Kathryn James describes as a growing field of adolescent literature in which death is not only present, but openly discussed (2009, 3). The strange landscape imagery, in deviating from the normal qualities of the topos, flags Hawkin's death as unusual. This green space diverges from the expected message of comfort and renewal which is canonically embedded in this topos. Hawkin's death does not reassure us that the world has order, but demands that we learn how to question that order.

David Calcutt's adaptation of *The Dark Is Rising* for BBC Radio 4 (November 1997) simplifies the narrative and omits a great many of Cooper's references to death. Some of this is purely pragmatic: the four thirty-minute episodes simply cannot depict the complexities of the novel in its entirety. For instance, it would be confusing to have all eight of Will's surviving siblings talking in the play so the number of siblings is cut to three. Hence, Will is not the seventh son of a seventh son and the references to Tom are taken out. Similarly, the conversation about the rabbits and hens with Farmer Dawson is cut, as is the sequence with the Wren-Boys, both perhaps seen as atmospheric rather than essential to the plot. However, Calcutt exploits the radio-play format by including references to death which the novel could not draw on. In the opening scene, which takes place in the noisy kitchen, we hear Wagner's *Ride of the Valkyries*, which carries strong suggestions of death and resurrection. Indeed, the soundscape of the play, with crows chattering throughout and Martin Alcock's sinister score, is richly connotative of death.

Calcutt is also supremely aware of the significance of greenery in Cooper's text and goes to great lengths to allude to it in the play. For instance, he adds in a reference to a Green Man carved in the

Huntercombe Church and in the scene when Will has a vision of the Lady, he describes her standing in a stone circle with a spear in one hand and a cup in the other, uniting symbols of violence and sustenance. Calcutt makes her connection with greenery and with vernal renewal explicit. She tells Will that this "is the world as it was. The world as it will be. I shall return and it shall return." The scene with Herne the Hunter is especially significant in the radio-play and Calcutt adds lines of dialogue to make Herne's appearance and his function within the text more explicit. Merriman says that Herne is "the power of nature in human form. It knows neither good nor bad, only the wildness of the world and the joy of the kill." Thus, Calcutt presents Herne as entwining the paradoxical functions of the green topos; in him death and life are inextricably linked.

However, unlike Cooper, Calcutt does not subvert the expected forms and functions of topoi. In the radio-play Hawkin's death is depicted, not as a great moment of crisis, but as a moment of true reconciliation between Merriman and his estranged servant. Here, rather than standing aloof, Merriman uses his powers to end Hawkin's suffering. He says "Hawkin, your journey is at an end. It's time for you to rest [...] I give you your death." There is great tenderness in Merriman's voice and Hawkin too demonstrates far greater magnanimity than Cooper's original character. His final words to Will impart both a blessing and advice for the future: "You have the signs... use them well." His death comes as a gentle release. Will describes it as "nothing...only dust on the earth, taken and scattered by the wind." The physicality and the brutality of Hawkin's death are much reduced. So, though Calcutt demonstrates awareness of the significance of landscape in Cooper's work, he stops short of engaging with the topoi in the same way. He does not include the subversive and unsettling elements of landscape which make Cooper's texts so powerful. His decision to reconcile Merriman and Hawkin at the end of the radio-play reinforces rather than redresses the stark binaries of Light and Dark, good and evil.

The 2007 Walden Media film adaptation of Cooper's text was also entitled *The Dark Is Rising* but, for the purposes of this discussion and to avoid unnecessary confusion, I will refer to the film as *The Seeker*, the title under which it was released in the United States of America. Scripted by John Hodge and directed by David L. Cunningham, the film diverges from Cooper's original text at many points. In an interview, Cooper claimed that "violence" had been done to her text in order to make *The Seeker* (see Adler 2007) but, although the film draws on technical and special effects to produce a sense of immediacy and vivacity, it is actually far less violent and disturbing than Cooper's original. While death and human suffering are very much a part of the world of Cooper's text and both Will and the reader have to come to terms with this kind of pain over the course of the narrative, there is no equivalent place for death in *The Seeker*. Although the novel opens in a cold, wintry landscape, full of signs and symbols of death and decay, the film bursts open with light and colour. The opening scene is, quite literally, quick. The sequence shows Will's last day of school before the Christmas holidays; students of all ages move quickly through the corridors, laughing and jostling, frantically clicking away on mobile telephones, personal stereos and digital cameras. The buzz of conversation and technology fills the screen. The speed of the sequence is enhanced by short shots and rapid cuts between images. There is a great sense of energy and immediacy here, as well as a sexual undercurrent provided by Maggie Burns with her red scarf and her equally red lips. The mood is utterly different to the quiet and contemplative opening of *The Dark Is Rising*.

Though there are several shots of rooks in the early part of the film, indicating perhaps that death is part of the world, Will is cut off from that world by listening almost continuously to a personal stereo. Will's separation from his environment is the first indication that landscape has no importance in *The Seeker*. Indeed, the green topos, along with the cycle of life, death and rebirth which it entails, is all but absent. This modern, urbanized world is far removed from the harsh realities of slaughter and harvest and although traditional carols may be heard through the speakers in the shopping centre Will visits, there is no sense that the festivities are celebrations of the cycle of decay and regeneration. Here, death is not a part of any natural or ecological cycle but is presented as something distinctly unnatural. Or, rather, supernatural, for death in *The Seeker* is shown as the direct consequence of the actions of the Dark.

It is a mark of Hodge and Cunningham's misinterpretation of Cooper's text and of their lack of engagement with landscape tropes, that they ascribe all of the deaths to the Dark. Death is always totally malignant. When Will is shown a glimpse of what the world will be like if he fails to collect the six signs in time, there is a montage of accidents, car crashes, storms and sickness. The crumbling of national icons such as Big Ben and, tellingly, the Statue of Liberty, indicates the extent of the damage caused by the Dark. The Dark will bring destruction—not the subtle wearing down of human spirit promised by Cooper's Mitothin—but outright chaos. In the world of *The Seeker* there is no such thing as a necessary death, or of a quiet death. Death is something to be resisted and even rejected outright. Indeed, the two apparent deaths in the film are both the result of direct and malicious action by the Dark and both are magically deferred at the end of the film. So while there is a suggestion, or perhaps the illusion, of death, the suffering it causes is mitigated over the course of the film.

The first of these supernatural pseudo-deaths unfolds when Farmer Dawson and his companion, George, enter a public house in Huntercombe village. Once inside, they are trapped by the Rider. A violent fight breaks out and the farmer is seen to be thrown backwards by the force of an explosion as a thousand rooks rush towards the two men. Farmer Dawson is seen to escape but George fails to emerge from the building. His absence and Dawson's distress lead us to believe that he has been killed by the forces of the Dark. After the final stand-off between Will and the Rider, however, George walks out from behind a wall, smiling wryly at Will and the camera, then comically spits out a crow's feather. He is unscathed, unchanged in manner or appearance. The message here is clear: the Light, in defeating the power of the Dark, has also thwarted death. In the world of *The Seeker*, death is neither final nor absolute.

The other cancelled death in the film is that of Tom. Tom plays a far greater role in *The Seeker* than in *The Dark Is Rising*. In *The Seeker*, Will stumbles across a box of photographs and letters and, by quizzing his mother, finds out that he had a twin brother, Tom, born only a few moments before him. Although this conversation takes place out of doors and therefore hints at a connection with the green topos, this connection is not properly extrapolated. Here, Mrs. Stanton weeps openly, unable to accept the reality of her loss. But though her tears are an open and outward sign of grief, the reality underlying this grief is not that of death. Mrs. Stanton says simply, "he was gone". Tom has not died, but vanished. "Gone" is a common euphemism for the word and the reality of death, but here Mrs. Stanton uses the word literally. Tom was kidnapped and though the knowledgeable reader may guess that the agents of the Dark are responsible, the Stantons do not know what exactly has happened to their son.

Tom's disappearance forms an integral part of the narrative of *The Seeker*, giving Will a very personal reason to defeat the Dark. At the very end of the film, the Rider demands the Six Signs in return for Tom's life. Tom, we now learn, was not killed at all but has been held hostage by the Dark for almost fourteen years. Will ultimately outwits the Rider and he and his brother return home to their delighted parents. So, although Hodge hints at death, he ultimately allows Tom to live and the family to be happily reunited. Yet this ending is problematic for several reasons. Firstly, the reappearance of Tom demands that Will's family find out something about his role as an Old One; and, secondly, Tom is completely unharmed by his time as the Rider's captive. This implies that the magical forces of the Light are accepted as everyday and that the Dark has no real and permanent effect on the world. All bad things come to an end and past events may be entirely forgotten. Thus, *The Seeker* actively avoids dealing with any emotional or psychological trauma. Death is deferred and then negated altogether. There is no natural cycle of life, death, decay and renewal. The passage of time does not have any lasting effect. Although Tom has grown up during his captivity, he is still instantly recognized and joyfully greeted by his family.

Perhaps the most obvious and significant omission in Hodge's text is that of Hawkin. As I have shown, in *The Dark Is Rising* Hawkin is a problematic figure who challenges the simple binary divisions of good and evil. He is both a traitor and a victim of circumstance and therefore draws complicated responses from the reader. His presence forces readers to re-examine the role of the Old Ones, denying the easy option of viewing Merriman as a simply-drawn, stock, good character and, by extension, demanding that we question the values Merriman stands for. By failing to include Hawkin in his screenplay, Hodge glosses over the questions Cooper posits in her text. The child viewer does not have to ask whether the Light can do evil or if the Dark can do good and, likewise, is not asked to question the rightness of the Light, or whether Merriman is deserving of trust and Will's loyalty. In contrast, the questions raised by Cooper's representation of Hawkin, and flagged by her treatment of landscape in his death-scene, prevent readers from being comfortable or complacent in their treatment of the Light.

It is possible that Hodge's refusal to ask these questions—never mind answer them—is potentially damaging to a young audience. Gibson and Zaidman suggest that "most psychologists and literary critics agree that ignoring death or at most whispering the word is unhealthy" (1991, 232). Indeed, some critics have even suggested that denying children's fears often increases them (Duncan et al. 1986, 28-44; Protinsky 1985, 11, 95-97). Several contemporary reviews of *The Seeker* point out that the film was aimed at a much younger audience than its source text (Adler 2007) but perhaps it is more accurate to say that the film was aimed at a more naïve audience than Cooper's text. In failing to problematize the relationship between good and evil, John Hodge fails to make his text suitable for a transitional audience who, aware of their own growth into maturity, will experience the "death" of their childhood and have a burgeoning awareness of their own mortality.

Although Hodge's screenplay is based on Cooper's text, *The Seeker* is totally cut away from the historical and literary intertexts which are integral to the original and therefore at a remove from the intertextually embedded landscape. Hodge "assiduously removed every trace of the pagan (i.e. non-Judeo-Christian) elements that were crucial to the original plot, all that fine old Celtic/Arthurian folklore—the Sleepers, Herne the Hunter, the Old Magic—presumably because they ran counter to the 'family values approach to positive messages' which the film's makers [Walden Media] seek to impart" (Danielsen 2007). Will's status as an American, an outsider to the folk traditions which inform *The Dark Is Rising*, could present an interesting opportunity to introduce and integrate these traditions for a new audience but this opportunity is put aside by Hodge's decision to omit Herne, Hawkin, the Lady and all of the other motifs and intertexts which allowed Cooper to open a dialogue on the meaning and function of death. As a result, neither the audience nor the characters in this text are made conscious of the passage of time, of change or of the inevitability of death.

In *The Dark Is Rising*, Cooper demonstrates that landscape is all-important as a space in which complex issues can be articulated. Through the medium of the green topos, she presents a view of death as integral to the natural world. Through her careful subversion of the expected criteria of the topos, she also raises complicated moral questions and encourages the reader to engage with, and to question, her representations of good and evil throughout the text. "In reducing her narrative to a simplistic good-versus-evil dialectic, the film contradicts the very spirit of her original books" (Danielsen 2007), and overlays a crude Christian paradigm—a deeply ironic move considering that Cooper's *Sequence* had been condemned by several major religious groups, including The Church of Scotland's Board of Social Responsibility, who accused Cooper of "undermining the Christian faith" (Mikkelsen 1998, 85). However, it has been argued here that by "experimenting with fantasy's inner core, breaking [...] its conventions" (Egoff 1988, 45) and by representing death in a variety of ways, Cooper encourages the reader to make the transition from naïve and unquestioning acceptance of the conventions of fantasy literature to a new kind of sophisticated and demanding readership wherein the values of good and evil, light and dark, may be analyzed and challenged. By encoding these issues in the landscape, she ensures that the messages are implicit rather than explicit, thereby shielding readers who are too inexperienced to interpret the signs for themselves from these issues. In his adaptation of Cooper's text, David Calcutt picks up on a lot—but not all—of these encoded ideas and presents a rather more straightforward version of the green space. On the other hand, John Hodge's screenplay has no engagement with landscape, and completely fails to articulate these difficult and complex ideas, resulting in a superficial view of landscape and a simplistic view of the struggle between the Light and the Dark.

Proper attention to the established canonical tropes in landscape representation allows authors like Cooper to use the landscape in their texts to supplement and support the narrative. In such texts, landscape is not simply the backdrop to the narrative action but "the very stuff from which the story will be woven" (Paterson 1995, 95). Treated in this way, landscape becomes a deeply significant medium whereby complex issues and ideas may be presented to the reader. Thus, though death may be continually "silence[d]" (Bronfen and Goodwin 1993, 3) in children's literature, landscape, and in particular the green space, allows it to be freshly articulated, explored, problematized and expressed.

References

Adler, Margot. 2007. Author Uncertain about 'Dark' Leap to Big Screen. http://www.npr.org/templates/story/story.php?storyId=14783609 . Date accessed 25 August 2011.

Bechmann, Paul. 1990; 1984. *Trees and Man: The Forest in the Middle Ages*. New York: Paragon House.

Bramwell, Peter. 2009. *Pagan Themes in Modern Children's Literature, Fiction: Green Man, Shamanism, Earth Mysteries*. Basingstoke and New York: Palgrave Macmillan.

Bronfen, Elisabeth and Sarah Webster Goodwin. 1993. *Death and Representation*. Baltimore, Maryland: John Hopkins University Press.

Calcutt, David. 1997. *The Dark Is Rising*, BBC Radio 4.

Cooper, Susan. 1973. *The Dark Is Rising*. London: Penguin.

—. 1975. *The Grey King*. London: Puffin Books.

—. 1977. *Silver on the Tree*. London: Puffin Books.

—. 1996. *Dreams and Wishes: Essays on Writing for Children*. New York: McElderry.

Cuirtius, Ernst Robert. 1953. *European Literature and The Latin Middle Ages*, trans. Willard R. Trask. London and Henley: Routledge and Kegan Paul.

Cullinan, Bernice E. and Diane Goetz Person, eds. 2005. *The Continuum Encyclopedia of Children's Literature*. London: Continuum.

Cunningham, David L.,dir. 2007. *The Seeker: The Dark Is Rising*. Walden Media.

Danielsen, Shane. 2007. The Dark is Rising, So Avoid It If You Can. *The Guardian* 9 October.
http://www.guardian.co.uk/film/filmblog/2007/oct/09/thedarkisrisingso avoidit . Date accessed 2 August 2011.

Davies, Sionad, trans. 2007. *The Mabinogion*. Oxford: Oxford University Press.

Duncan, B. L., M.A. Kraus, and M.B. Parks. 1986. Children's Fears and Nuclear War: A Systems Strategy for Change. *Youth and Society* 18(1): 28-44.

Egoff, Sheila. 1988. *Worlds Within, Children's Fantasy from the Middle Ages to Today*. New York: American Library Association.

Frazer, James. 1994;1922. *The Golden Bough: A Study in Magic and Religion*. Oxford: Oxford University Press.

Gibson, Lois Raunch and Laura M. Zaidman. 1991. Death in Children's Literature: Taboo or Not Taboo? *Children's Literature Association Quarterly* 16: 232-234.

James, Kathryn. 2009. *Death, Gender and Sexuality in Contemporary Adolescent Literature*. New York: Routledge.

Johnson, Matthew. 2007. *Ideas of Landscape*. Oxford: Blackwell.

Lawrence, Elizabeth Atwood. 1997. *Hunting the Wren: Transformation of Bird to Symbol: A Study in Human-Animal Relationships*. Tennessee: University of Tennessee Press.

Mikkelsen, Nina. 1998. *Susan Cooper*. New York: Twayne.

Nicholson, Janice I. and Quinn M. Pearson. 2003. Helping Children Cope with Fears: Using Children's Literature in Classroom Guidance. *American School Counsellor Association* 7(1): 15-19.
http://www.schoolcounselor.org/files/7-1-15%20Nicholson.pdf. Date accessed 20 August 2011.

Paterson. Katherine. 1995. *A Sense of Wonder: On Reading and Writing Books for Children*. New York: Plume.

Pennick, Nigel. 1996. *Celtic Sacred Spaces*. London: Thames and Hudson.

Protinsky, H. 1985. Treatment of Children's Fears: A Strategic Utilization Approach. *Journal of Marital and Family Therapy* 11: 95-97.

Robinson, Philip. 2007. *The Faber Book of Gardens*. London: Faber and Faber.

Wells, Rosemary. 1988. *Helping Children Cope with Grief*. London: Sheldon Press.

Wilhelm, James J. 1965. *The Cruelest Month: Spring, Nature, and Love in Classical and Medieval Lyrics*. New Haven and London: Yale University Press.

Wood, Naomi. 2004. (Em)bracing Icy Mothers: Ideology, Identity and Environment in Children's Fantasy. *Wild Things: Children's Culture and Ecocriticism*, eds. Sidney I. Dobrin and Kenneth B. Kidd, 198-214. Michigan: Wayne State University Press.

PART III

WHAT DO WE TELL THE CHILDREN ABOUT RACE AND NATIONAL IDENTITY?

THE 9/11 MEDIA AFTERMATH AND CULTURAL IDENTITY POLITICS IN ADOLESCENT FICTION: RESPONSES FROM THE SOUTH ASIAN DIASPORA

SHEHRAZADE EMMAMBOKUS

Following the World Trade Center and Pentagon attacks on 11 September 2001, the international news media was gripped by the events that took place. Television networks suspended their schedules to focus on these events; images of the Twin Towers collapsing were repeated on television; radio networks replayed eye-witness interviews and the front pages of newspapers were dominated with headlines and images of these attacks.

Sociologists (Arnett 1995; Lengua et al. 2005; Pechmann et al. 2005; Villani 2001) widely recognize that contemporary media play a significant role in influencing young people's identity development. Children, as Susan Villani (2001, 392) states, "learn their behaviours and have their value systems shaped by media". Within the genre of children's literature from the South Asian diaspora—texts written by and about people who are from, or whose ancestors are from, the Indian subcontinent: Bangladesh, Bhutan, India, Nepal, The Maldives, Pakistan and Sri Lanka—there are a number of books that explore the media's handling of 9/11. Marina Budhos's *Ask Me No Questions* (2006) and Mitali Perkins's *First Daughter: Extreme American Makeover* (2007) are two such novels. These books recognize the role that the media plays in shaping young people's self-identities and they critique the media's handling of 9/11 by exploring the reactions and responses of young individuals from the South Asian diaspora, not only to the events of 9/11, but more specifically, to the news media's coverage of these events (Cainkar 2002, 2004; Dreher 2006; Poynting and Noble 2004).

Ask Me No Questions and *First Daughter,* both published in America, were two of the earliest novels to depict life in the U.S. for South Asian diasporic youth following the events of 9/11. Perkins and Budhos, both of South Asian descent, grew up in America: Perkins was born in India and moved to the U.S. when she was seven years old and Budhos was born and raised in New York. Like all authors, Perkins and Budhos have their own ideological and cultural agendas that have influenced how they have chosen to construct their protagonists and both wanted to provide their readers with a voice that reflected the feelings and experiences of South Asian diasporic youths and communities post-9/11.

Ask Me No Questions tells the story of fourteen-year-old Nadira Hossain and her older sister, Aisha, who are living with their family in America in the wake of the 9/11 attacks. Nadira and Aisha's family, originally from Bangladesh, live in New York City. However, as their visas have expired, the Hossains flee to the Canadian border to apply for asylum for fear of how they will be treated in America for two reasons: firstly because they are illegal immigrants and, secondly, because they are Muslim. As expressed in the endnote of her novel, Budhos wanted to give a voice to the people who became the victims of racial profiling and harassment in America as a result of 9/11, and through Nadira and Aisha she is able to project this voice.

Similarly, Perkins asserts that her novel is "a story of celebrating and using your authentic voice" (Smith 2008, 23), and her protagonist Sameera, via Sameera's blog, is able to speak to and on behalf of individuals like herself. *First Daughter* tells the story of Sameera Righton, also known as "Sparrow" by her close friends and family, who, at the age of three, was adopted by American parents from an orphanage in Pakistan. Now sixteen years old, Sameera leaves school in Europe to join her parents in America to help promote her father's campaign for presidency and is given, as the subtitle of the novel indicates, a makeover to make her look and seem more "American". During her makeover, the PR firm that her father hires tries to repress Sameera's voice and identity. However, Sameera notably does not allow her voice to be censored, highlighting the fact that what she has to say is important and needs to be heard.

Through their protagonists, both Budhos and Perkins reassure their readers that, despite the reporting methods employed by the media during its 9/11 coverage and the subsequent pressure it placed on young individuals to reassess their cultural self-identities, young people ultimately have the right to choose their own cultural identities. Like Sameera, Nadira and Aisha, many of those who identify with these characters and are part of a diaspora have been enculturated with both their "home" (the country in which they live) and "homeland" (the country where their family and ancestors are from) cultures; that is, they have been raised within two (or more) different cultural spheres and have consequently absorbed the traits and values of these cultures. This process enables diasporic individuals to determine their hybrid cultural identities as they simultaneously embody and project different aspects of the different cultures that they have been enculturated with. These cultural traits overlap with one another and the cultural identity that the individual chooses to project is never fixed and is constantly being renegotiated. As there is no definitive cultural identity model that takes enculturation into account, I have labelled this negotiation of cultural self-identities as "Overlapping Space" (Emmambokus 2011).

Borrowing from Homi Bhabha (1994), Avtar Brah (1996), and Stuart Hall (1996), the concept of Overlapping Space respectively fuses ideas of third space, diaspora space and translation: it recognizes that when two cultures hybridize, a third emerges, that hybridized cultures and individuals are influenced by multiple subject positions (Brah 1996, 208), and that individuals who belong to cultures of hybridity (Hall 1996, 310) translate and reinterpret their cultures of origin. However, the Overlapping Space model recognizes that although cultures are reinvented and redefined during hybridization, in order for people to maintain their identification(s) with their "home" and "homeland" cultures, some cultural elements and codes are faithfully reproduced. So whereas Bhabha claims that the hybrid product is "neither the one nor the other" (Bhabha 1994, 25), this theory cannot be fully applied to identities. Using myself as an example, I am *not* happy to say that I am *neither* British *nor* South Asian for two reasons. Firstly, the suggestion that I am "neither the one nor the other" implies that I do not fit in or belong to either culture. Secondly, as a result of enculturation, I consider myself to be part of both cultures. Within the British context I class myself as British-Asian. Hybrid Overlapping Space identities embody both "home" and "homeland" cultures and are the one *and* the other, and the characters Sameera, Nadira and Aisha exemplify this.

Drawing on media, cultural and children's literature theory, this chapter argues that *Ask Me No Questions* and *First Daughter* foreground the importance of autonomy. It begins by exploring how both Muslim individuals and those labelled "Muslim" because of their real or imagined associations with Islam (hereafter referred to as "Muslim") felt scapegoated and singled out as a result of the media's focus on 9/11. By closely analyzing the texts, and drawing from the works of W. E. B. Du Bois (1989) and Frantz Fanon (1986), I will argue that these novels establish how the media helped facilitate the development of multi-person consciousness which, in turn, left many young people feeling "visible", vulnerable and open to racial and cultural discrimination and attack. To counter these feelings some young people, post-9/11, chose either to assimilate into the dominant culture or to exhibit what are referred to as reactive ethnicity techniques. Engaging with sociological investigations analyzing this phenomenon, this chapter also traces how the characters work against the external pressures placed on them to reform their cultural identities. I therefore suggest that the characters' struggles are potentially able to offer readers who relate to these texts a form of bibliotherapy, which, as John Pardeck (1995, 83) argues, aims:

> "(a) to provide information on problems, (b) to provide insight into problems, (c) to stimulate discussion about problems, (d) to communicate new values and attitudes, (e) to create an awareness that others have dealt with similar problems, and (f) to provide solutions to problems".

Bibliotherapy tries to "impart a sense of normality" (Coleman and Ganong 1990, 327) upon the reader "that otherwise might be absent" (ibid.) and studies (Hayes and Amer 1999; Shechtman 2000; Betzalel and Shechtman 2010) have shown that literature can be used successfully to help young people cope with their emotional problems and concerns. Children's literature theorists and critics have also discussed the bibliotherapeutic potential of stories aimed at younger readers. Bruno Bettelheim, for example, argues that fairy tales can be used to help children "master the psychological problems of growing up" (1976,7) and Kenneth Kidd contends that "there seems to be a consensus now that children's literature is the most rather than the least appropriate literary forum for trauma work" (2005, 120).

There are several different forms of bibliotherapy; however this chapter is primarily interested in the potential effects of cognitive bibliotherapy. Cognitive bibliotherapy is a self-administered form of bibliotherapy which involves little or no contact with a therapist (Shechtman 2000), and a recent study (Betzalel and Shechtman 2010) has shown that cognitive bibliotherapy can be effective in reducing social anxiety in children. *Ask Me No Questions* and *First Daughter* have the potential to offer readers a form of cognitive bibliotherapy. Readers can see how, following the events of 9/11, Sameera, Nadira and Aisha coped with their new visibilities, how these new visibilities impacted their hybrid Overlapping Space identities and how they resolved the cultural self-identity tensions that emerged from these new visibilities. Furthermore, by acknowledging these tensions, these texts recognize and in turn legitimize readers' own potential responses to the media's coverage of 9/11. Ultimately, these novels, by exploring the cultural self-identity tensions that the media helped fuel, not only acknowledge and legitimize

Overlapping Space identities, they support the readers' right to choose how they negotiate this identity.

Media attacks post-9/11

As a result of the negative news focus on Islam post-9/11, many Muslim/"Muslim" individuals felt victimized (Cainkar 2002, 2004; Dreher 2006; Poynting and Noble 2004). *Ask Me No Questions* and *First Daughter* explore how such individuals felt scapegoated, targeted and attacked by the media in the wake of 9/11. Throughout *Ask Me No Questions*, Nadira makes frequent references to television. For example, when her family are stopped at the Canadian border, Nadira states: "It's funny how long it can take to arrest a person. You'd think it would be like on TV" (14); when the police come to arrest Uncle, she observes: "The other man is young and is wearing a quilted vest. I've only ever seen one of those on TV" (80-81); when Nadira goes with Tareq to buy a social security card from an underground resistance group she makes three references to television: "I can hear the low warble of a TV" (121), "I want everything to be the way it was before we went to Canada, when Ma and Abba let me watch TV for an hour every night" (122) and "I can see Tareq's silhouette looming in the doorway, the blue light of the TV through the lace curtains" (123); and finally whilst waiting for her father's case to be heard in court, Nadira asserts: "I keep expecting to enter some kind of huge courtroom, just like on TV" (129). Significantly, all these references to television are made when Nadira is in danger or feels threatened. For Nadira, television has come to symbolize danger and, by extension, the news media as aggressor. *First Daughter*, like *Ask Me No Questions*, also focuses on the news media's aggressive handling of 9/11:

> "She was only a few steps from the limo when someone blocked her way. 'Are you an American citizen, young lady?' a gruff voice barked....
> 'Don't answer him,' Tara called sharply from inside the limo. *Don't worry, I won't*, Sameera thought, trying to get around the foul-smelling man, who seemed about three times her size. *If I open my mouth I'll hurl on him.*
> 'I asked: ARE YOU A CITIZEN OF THE UNITED STATES?'" (22).

The reporter's questions are extremely invasive and his intrusion is reinforced via his repulsive physical presence: he is physically too close, his offensive smell and breath overwhelm Sameera, and his size blocks her from getting away. Her nausea symbolically reflects the discomfort felt by those classed as "them"—those who felt that their national loyalties and ties were being questioned by the media post-9/11. This encounter with "Mr. Halitosis" positions Sameera as the "eternal" immigrant: someone who, regardless of her ties to her country of residence, will always be an outsider or have her "home" affiliations called into question. Furthermore, Mr. Halitosis reflects some of the sentiments actually expressed in the news media; for example, John Mackinlay (2001, para. 13), writing for the *Observer*, states that Osama bin Laden's

"constituency is the immigrant and dispossessed, the internally displaced, second-generation migrants, refugees and rural communities which have fled from war and famine to unhappy and overcrowded metropolitan areas".

Mackinlay clearly groups all immigrants—including second generations—as "them", as Other, as eternal immigrants. Sameera's encounter with Mr. Halitosis highlights not only how the media questioned the loyalties of Muslim/"Muslim" individuals and groups following the 9/11 attacks, but also how these individuals and groups felt scapegoated by the media post 9/11.

By depicting the news media as aggressors, both novels highlight the discriminatory reporting techniques and styles that were employed. This may enable young readers to appreciate how some Muslim/"Muslim" people, because of their real or imagined links to Islam, and, by extension, to the terror threats of 9/11, felt as though they were being attacked by the news media. These novels, therefore, draw attention to the detrimental effects the media's focus had on hybrid Overlapping Space identities, and, more importantly, by engaging directly with these experiences these texts have the potential to offer those who relate to these experiences a form of bibliotherapy. Discussing young adult fiction, Janet Alsup (2010, 10) argues that

"identifying or relating to a character involves a mental and emotional grappling with what the character represents—an ongoing interaction between the reader's lived experience and the narrative with which he or she is engaging. While reading can and does evoke emotion and memory, the reader uses the narrative experience to reconsider personal responses in a new, various context".

First Daughter and *Ask Me No Questions* demonstrate to the readers who relate to these texts that they are not alone in their experiences, that, following the events of 9/11, there were other young people who also felt as though the media's focus on 9/11 was pointing at them. The characters in these novels experience a variety of emotions and exhibit different ways of dealing with the news media's handling of the events of 9/11. By offering readers a range of emotional responses, these texts allow for a wide range of identification with the differing experiences of individual readers, and it is this range that opens these books' bibliotherapeutic potential.

Multi-person consciousness: feeling visible

The aggressive reporting methods employed by the news media post-9/11 helped fuel tensions among the public and disseminated fear about the Muslim/"Muslim" Other. *First Daughter* and *Ask Me No Questions* present the reader with the voice of this feared Other: voices, as Roderick McGillis (2000, xxi) points out, that are "more written about than writing, more spoken about than speaking". These two novels speak on behalf of this feared Muslim/"Muslim" Other and highlight that although the general public became increasingly afraid of Islam, they were not the only ones who were afraid. The reporting methods employed by the news media spread fear amongst Muslim/"Muslim" communities as well. These communities were frightened, like everyone else, by the threat of terrorism. They were also frightened, due to "multi-person consciousness", of how they might be treated because of their real or imagined relationship to Islam (Anonymous 2006; Committee on Religious Offences in England and Wales 2003; Civil Rights Organization 2003; Casciani 2002; Maira 2004; Rayner 2005). Multi-person consciousness borrows and fuses the ideas of what W. E. B. Du Bois (1989, 5) and Frantz Fanon (1986, 110) refer to as "double-consciousness" and "third-person consciousness" respectively. Du Bois and Fanon argue that racism forces minority individuals to recognize the stereotypes ascribed to their bodies. In terms of 9/11, these novels suggest that the media has helped elevate people's levels of multi-person consciousness, as those associated with Islam (regardless whether the association is real or perceived by others to be real) recognize that their bodies have become symbolically linked with terrorism.

Explicitly highlighting the news media's role in the dissemination of fear amongst Muslim/"Muslim" minority groups post-9/11, and the subsequent heightened development of multi-person consciousness, Nadira states:

> "Even after September 11, we carried on. We heard about how bad it had gotten. Friends of my parents had lost their jobs or couldn't make money....We heard about a man who had one side of his face bashed in,

and another who was run off the road in his taxi and called bad names.... *But things got worse* [my italics]. We began to feel as if the air had frozen around us, trapping us between two jagged ice floes. Each bit of news was like a piece of hail flung at us, stinging our skins. *Homeland Security. Patriot Act. Code Orange. Special Registration....* We watched the news of the war and saw ourselves as others saw us: dark, flitting shadows, grenades blooming in our fists. Dangerous" (9).

Nadira's claim that the news media made things worse for Muslim/"Muslim" individuals post-9/11 is substantiated by sociological investigations and reports (Cainkar 2002, 2004; Dreher 2006; Poynting and Noble 2004). The references to the hate crimes that targeted these individuals not only reflect the real after effects of 9/11 but highlight, as argued, that this community was doubly frightened: frightened by the threat of terrorism and, because of multi-person consciousness, frightened by how they might be treated because of their real or imagined associations to Islam.

Nadira and the community for whom she speaks blame the news media for their increased victimization. Her hailstones metaphor reinforces this idea and the word "dark" has obvious racial connotations. Within the context of the passage above, however, this word is used synonymously with the word "dangerous". Although, as Edward Said (1997) has argued, the media often tried to demonize Islam prior to 9/11, the double meaning behind the word "dark" demonstrates how Muslim/"Muslim" individuals and communities were negatively branded by the media post-9/11. Nadira and her community are forced via their multi-person consciousness to recognize that the negatively stereotyped Islamic images presented in the news media are supposedly meant to represent them. This heightens not only their apprehension and sense of cultural alienation from their "home" country, but also their feelings of perceived visibility within the scrutiny of the public gaze.

Perkins's *First Daughter* offers similar reflections. During her father's presidential campaign, the Rightons become the victims of smear campaigns and, through Sameera's experience, readers are made aware of how the media helped generate and reinforce multi-person consciousness:

"The worst was a photo of Dad smiling down into Sparrow's face as they walked on the dance floor. 'Righton: Soft on Muslims?' read the caption. 'As he clutched his Pakistani daughter in his arms, observers wondered if James Righton's foreigner-friendly approach during these frightening times might not be tough enough to fight the war on terror. We interviewed...' Sameera stopped reading" (106-107).

The article headline, the photograph, and the references to Pakistan and the "war on terror" align Sameera with Islamic extremism and highlight how the news media post-9/11 not only demonized Islam but, by Othering Muslims, forced some young Muslim individuals to feel alienated from their "home" country. Ironically, Sameera, though born in Pakistan which is largely an Islamic country, is not Muslim. Nonetheless, because she is loosely associated with Islam she, via the article, becomes the victim of negative media stereotypes, illustrating how Muslim/"Muslim" images were negatively used post-9/11.

Having read this article Sameera, like Nadira, develops a heightened awareness of multi-person consciousness. This article forces her to recognize that she has no control over how she is represented or how others perceive her. Though Sameera freely accepts—and in fact embraces—her Pakistani heritage, the article forces her to acknowledge that her body is ascribed labels which are beyond her control: in this instance her body, for the American news media, symbolizes terror.

As a result of multi-person consciousness, the characters in *Ask Me No Questions* and *First Daughter* feel visible, exposed and vulnerable, reflecting the real-life experiences of many Muslim and "Muslim" youths post-9/11. As stated, because of the media focus on Islam, Muslim/"Muslim" individuals became figures of suspicion and, as such, many became victims of race-hate crimes and attacks. In a 2006 study of Sikh youth in the UK, Rita Verma (2006, 89) concluded that their new visibility after the events of 9/11 "created more barriers for the youth in their schools as they became the victims of racist slurs, threats and physical assault that were treated with apathy from teachers and administrators." *Ask Me No Questions* and *First Daughter* explore the impact that these new visibilities have on their protagonists and in turn on young hybrid Overlapping Space identities after 9/11.

Sameera, in an attempt to evade the paparazzi and the PR firm her father has hired, decides that the best way to conceal her identity so that she can go out is to wear her salwar kameez and hijab. However, although she succeeds in her covert mission and is not recognized as "Sameera Righton: First Daughter-in-waiting", she actually draws more attention than intended. On the train, one woman regards Sameera with a "suspicious look" (182) and another tries to be overly friendly in what seems to be an attempt to stop a potential terrorist in the making. Sameera recognizes that these women are reacting to her in this way because of her "veiled head" (182), and here we can clearly see the type of Othering that Edward Said (1978) offers in *Orientalism*: Sameera, for these women, is the feared Other. Engaging with Said's concepts of the Othering process and drawing on Leila Ahmed's (2005) work, Clare Bradford (2007) interrogates the ways in which some children's novels propagate imperial feminist views about the veil: that it symbolizes the Muslim female's oppression and is a sign of her obedience and subservience from which she must be saved. In the books that Bradford critiques, the veiled female is portrayed as a victim. However, the women that Sameera encounters see her as a threat: someone whom *they* need protecting from. The reactions of these women suggest that the news media's use of sensationalism was successful in vilifying Muslim images; news headlines, such as the *Washington Times*' (2010) "Terrorists Hiding in Hijabs", extended the symbol of the veil to include the threat of terrorism. Clearly Sameera is not a victim: she is not subservient, does not need saving and her hijab actually offers her a sense of freedom, nor is she a terrorist. *First Daughter*, therefore, undermines some of the myths the news media disseminated about the Muslim Other. Nonetheless, what Sameera's encounter with these two women highlights is the increased Muslim visibility in the public gaze.

Like Sameera, Nadira's sister, Aisha, not only displays multi-person consciousness but is also forced to acknowledge her new and uncomfortable "visible" status. Before 9/11 Aisha was a very confident and popular teenager and she enjoyed being "visible" in this respect. However, Aisha's persona changes post-9/11 and Nadira sees her sister "falling away into a corner" (91). Aisha clearly no longer enjoys being in the limelight and the text indicates that her new introvert personality is a result of the events of 9/11. Aisha, at the end of the novel claims that "we, the invisible people, became visible" (151), which suggests that Aisha's retreat into a corner is her attempt at trying to make herself "invisible" once more. However, because of the media focus on 9/11, her multi-person consciousness forces her to acknowledge that her body, for many people, has become associated with the image of a terrorist: she no longer draws attention because she is "Aisha, the popular girl at school"; Aisha feels that people are looking at her and judging her because she looks and is Muslim.

Like Aisha, Nadira makes concerted efforts to be "invisible". Although *Ask Me No Questions* is written from Nadira's perspective, Nadira seems more like an omniscient narrator than an actual character. As narrator and commentator, Nadira places herself on the margins of her story which is highly significant. On the margins, Nadira is detached from the events that unfold, reflecting how some people post-9/11 had no control of what was going on around them. Equally, and perhaps ironically, on the margins

Nadira can watch her life in the third person which enables her to re-appropriate a certain sense of invisibility.

Sameera's, Nadira's and Aisha's experiences with new visibilities and multi-person consciousness, foreground the disparity between what is real and what is perceived as "real": none of these characters are dangerous yet their bodies become labelled as such by the news media. These texts, therefore, lend themselves to Christine Wilkie-Stibbs's ideas of the "*féminine* postmodern" within children's literature:

> "These kinds of *féminine* postmodern texts exhibit tensions between unity and disunity and between interiority and exteriority. On the one hand, they manifest the kinds of 'classic' postmodern features... such as fragmentation, dissolution, marginality....On the other hand, paradoxically, they sustain notions of 'centeredness,' 'truth,' 'reality,' the presence of human agency, and intersubjectivity" (2006, 76).

Sameera, Nadira and Aisha, because of multi-person consciousness, become increasingly aware that their appearances make them more visible. Furthermore, in trying to avoid scrutiny, Nadira and Aisha both try to make themselves invisible. Their feelings of exposure and isolation reflect how some of the candidates from Verma's study felt post-9/11. However, all three girls also exhibit the *féminine* postmodern. Although their new visibilities make them feel vulnerable and alienated from their "home" cultures, they simultaneously display a level of centeredness and agency: they eventually lay claim to their new visibilities, not only to highlight their hybrid Overlapping Space identities, but also to challenge the negative self-images used in the news media.

Claiming new visibilities

Since 9/11, the word "Muslim", as Vijay Prashad (2005, 586) argues, "has come to stand in for those who look or sound like immigrants", and, as Pnina Werbner (2004, 907) highlights, because most South Asian individuals are often racialized as "Pakis" they are, by extension, associated with Islam. Consequently, many Muslim/"Muslim" individuals have felt as though they have been placed under public scrutiny after 9/11. Discussing the effects of 9/11, Sunaina Maira (2004, 119) writes that, "questions of citizenship and racialization have taken on new urgent meanings for South Asian immigrant youth," as many members of this diaspora began to reassess their cultural identities in response to these questions. Looking at studies which specifically explore identity formation of ethnic minority children, one can see how this is possible. Discussing the work of child psychoanalyst E. H. Erikson, Margaret Beale Spencer and Carol Markstrom-Adams (1990, 299) write:

"Erikson speculates that minority and oppressed individuals may be prone to develop a negative identity as a result of accepting negative self-images projected onto them, not only by the larger society, but by their own group as well".

Spencer and Markstrom-Adams argue that Erikson's theory does not solely explain the development of negative self-identities; however, when applying Erikson's ideas to Muslim/"Muslim" children and adolescents post-9/11, one can speculate that as a result of the negative media focus, the heightened development of multi-person consciousness coupled with the sensation of feeling "visible" could explain why some young people, in order to recreate/re-appropriate feelings of belonging, felt compelled to reassess their cultural self-identities.

Reviewing almost twenty years of material exploring ethnic and social identity well-being, Jean S. Phinney (1990, 501) asserts that "being a member of a group provides individuals with a sense of belonging that contributes to a positive self-concept"; as such, "members of low-status groups seek to improve their status by 'passing' as members of the dominant group... [or] develop pride in one's group" (ibid.). These types of reactions are observed post-9/11. In her study of Sikh youths after 9/11, for example, Verma (2006) observes that some of the individuals either intensified their association with their "homeland" cultures and/or religion, which Alejandro Portes and Rubén G. Rumbaut (2001, 284) refer to as "reactive ethnicity", or they tried to assimilate into the dominant culture.

Jo Lampert (2010) observes that children's books about 9/11 that engage with ethnicity seem to privilege "white" cultural positions. For example, in the picture books that she discusses, Lampert (2010, 58) argues that "fear of the Other is given final privilege over tolerance" and that the *Parvana* trilogy promotes "Western" imperial feminist perspectives. Her analysis of Joseph Geha's short story "Alone and All Together" reveals "how the American cultural identity is largely privileged over the Arab identity" (2010, 75). The 9/11 texts that Lampert explores appear to promote assimilationist ideas. In doing so, these texts indirectly inform their ethnic minority readers that they should do the same: that they should abandon their "homeland" identities in favour of a more "Western" one. In effect, by promoting more "Westernized" identities, these books attempt to negate readers' rights to choose their own cultural identities.

Interestingly, however, the protagonists from *Ask Me No Questions* and *First Daughter* do not ultimately employ assimilation or reactive ethnicity techniques despite the media's use of negative self-identities and their heightened awareness of multi-person consciousness. In the end Sameera, Nadira and Aisha, unlike the protagonist in Geha's story, remain culturally plural and do not favour one cultural identity over another. These characters exhibit the "*féminine* postmodern" that Wilkie-Stibbs (2000) describes: despite their experiences with multi-person consciousness they also employ human agency. These characters find self-empowerment by choosing their own identities and, by deciding to remain culturally plural, they acknowledge that there is a range of cultural identity positionings that they, and in turn the reader, can choose from. By not being prescriptive, these texts empower their readers to choose their own cultural self-identities and thus offer an optimistic perspective on cultural identity:

> "The message of hope that the reader might take from these narratives of outsiderness…is the idea of the palimpsest: of cultural and ethnic identities not as monoliths but comprising histories of cultural superimpositions eroding the very idea of essentialist discourse that would dictate, determine, and command a center of dominance to be aspired to or assimilated into" (Wilkie-Stibbs 2008, 46).

Novels that support cultural pluralism, like *Ask Me No Questions* and *First Daughter*, offer readers a positive reading of hybrid Overlapping Space identities, and the cultural identities which Sameera, Nadira and Aisha project at the end of each novel help to promote the optimism that Wilkie-Stibbs describes.

In order to assert their hybrid Overlapping Space identities, Sameera, Nadira and Aisha actually *claim and re-appropriate* their new visibilities. They take advantage of their new visibilities to foreground *their actual identities*: identities which stand in contrast to the negative self-identities presented in the media. Unlike the texts explored in Lampert's study, these novels present readers with an alternative way of dealing with the media's use of negative self-imagery. Instead of denying parts of one's cultural identity, these texts suggest that one can embrace one's plurality and hybridity. Although assimilation and reactive ethnicity techniques may help compensate for, or even resolve, one's feelings of alienation, equally, as the characters from these novels demonstrate, embracing one's cultural plurality can also help foster feelings of acceptance.

First Daughter deals directly with how the American media appeared to encourage assimilation tendencies post-9/11. As part of his campaign trail, James Righton's office employs a public relations officer, Tara Colby. Tara and her team are put "in charge of spinning James Righton's personal life for the media" (10). As such, explicit connections are drawn between Tara and the media. When put in charge of Sameera's public image, Tara insists that Sameera should be called "Sammy" instead of "Sameera" or "Sparrow" because "Sammy" sounds more "American". Additionally, as part of her makeover and to promote Sameera's "Americanness", Tara suggests that she throw away her salwar kameezes. According to Tara, it would be in Sameera's interest if she were to disassociate herself from her Pakistani culture and assimilate into the dominant American mainstream as it would make her life easier. The rationale behind Tara's thinking helps highlight why some of the candidates in Verma's and Phinney's studies, in order to escape discrimination, chose to embrace assimilation techniques. Equally, because it is Tara who puts pressure on Sameera to change, the novel highlights how the media helped influence young people to reassess their cultural identity choices after 9/11.

Despite Tara's efforts and the fact that her new "American" look instils Sameera with a new-found confidence, Sameera defies Tara and wears her salwar kameezes and headscarf regardless. In fact Sameera finds wearing her traditional Pakistani outfits equally empowering as her makeover. She claims that these clothes make her feel "free and powerful" (197) and "extra safe" (229). Since Sameera's confidence is increased by both looks, she asserts that she wants to embody a Pakistani-American identity, and her interest in a group of girls called the "Covered Girls"—Muslim girls who sport "tight jeans and head coverings" (188)—affirms this. These girls have become a new type of role-model for Sameera. Their "new all-American look" (188) synthesizes both American and Pakistani styles together, and evidently their hybrid look appeals to Sameera.

Sameera's desire for a hybrid cultural identity is further emphasized when having the freedom to choose between American clothes or Pakistani clothes is proven essential: "What Sameera really needed was the power to shift from visible to invisible, from elegant to funky, from modest to sexy—and to stay in charge of when, where, how and why" (216). Note that the word "visible" is aligned with Sameera's Pakistani identity. Sameera's need to be able to shift from invisible to visible suggests that Sameera's experiences with new visibilities and multi-person consciousness have not affected her affiliation with her Pakistani identity. Ironically, in fact, when Sameera claims her new visibilities she also feels invisible as well. Although wearing her Pakistani clothes makes her stand out and visible in this respect, because nobody recognizes her as America's First Daughter-in-waiting, Sameera actually feels invisible at the same time. Embracing her Pakistani heritage allows Sameera to feel safe and hidden. By claiming her new visibilities, Sameera not only transforms the negative sensations that she experiences with multi-person consciousness into positive ones, but is actually able to re-appropriate a sense of power.

Though Sameera makes explicit efforts throughout the novel to embrace her cultural plurality, both Nadira and Aisha *initially* demonstrate reactive ethnicity techniques: Aisha moves away from the cultural mainstream at school and Nadira seeks assistance from a group who reject American culture. Nadira's and Aisha's actions, however, not only coincide with Verma's (2006) findings but also acknowledge that the employment of these techniques, given the circumstances, is understandable. Nonetheless, although both girls demonstrate reactive ethnicity tendencies, they both finally choose to reject this type of cultural identity reframing by embracing their cultural plurality: Nadira rejects the underground resistance group and Aisha resumes her position in her school. In fact, both characters embrace their new visibilities in order to affirm their hybrid Overlapping Space identities, and, like Sameera, they both feel empowered as a result. Nadira eventually moves from the margins of her story to claim her place as the novel's protagonist when the situation with her father, Abba, worsens and he is accused of a crime he never committed:

> "I press my palms on the table and stand. 'May I speak? … You've got the wrong person.' … I push all the papers toward them and start pointing…. I made them stop and see me—see *us*. Take a second look" (132-136).

Nadira stops her father from being sent to prison and as Nadira stands up in court to get her voice heard she demonstrates that she is no longer happy to stand on the sidelines: she wants to be visible—but on her own terms. She forces the court to see the Hossain family independently from all the other images that they may have "seen". Significantly, here, the collective pronoun "us", within the context of the novel, not only refers to the Hossain family, but to Muslim/"Muslim" communities as well. Nadira's use of this word indicates that she has not assimilated into the American mainstream; however, it simultaneously suggests that she has *not* employed reactive ethnicity techniques either. In fact, Nadira negotiates her cultural identities by embracing her cultural plurality. The images presented in the news represent a small minority of individuals and not the "us" whom Nadira wants to represent; not the "us" who have successfully integrated and hybridized with American culture. By calling attention to herself and ultimately re-appropriating her visibility, Nadira forces people to recognize that the negatively stereotyped images seen in the news do not fully represent her or the "us" communities. So, as Nadira helps win Abba's case, the novel illustrates that by embracing her new visibility she is able to affirm her hybrid Overlapping Space identity, which, in turn, empowers her.

Equally, Aisha gains more confidence when she takes advantage of her new visibilities and affirms her hybrid Overlapping Space identity during her valedictorian speech at her high school graduation ceremony:

> "Aisha's stepping onto the stage, and as she lifts the bottom of her gown, I can see the high heels Ma let her buy…bright, shiny red satin heels with skinny straps….
>
> 'My name is Aisha Hossain. And I am an illegal alien….My family came here eight years ago on a tourist visa and stayed….In those days they didn't enforce the laws. We were the people you didn't always see….And then one day two planes came and smashed into two towers. A war started. Overnight, we, the invisible people, became visible. We became dangerous. We became terrorists, people with bombs in our luggage, poison in our homes….All I ask of you is to see me for who I am. Aisha. I spell my name not with a *y* or an *e*, but with an *i*. See me. I live with you. I live near you. I go to your school; I eat in your cafeteria; I take the same classes. Now I am your valedictorian. I want what you want. I want a future'" (150-152).

Aisha's shoes link her to Dorothy from the iconic American movie *The Wizard of Oz* (1939) and symbolically affirm Aisha's "Americanness". Simultaneously, however, by using the collective pronoun "we", Aisha also aligns herself with Muslim/"Muslim" minority groups. In her speech Aisha draws attention to her multi-person consciousness and repeats the phrase "we became": "we…became visible"; "we became dangerous"; "we became terrorists". Her sad tone asserts that this "becoming" is not meant in the literal sense: people did not suddenly become terrorists. They did, however, involuntarily fulfil the image of the feared Other presented in the news. The subtly ironic way that Aisha describes this "becoming" actually affirms Aisha's disassociation from these terrorist images which, in turn, illustrates that a terrorist identity is not part of the repertoire of Bangladeshi or Islamic identities that Aisha has, through enculturation, been taught to embody.

Aisha, therefore, challenges the image of the feared Muslim Other post-9/11, and when she demands that her audience "see" *her*, she, like Nadira, is asking them to perceive her as a representative of Islamic-American culture and to ignore the negative images presented in the news media. Aisha, like Nadira and Sameera, also reappropriates her new visibilities to empower both herself *and* her community.

Conclusion

First Daughter and *Ask Me No Questions* explore the effect that the American news media's attention on 9/11 had on Muslim/"Muslim" individuals and communities living in the U.S. Both novels reflect the findings and observations made by sociological studies into the after-effects of 9/11. They help draw attention to the fact that many individuals felt targeted, scapegoated and attacked by the media because of their real or imagined relations to Islam which not only made people feel alienated from their "home" cultures but forced some people to develop a heightened sense of multi-person consciousness. As a result of this consciousness, many individuals felt vulnerable, exposed and visible and some experienced abuse or discrimination because of these associations with Islam. However, although Sameera, Aisha and Nadira initially find their new visibilities oppressive, none of the characters demonstrates a permanent shift in cultural identity. In fact, despite the media's use of negative self-imagery, the characters learn to take advantage of their new visibilities and they feel more empowered when they reassert and reaffirm their culturally plural hybrid Overlapping Space identities.

The cultural identity tensions presented in these novels become important for a number of reasons. Firstly, readers who identify with the characters may potentially find these books a source of bibliotherapy. Some readers might find comfort and even inspiration from the ultimately empowering ways in which Sameera, Nadira and Aisha deal with the media aftermath of 9/11. Secondly, these texts illustrate that Muslim/"Muslim" communities and individuals were also victims of the 9/11 events and they raise awareness about how the media helped fuel tensions—tensions which ultimately forced some people to feel alienated from their "home" cultures, which, in turn, put pressure on many young individuals to reassess their cultural identities. Finally, because of these cultural identity tensions, readers can see how the characters make their cultural identity choices by emphasizing their cultural plurality; this not only helps legitimize readers' own hybrid Overlapping Space identities, but makes these books significant contributors to the understanding of cultural identity negotiation. These books tell their readers that despite prejudice, "home"(land) cultural alienation and the consequential pressures to change one's cultural identity, young people enculturated with two or more cultures should, and have the right to, choose who *they* want to be.

References

Ahmed. Leila. 2005. The Veil Debate – Again. *On Shifting Ground: Muslim Women in the Global Era,* ed. Fereshteh Nouraie-Simone, 153-171. New York: Feminist Press.

Alsup, Janet. 2010. Identification, Actualization, or Education: Why Read YAL? *Young Adult Literature and Adolescent Identity Across Cultures and Classrooms: The Literary Life of Teens*, ed. Janet Alsup, 1-16. New York: Routledge.

Anonymous. 2006. "Islamophobia" Felt 5 Years After 9/11. *ABC News*, September 9. http://abcnews.go.com/print?id=2413473. Date accessed 12 October 2007.

Anonymous. 2010. Hiding in Hijabs: Muslims Seek Special Treatment to Elude TSA Groping. *Washington Times*, November 17. http://www.washingtontimes.com/news/2010/nov/17/terrorists-hiding-in-hijabs/. Date accessed 23 November 2011.

Arnett, Jeffrey Jensen. 1995. Adolescents' Use of Media for Self-Socialisation. *Journal of Youth and Adolescence* 24 (5): 519-533.

Bettelheim, Bruno. 1976. *The Uses of Enchantment: The Meaning and Importance of Fairy Tales*. New York: Knopf.

Betzalel, Nurit and Zipora Shechtman. 2010. Bibliotherapy Treatment for Children With Adjustment Difficulties: A Comparison of Affective and Cognitive Bibliotherapy. *Journal of Creativity in Mental Health* 5 (4): 426-439.

Bhabha, Homi K. 1994. *The Location of Culture*. London: Routledge.

Bradford, Clare. 2007. Representing Islam: Female Subjects in Suzanne Fisher Staples's Novels. *Children's Literature Association Quarterly* 31 (1): 47-62.

Brah, Avtar. 1996. *Cartographies of Diaspora: Contesting Identities.* London; New York: Routledge.

Budhos, Marina. 2006. *Ask Me No Questions*. New York: Atheneum Books for Young Readers.

Cainkar, Louise. 2004. The Impact of the September 11 Attacks and Their Aftermath on Arab and Muslim Communities in the United States. *GSC Quarterly* 13 (Summer/Fall). http://programs.ssrc.org/gsc/publications/quarterly13/cainkar.pdf. Date accessed 15 October 2007.

—. 2002. No Longer Invisible: Arab and Muslim Exclusion After September 11. *Middle East Report* 224 (Fall): 22-29.

Casciani, Dominic. 2002. UK "Islamophobia" Rises After 11 September. *BBC*, August 29. http://news.bbc.co.uk/1hi/uk/2223301.stm. Date accessed 12 October 2007.

Civil Rights Organization. 2003. Wrong Then, Wrong Now: Racial Profiling Before & After September 11, 2001. *Leadership Conference on Civil Rights.* http://www.civilrights.org/publications/reports/racial_profiling/. Date accessed 14 September 2007.

Coleman, Marilyn, and Lawrence H. Ganong. 1990. The Uses of Juvenile Fiction and Self-Help Books with Stepfamilies. *Journal of Counselling & Development* 68 (3): 327-331.

Committee on Religious Offences in England and Wales. 2003. Islamophobic Attacks in the Wake of September 11. *The United Kingdom Parliament.* http://www.parliament.the-stationery-office.co. uk/pa/ld200203/ldselect/ldrelof/95/2102304.htm. Date accessed 15 October 2007.

Dreher, Tanja. 2006. *'Targeted': Experiences of Racism in NSW after September 11, 2001.* UTSePress. http://hdl.handle.net/2100/46. Date accessed 15 October 2007.

Du Bois, W. E. B. 1989. *The Souls of Black Folk.* New York: Penguin Books.

Emmambokus, Shehrazade. 2011. Overlapping Space and the Negotiation of Cultural Identity: Children's Literature from the South Asian Diaspora. *Postcolonial Spaces: The Politics of Place in Contemporary Culture*, eds. Andrew Teverson and Sara Upstone, 83-96. Basingstoke: Palgrave Macmillan.

Fanon, Frantz. 1986. *Black Skin, White Masks*, trans. Charles Lam Markmann. London: Pluto Press.

Fleming, Victor, dir. 1939. *The Wizard of Oz.* Metro-Goldwyn-Mayer.

Hall, Stuart. 1996. The Question of Cultural Identity. *Modernity and its Futures*, eds. Stuart Hall, David Held, and Tony McGrew, 273-325. Oxford: Polity Press.

Hayes, J. S., and Amer, K. 1999. Bibliotherapy: Using Fiction to Help Children in Two Populations Discuss Feelings. *Pediatric Nursing* 25: 91–95.

Kidd, Kenneth B. (2005). "A" is for Auschwitz: Psychoanalysis, Trauma Theory, and the "Children's Literature of Atrocity". *Children's Literature* 33: 120-149.

Lampert, Jo. 2010. *Children's Fiction about 9/11: Ethnic, National and Heroic Identities.* New York: Routledge.

Lengua, Liliana J., Anna C. Long, Kimberlee I. Smith, and Andrew N. Meltzoff. 2005. Pre-Attack Symptomatology and Temperament as Predictors of Children's Responses to the September 11 Terrorist Attacks. *Journal of Child Psychology and Psychiatry* 46 (6): 631-645.

McGillis, Roderick. 2000. Introduction. *Voices of the Other: Children's Literature and the Postcolonial Context*, ed. Roderick McGillis, xix-xxxi. New York: Garland Publishing.

Mackinlay, John. 2001. Tackling Bin Laden: Lessons from History. *Observer*, October 28. http://www.guardian.co.uk/world/2001/oct/28/afghanistan.religion. Date accessed 13 October 2007.

Maira, Sunaina. 2004. Youth Culture, Citizenship and Globalization: South Asian Muslim Youth in the United States after September 11th. *Comparative Studies of South Asia, Africa and the Middle East* 24 (1): 219-231.

Pardeck, John T. 1995. Bibliotherapy: An Innovative Approach for Helping Children. *Early Child Development and Care* 110 (1): 83-88.

Pardeck, John T. and Martha Markward. 1995. Bibliotherapy: Using Books to Help Children Deal with Problems. *Early Child Development and Care* 106 (1): 75-90.

Pechmann, Cornelia, Linda Levine, Sandra Loughlin and Frances Leslie. 2005. Impulsive and Self-Conscious: Adolescents' Vulnerability to Advertising and Promotion. *Journal of Public Policy & Marketing* 24 (2): 202-221.

Perkins, Mitali. 2007. *First Daughter: Extreme American Makeover*. New York: Dutton Children's Books.

Phinney, Jean S. 1990. Ethnic Identity in Adolescents and Adults: Review of Research. *Psychological Bulletin* 108 (3): 499-514.

Portes, Alejandro, and Rubén G. Rumbaut. 2001. *Legacies: The Story of the Immigrant Second Generation*. Berkeley: University of California Press.

Poynting, Scott and Greg Noble. 2004. Living With Racism: The Experience and Reporting by Arab and Muslim Australians of Discrimination, Abuse and Violence Since 11 September 2001. *Human Rights and Equal Opportunity Commission*. http://www.hreoc.gov.au/racial_discrimination/isma/research/UWS Report.pdf. Date accessed 9 July 2010.

Prashad, Vijay. 2005. How the Hindus Became Jews: American Racism after 9/11. *South Atlantic Quarterly* 104 (3): 583-606.

Rayner, Jay. 2005. Grim Truth About Race Hate. *Guardian*, March 27.

http://www.guardian.co.uk/uk/2005/mar/27/race.foodanddrink.   Date accessed 15 October 2007.

Said, Edward W. 1978. *Orientalism*. New York: Vintage.

—. 1997. *Covering Islam: How the Media and the Experts Determine How We See the Rest of the World*. London: Vintage.

Shechtman, Zipora. 2000. An Innovative Intervention for Treatment of Child and Adolescent Aggression: An Outcome Study. *Psychology in the Schools* 37 (2): 157–167.

Smith, Cynthia Leitich. 2008. Author Interview: Mitali Perkins on the First Daughter Books. *Cynsations*. http://cynthialeitichsmith.blogspot.com/2008/06/author-interview-mitali-perkins-on.html. Date accessed 17 November 2011.

Spencer, Margaret, and Carol Markstrom-Adams. 1990. Identity Processes Among Racial and Ethnic Minority Children in America. *Child Development* 61 (2): 290-310.

Villani, Susan. 2001. Impact of Media on Children and Adolescents: A 10-Year Review of the Research. *Journal of the American Academy of Child and Adolescent Psychiatry* 40 (4): 392-401.

Verma, Rita. 2006. Trauma, Cultural Survival and Identity Politics in a Post-9/11 Era: Reflections by Sikh Youth. *Sikh Formations* 2 (1): 89-101.

Werbner, Pnina. 2004. Theorising Complex Diasporas: Purity and Hybridity in the South Asian Public Sphere in Britain. *Journal of Ethnic Migration Studies* 30 (5): 895-911.

Wilkie-Stibbs, Christine. 2000. "Body Language": Speaking the *Féminine* in Young Adult Fiction. *Children's Literature Association Quarterly* 25 (2): 76-87.

—. 2008. *The Outside Child In and Out of the Book*. New York: Routledge.

COMING OF AGE AND NATIONAL CHARACTER AT HOME AND ABROAD

ANNE MARKEY

It is generally recognized that children's literature, since its emergence as a distinctive genre over the course of the eighteenth century, has reflected broader adult anxieties and social values (Müller 2006; Hilton and Sheffrin (2009). Narratives about youth and childhood are often nostalgic recreations of the past, but they also reflect ambiguous reactions to present conditions and future uncertainties and so can illuminate more general cultural concerns and ambivalences. It is over fifty years since Philippe Ariès (1960) claimed that in medieval society the idea of childhood, at least as that term was understood by Western cultures in the middle of the twentieth century, did not exist. That assertion has been challenged by subsequent scholarship but Ariès's more fundamental thesis, that understandings of, and approaches to, childhood vary radically between societies and over time, has gained widespread acceptance (Hutton 2004, 92-112). Childhood is not a universal condition but a cultural construct that can be viewed either positively, as a time of innocence and freedom, or negatively, as a time of unruliness and dependence. Post-colonial critics have explored links between constructions of childhood and discourses of imperialism, recognizing that "the invention of childhood itself in European society was coterminous with the invention of that other notion of supreme importance to imperialism—race" (Ashcroft 2001, 37). Viewing colonized, native cultures as childlike and therefore as undeveloped and in need of guidance and protection is a basic strategy of imperialism. Over forty years ago, the historian, LP. Curtis (1968, 54-62) drew attention to the ways in which English representations of the Irish as childlike during the nineteenth century reflected the belief that the Irish were incapable of self-government and were thereby used to justify the imperial project in Ireland. During the course of the twentieth century, both before and after Independence, the figure of the child became such a crucial component of Irish self-definition and such a recurrent trope in Irish writing that it became an emblem of the nascent, emerging, and established nation state (Haslam 1999; Young 2006). More recently, Jarlath Killeen (2011, 125) has persuasively demonstrated that contemporary Irish writing draws attention to "inadequate understandings of Irish nationhood and childhood".

Given that the representation of childhood in texts about Ireland has always carried, and continues to bear, a political charge heightened by the country's colonial past and post-colonial present, this essay examines the representation of Ireland and the construction of Irish national identity in two recent award-winning, coming-of-age novels. Kate Thompson's *The New Policeman*, first published in London in 2005, was an international critical and commercial success, winning the Dublin Airport Authorities Irish Children's Book of the Year (2005), the Guardian Children's Fiction Prize (2005), the Whitbread [Costa] Children's Book Award (2005), and the Children's Books Ireland Bisto Book of the Year (2006). Éilís Ní Dhuibhne's *Hurlamaboc*, written in the Irish language and first published in Dublin in 2006, was well received in Ireland, winning first prize in the fiction for young people (13-15) category of the Oireachtas literary competition (2006) and a Children's Books Ireland Bisto Honour's Award (2007). It would be wrong to extrapolate general principles from an analysis of just two novels, but investigation of *Hurlamaboc* and *The New Policeman* points towards an intriguing duality in the development of Irish children's literature in the era of twenty-first century globalization. In particular, the varying ways in which Thompson and Ní Dhuibhne portray the coming of age of their young Irish protagonists highlight some significant differences in how Irish identity is constructed for readers at home and abroad.

The New Policeman, set in Kinvara, Co. Galway intertwines the adventures of Larry O'Dwyer, the village's new policeman, and those of 15 year-old J.J. Liddy, a gifted fiddler who comes from a family of traditional musicians. J.J., like everyone else in Kinvara, finds that there no longer seem to be enough hours in the day to do all that has to be done, let alone to relax. Two shadows hang over J.J.'s family: his grandmother was abandoned by her handsome, feckless lover in the days when being a single mother was frowned on by the narrow-minded parish priest, and there is a persistent rumour that his great-grandfather killed that intolerant cleric. Torn between the desire to play his fiddle at the next family céilí [a gathering featuring traditional music and dance] or to go clubbing with his friends, J.J. eventually decides that family loyalty and tradition are more important than the approval of his peers. Determined to solve the mystery surrounding his grandfather and to discover where time is going, he walks through the wall of an underground cave and finds himself in Tír na nÓg, the land of eternal youth. There he meets Aengus Óg, a charming, talented fiddler who tells him that time is leaking from the actual world into this parallel, mythical one. By the end of the novel, J.J. has fixed the leak, cleared his grandfather's name and discovered that Larry O'Dwyer, Aengus Óg, and his grandmother's feckless lover are one and the same. Reconciled with his family and his heritage, J.J. is set to live happily ever after—just like his fairy grandfather! For Thompson's young protagonist, coming of age involves a rapprochement with the past and a happy acceptance of one's heritage.

Hurlamaboc, set in the affluent, fictional Dublin suburb of Rathcormac, presents a complacently competitive, class-ridden society, where those who have money flaunt it and want more, and where those who have nothing get nothing. The Irish word "hurlamaboc" translates into English as "commotion" or "uproar". The novel lives up to its title by interweaving the stories of three contemporary young Dubliners who negotiate various personal upheavals during the period leading up to, and just after, the Leaving Certificate examination. The action opens as Ruán's comfortably middle-class parents are about to celebrate their twentieth wedding anniversary with their friends and neighbours on Ashtree Avenue. The next few chapters introduce the two other principal young characters: Emma, who is regarded condescendingly by her neighbours on the Avenue because her single mother is living with a much younger partner, and Colm, who lives with his abusive father and weary mother in the local Council estate. As the action develops, there is a domestic dispute in which Colm intervenes to protect his mother. The police believe that he, not his father, is the violent one and Colm runs away, ending up in Bangor in Wales. Ruán's parents die in a road accident and he slowly learns how to cope with his unexpected and not entirely welcome independence. Finally, Emma, who despises her mother's young lover, discovers, to her delight, that her attraction to Ruán is reciprocated. These three young characters learn that coming of age involves moving beyond the confinement or contentment of early family life, learning to make one's own independent decisions, and looking towards the future regardless of the challenges that life throws in one's path.

Irish critics generally acknowledge the merits of both novels, but concerns have been expressed about Thompson's nostalgic conservatism and Ní Dhuibhne's radical use of a modern Irish-language idiom. Shortly after its publication, Robert Dunbar (2007, 140) drew attention to Celia Keenan's prediction that *The New Policeman* would become a classic, and himself described the novel as "Thompson's finest achievement, a worthy winner of its many awards". More recent criticism, though, has been less enthusiastic. Patricia Kennon (2011, 149), for example, argued that although Thompson is committed "to charting the layering and sedimentation of history, culture, and individual identity", the novel endorses "a conservative and politically passive status quo". Ciara Ní Bhroin (2011, 24, 23), meanwhile, commented on Thompson's disdain for "philistine modernity", as evidenced in the evocation of "a pastoral, pre-technological, and pre-industrial" Kinvara. By contrast, *Hurlamaboc*'s embrace of modernity delighted Mary Shine Thompson (2009, 131-132), who lauded Ní Dhuibhne's "cool appraisal of contemporary suburban Ireland in a contemporary sassy idiom". That idiom, as Ní Dhuibhne (2006) explained, is based on the type of Irish spoken by urban, non-native speakers of the language who have been educated in Gaelscoileanna [Irish medium schools]:

> "The Irish language of the Gaelscoils has almost developed into a dialect in its own right. It has its own characteristics, with a strong relationship to English in terms of the children mixing the syntax of English to a certain extent with that of Irish".

Fellow Irish-language novelist, Ruaidhrí Ó Báille (2006, 73), though, was not impressed with Ní Dhuibhne's incorporation of English words and phrases into the dialogue, arguing that "the technique actually took from the overall impact of the book". Another Irish-language critic, however, pointed out that the use of a contemporary teenage idiom would appeal to young readers (Mac Murchaidh, 2006). Although critical opinion of *The New Policeman* and *Hurlamaboc* has generally been favourable, it is telling that the issues of conservatism and innovation have been central to the reception of both novels.

In *The New Policeman*, Ireland is a magical place that has changed little over the centuries and Irishness is linked to the landscape and tradition. The novel's title, taken from a variant of a traditional Irish reel, gestures towards Flann O'Brien's *The Third Policeman* (1967), which has been described by Keith Hopper (1995, 15) as "the first great masterpiece [...] of what we generally refer to now as post-modernism". Although both novels share a rural Irish setting, Thompson's portrayal of rural life is considerably less disturbing than O'Brien's bleak investigation of existential angst. As Jan Mark (2005) observed, O'Brien provides a vision of hell while Thompson's novel exudes a "robust sense of fun". Tír na nÓg, where the sun always shines, is effectively a prelapsarian version of the real world but Kinvara itself, as described in the novel, despite the rain, the necessity for work, and the chronic shortage of time, is fairly idyllic: people meet in pubs and houses to play music and dance; families work together to save the hay; and there is "nothing whatsoever for a policeman to do" (Thompson 2005, 245). It is a welcoming place, where outsiders, like J.J.'s Dublin-born father, Ciaran Byrne, and the German publisher, Anne Korff, feel at home and so blend into the fabric of communal life. Korff is a real person and a resident of Kinvara, and the novel's cast of characters, as Thompson (2005, n.p.) has explained, also includes "Séadna Tobín, Kinvara's fiddle-playing pharmacist, and Mary Green, landlady of Green's pub". Ní Dhuibhne (2011, 36) praised Thompson's focus "on the specific human geography of Kinvara and its immediate hinterland", but the novel presents the village as an idealized, mythical place. Although there is one brief mention of "ubiquitous televisions and computers" (Thompson 2005, 34), there is little indication that Kinvara is connected to the outside, modern world; there are no satellite dishes blemishing the skyline, no mobile phones interrupting traditional music sessions, and no-one downloads music from the internet. As Ciara Ní Bhroin (2011, 23) observed, "the Kinvara of Thompson's Tír na nÓg is a tourist's paradise: a sunny Irish Eden, where rousing musical sessions, dancing in the streets, and drinking Guinness are the order of the day". Other parts of Ireland are not so Edenic—"a few miles away in Galway city violent crime was escalating dramatically" (Thompson 2005, 10)—but Thompson's Kinvara is a special place, untouched by urban alienation or degradation.

In *Hurlamaboc*, the fictional suburb of Rathcormac provides a microcosm of twenty-first century Irish society. Judging by the behaviour of the adults, both in middle-class Ashtree Avenue and the working-class Council estate, Ireland is a soulless, materialistic place and Irishness seems to be characterized by selfishness, competitiveness, and class-consciousness. Humorous references to recognizable aspects of Dublin life enhance the credibility and topicality of the narrative: the superiority of clothes from Kilkenny Design and the House of Fraser over those from Penneys, the difficulty of getting a seat on the DART train system at rush hour, the convenience of Trinity College Dublin's proximity to the DART and the Luas tram line and this university's consequent superiority to University College Dublin, served only by irregular buses, and the popularity of Church of Ireland primary schools with liberal Catholic parents. At the same time, the interconnecting stories of Ruán, Colm and Emma enable Ní Dhuibhne to cast a keen and scathing eye on serious issues in modern Ireland, including social disadvantage and prejudice, familial disharmony, alcoholism, under-age drinking, and the drawbacks of a narrowly-focused, exam-based educational system. The real sense of inter-generational conflict in the novel suggests that a new form of Irishness is being forged as Ruán, Colm and Emma move beyond parental control to take charge of their own lives. By the end of the novel, the behaviour of these three young adults suggests that Ireland is set to become a more tolerant, compassionate place and that the Irishness of the future will be characterized by an increased sense of inter-dependence and generosity.

The varying approaches to Ireland, Irishness and tradition in these two novels are partly attributable to their differing narrative modes; *The New Policeman* is a fantasy addressed primarily to pre-teen readers, whereas *Hurlamaboc* is a more realistic story addressed primarily to teenagers. Recent criticism has interpreted the adult nostalgia that pervades children's fantasy as a regressive yearning for an imagined period of innocence (Ní Bhroin 2011, 23). Arguing that the genre has changed since the publication of Rosemary Jackson's *Fantasy: The Literature of Subversion* (1975), Jack Zipes (2009, 53) claimed that development of a global culture industry has resulted in a situation where "delusion has become the goal of fantasy, not illumination". Thompson's recourse to fantasy is tinged with nostalgia and so presents a misleading, rather than illuminating, picture of contemporary Ireland. As J.J. Liddy moves between contemporary Kinvara and the legendary Tír na nÓg, *The New Policeman* can be regarded as a time-slip novel, a form of fiction in which, as Humphrey Carpenter (1985, 218) observed, the plot is "likely to concern one or two children who stumble across some feature of history or mythology which concerns their own family or the place where they are living or staying".

In her study of a group of twentieth-century English children's novels featuring the time-slip device, Tess Cosslett (2002, 251) traced the ways in which authors increasingly evaded the dangers of nostalgia by using that narrative trope to stress the horrors of the past, "in contrast to which the present is undeniably better". *The New Policeman*, though, has more in common with earlier examples of the form, such as Rudyard Kipling's *Puck of Pook's Hill* (1906), in which a nostalgic evocation of the past "adds up to a grand narrative of Englishness" (Cosslett 2005, 245). As Patricia Kennon (2011, 149, 150) has argued, Thompson uses "the chronotopic device of the timeskin, a two-way permeable membrane both separating and linking the human sphere with Tír na nÓg" to align "the worlds of magical and mortal experience [...] rather than actually interrogating the ongoing nostalgic hunger for an Arcadian Celtic past". *The New Policeman*, then, through its use of the timeslip device, presents modern Ireland as a harmonious place in tune with its mythological past, thereby offering a static, essentialist version of Irish national identity. *Hurlamaboc*, by contrast, through its embrace of what Charles May (1999, 151) described as "the specific detail of realism" characteristic of modern fiction, presents Irish identity as fractured along class lines. Ruán, Emma and Colm all live near each other in suburban Rathcormac, but inhabit different worlds. The County Council housing estate, where Colm lives, lies to the north of Rathcormac; private estates of three-bedroomed semi-detached houses lie to the south; large, grand houses surrounded by walls and protected by gates lie to the west in the foothills of the mountains, while to the east more modest, detached houses line streets like Ashtree Avenue where Ruán and Emma live. People who live in the east and the south intermingle but avoid those who live in the north, while those rich enough to live in the west do not mix, even amongst themselves (Ní Dhuibhne 2006, 46-47).

Class differences, as reflected in the suburban landscape, affect the aspirations of the three main characters and influence relationships between them. Although Ruán and Colm attended the same primary school, a social gulf separates them at the outset of the novel. Ruán, who now attends a private secondary school, has parents who do all in their power to ensure his academic success. By contrast, Colm, who now attends the local comprehensive school, has to work part-time in an off-licence to supplement the meagre income of his long-suffering mother and abusive father. Emma's father, who is estranged from her mother, is an Irish-language poet who ekes out a living giving classes in creative writing while aided by a small grant from the Arts Council, and the girl herself, craving the recognition denied her father, longs to become a Booker Prize winner. After the death of his parents, Ruán follows his dream to study film, a possibility that his late mother did all in her power to prevent. Having stood up to his father only to be let down by his mother, Colm runs away from home and makes a new life for himself in Wales, where he meets Emma. At the end of the novel, Emma becomes romantically involved with Ruán, while taking the first steps towards achieving her ambition to become a writer. Through her realistic accounts of the differing, but interlinking, experiences of these three young characters, Ní Dhuibhne presents modern Ireland as a place where the legacy of the past does not overshadow the promise of the future.

Undoubtedly, the backgrounds of the respective authors contribute to their representation of Ireland in *The New Policeman* and *Hurlamaboc*. Kate Thompson, born in Yorkshire in 1956, has described her move to Ireland in the 1980s as a way of moving beyond the family shadow and "of clearing space for myself" (cited in Rabinovitch, 2006). Her father, E.P. Thompson, was a committed socialist, peace campaigner and pioneering Marxist historian, while her mother, Dorothy Thompson, was a highly-regarded radical historian and expert on the Chartist movement.

Thompson has spoken about her feelings about not following the family tradition of writing about actual social conditions: "I'm not my dad, I'll never write polemic, as he did. And at times I feel a bit guilty about that" (ibid.). Thompson's perception of Ireland as a place where she could meet life on her own terms, free of the political involvement and social commitment that characterized her parents' work and life, is reflected in her portrayal of Ireland and Irishness in *The New Policeman*. Kinvara, as it is presented in the novel, is an idealized, mythical place that reveals perhaps more about the author's perceptions of rural Ireland than it does about actual Irishness. Éilís Ní Dhuibhne was born in 1954 in Dublin, where she has spent most of her adult life. Her father was a native Irish speaker from Donegal who settled in Dublin and married an English-speaking woman. Growing up between the two places and the two languages, Ní Dhuibhne has been aware, since early childhood, that Irishness is not essential, but variable and negotiable. Speaking of her own early sense of the rural/urban divide and of the significance of language and class to the creation of identity, she outlined how these personal impressions reflect "other dualities and conflicts and ambiguities in Irish society" (Moloney and Thompson 2003, 106). In Ní Dhuibhne's view: "Stability can't happen in any society, but it's impossible for a postcolonial society to have cultural stability. Many reactions have to occur before Ireland is a place where a constant, stable identity can be established" (Moloney and Thompson 2003, 115). Her sense both of the interconnection of personal and national identity and of Ireland as a place where such identities are never stable is reflected in *Hurlamaboc*. Rathcormac, the fictional setting for much of the novel's action, combines aspects of actual, predominantly middle-class Dublin suburbs, such as Shankill and Malahide, served by the DART and largely untouched by immigration. In other words, it is a credible place that provides a humorously unflinching and largely unflattering portrait of suburban Irishness at the beginning of the twenty-first century. While Thompson presents Ireland, through the lens of rural Kinvara, as a welcoming place steeped in magical tradition, Ní Dhuibhne's portrayal of Dublin acknowledges that self-absorption and ambition are ineluctable, albeit not completely pervasive, characteristics of modern Irish life.

Thompson and Ní Dhuibhne both draw on strands of the Irish folk tradition in their portrayal of life in Ireland in the early years of the twenty-first century, but the literary uses to which they put that material vary considerably. Jennifer Schacker (2003, 2) has noted that the roots of folklore study can be traced back "to the quest for national identity and cultural purity that began in late eighteenth century [...] nationalist movements, particularly in Europe". When the English antiquarian, William John Thoms, coined the word "folklore", in 1846, he described it as "a good Saxon compound" that denoted "the manners, customs, observances, superstitions, ballads, proverbs, &c of the olden time" (Dundes 1965, 4-5). As collections of national folklore, including Edgar Taylor's *German Popular Stories* (1823) and Thomas Crofton Croker's *Fairy Legends and Traditions of the South of Ireland* (1825), became available to English readers, they "were cast as sources of insight to the national character of their respective places of origin, drawing on the rhetoric and ideology of Romantic nationalism, social evolutionism, and comparative philology" (Schacker 2003, 11). Although folklore scholarship, as it developed after 1846, drew attention to the international nature of much of the material that formed the basis of its inquiry, it also stressed the significance of local variations so that the perceived link between traditional art forms and national identity remained tenacious. Commenting on folkloristics in the twenty-first century, Linda Dégh (2001, 419) observed: "The discipline of folklore reached its maturity when it was weaned from its romantic nationalistic roots". The reading public, though, unaware of how modern scholarship has developed, continues to believe that folklore is invariably linked to national character and identity. The reason for this misconception, according to Dégh (ibid.) lies with "modern booksellers and publishers" who "continue to shun the rich authentic texts of present day people which are collected by academic authors", and instead "prefer to market the older classics and newer folklore collections that have been rewritten by their collectors and editors".

Folklore, as defined by Thoms, consists of the beliefs, practices and communal expressions of a bygone age. A more recent, authoritative definition within a specifically Irish context expands on Thoms's acknowledgement of the variety of topics involved while refuting the perceived link between these materials and the past; in answer to the question "What is Irish folklore", Bo Almqvist (1977-1979, 11) explained:

> "our definition is: 'All such things as are mentioned and enquired about in *A Handbook of Irish Folklore*.' And the section headings in that book, from Settlement and Dwelling, to Livelihood and Household Support, Communications and Trade, The Community, Human Life, Nature, Folk Medicine, Time, Principles and Rules of Popular Belief and Practice, Mythological Tradition, Historical Tradition, Religious Tradition, Popular Oral Literature and Sports and Pastimes, will make you understand that what is covered is the totality of folk culture, spiritual and material, including everything human and everything supernatural".

That *Hurlamaboc* and *The New Policeman* draw on dissimilar folkloric sources while revealing differing authorial awareness of "the totality of folk culture" goes some way towards accounting for their varying representations of Irish national character.

In addition to being an accomplished and acclaimed novelist and short-story writer in both Irish and English, Éilís Ní Dhuibhne is a respected folklorist who has collected tales and legends from living informants and who has published widely on several aspects of the Irish folk tradition. Recalling that she first heard the word "hurlamaboc" from Bab Feirtéar, a traditional Irish-language storyteller, in Dunquin, Co. Kerry, Ní Dhuibhne has described how she was determined to use it in some way (Ó Dónaill, 2006). Her experience of folklore collection was not confined to Irish-speaking regions as she contributed to the Urban Folklore Project, undertaken by the Department of Irish Folklore in University College Dublin from 1979 to 1980. That pioneering project, reflecting an awareness that folklore was not a thing of the past or confined to rural Ireland, consisted of interviews and field recordings made at various locations throughout Dublin and its environs. As her fellow folklorist, Anne O'Connor (2009, 272), observed, "Ní Dhuibhne learned a great deal about Dublin and its people [...] during that collecting year". In *Hurlamaboc*, Ní Dhuibhne's impressive knowledge of a broadly conceived Irish folk tradition and modern folkloristics come together in her portrayal of suburban Dublin, in which she explores, *inter alia*, contemporary patterns of suburban settlement and dwelling, livelihood and household support, trade, communication, human life and the community. Throughout the novel, her unobtrusive recourse to oral narrative tradition enriches her exploration of coming of age in modern Ireland. Not only is the triadic patterning associated with the folktale evident in the focus on three young characters but it is also apparent in a series of three knocks at the door, which all occur at significant periods in Ruán's life. The first knock results in the disclosure that his parents have been killed; the second signals the ghostly reappearance of his mother, Lisín, who reaches from beyond the grave to help a child in trouble, while the third is heard by Emma as she kisses Ruán, who chooses to ignore it, thus signalling his independence and desire to look towards the future rather than the past. In addition, a number of chapters, including "Trasna na dtonnta" [Across the waves] and "Thugamar féin an samhradh linn" [We took the summer with us], take their titles from traditional songs, while another "Ar scáth a chéile" refers to the proverb "ar scáth a chéile a mhaireann na daoine" [people survive in each other's shelter]. These references to folk tradition encompass and enhance a number of thematic concerns, such as emigration, nostalgia, and interdependency. As a result, Ní Dhuibhne's oblique recourse to Irish folklore in a novel remarkable for its social realism enables her to present Irishness as a continually evolving construct that is linked to tradition but not confined by it.

By contrast, Kate Thompson's overt recourse to Irish folklore in *The New Policeman* contributes to the construction of an imaginatively appealing, but fundamentally static, brand of Irishness that is rooted in tradition. Having been awarded an MA in Irish Traditional Music Performance by the University of Limerick, it is unsurprising that Thompson's love for that music permeates her novel, where transcriptions of traditional Irish melodies at the end of each chapter bridge the distance between Tír na nÓg and Kinvara. Passing between these two locations, the young protagonist, J.J. Liddy, embodies the continuum between past and present and so represents the enduring power of tradition. Although J.J. is aware of a pull between the lure of contemporary teenage pursuits and the call of his heritage, there is no real sense of inter-generational conflict in this novel. Irishness is portrayed as an essentially unchanging quality that is characterized by generosity, tolerance, love of music, and loyalty to family. J.J.'s desire to clear his grandfather's name, his devotion to his mother, and his love for traditional music ensure that his coming of age represents an emotionally satisfying reconciliation between past and present rather than an independent orientation towards the future. A bibliography on the final page of *The New Policeman* reveals that Thompson (2005, [409]) drew on the following folkloristic sources while writing the novel:

> Lady Augusta Gregory, *Gods and Fighting Men* (Kissinger Publishing Co., 2004);
> —. *Cuchulain of Muirthemne* (Dover Publications, 2001);
> —. *Visions and Beliefs* (Colin Smythe Ltd., 1976);
> James Stephens, *Irish Fairy Tales* (Lightning Source UK Ltd., 2004);
> Lady Wilde, *Ancient Legends, Mystic Charms and Superstitions of Ireland* (1925; reprinted: Lemma Publishing Corporation, New York, 1973).

Lady Gregory's three collections of traditional tales were respectively first published in 1904, 1902, and 1920; James Stephen's book of fairy tales was first published in 1920; Lady Wilde's two-volume set of legends was first published in 1887. In other words, all three authors produced collections of Irish folklore in the period associated with the Irish literary revival, during which the Romantic, nationalist approach to folklore dominated. That Thompson drew on recent American and English re-issues of these collections testifies to the validity of Dégh's criticism of modern publishers and booksellers who perpetuate anachronistic approaches to folklore by marketing new editions of old classics instead of producing volumes that reflect current trends in folkloristics. That misleadingly anachronistic presentation of folklore informs Thompson's portrayal of Ireland and the Irish in *The New Policeman*.

Stuart Hall's identification of two differing ways of thinking about the complex processes involved in the construction and representation of cultural identity provides a useful framework for analyzing and evaluating the differences between Ní Dhuibhne's and Thompson's recourse to folklore and representation of Ireland in their coming-of-age novels. The first position, according to Hall (1990, 300), looks for and finds "shared cultural codes which provide us, as 'one people', with stable, unchanging and continuous frames of reference and meaning, beneath the shifting divisions and vicissitudes of our actual history". For Lady Wilde, Lady Gregory and James Stephens, folklore represented just such a set of shared codes, capable of transcending social, ethnic and religious differences. By drawing on an indigenous resource to produce a unifying and coherent sense of cultural identity, the collection and publication of Irish folklore by these writers constituted an act of national resistance to colonial subjugation. Although the imaginative rediscovery of Irish folklore by late-nineteenth- and early-twentieth-century writers was undoubtedly significant, times change and national culture develops. Thompson's dependence on the work of Wilde, Gregory and Stephens is problematic because her endorsement of an essential Irish identity not only overlooks the shifting divisions of actual history but also the complicated realities of contemporary Ireland. As an alternative to this type of essentializing approach to the construction of identity, Hall (1990, 302) identified a more liberational position, in which identity "is a matter of 'becoming' as well as of 'being'", so "is not something which already exists, transcending place, time, history and culture". In *Hurlamaboc*, Ní Dhuibhne draws on Irish folklore to chart the maturation of her three young characters, and so portrays the construction of identity as a dynamic process that belongs to the future as much as the past.

The differing presentation of Ireland and Irishness in *Hurlamaboc* and *The New Policeman* reflects a variety of factors including language of composition; narrative mode; differing authorial backgrounds, aspirations, knowledge of, and approach to, Irish folklore; and, most importantly, target audience. As a result, these two novels draw attention to a crux at the heart of contemporary Irish writing for children: because the Irish market is limited and because Irish publishers make little impact on the lucrative British market, Irish authors who want to make a living from their writing need a British or international publisher. There has been a dramatic decline in Irish publishing for children since the year 2000, while the number of British and international publishers bringing out work by Irish writers has increased (Webb 2003). Critics disagree on the extent to which Irish authors of young adult or children's fiction published by international houses find themselves obliged to produce work that conforms to the imperatives of a global market. Celia Keenan (2007), for example, commented on the losses incurred when Irish writers switch to non-Irish publishers, arguing that their work becomes increasingly bland as local markers, including use of dialect and specific contemporary cultural references, disappear. More recently, Valerie Coghlan (2009, 101) challenged this view, drawing attention to the success of *The New Policeman*, "where the Irish landscape and protagonist switch between past and present". Coghlan (ibid.) concluded: "It seems that international audiences want to read about Ireland, despite earlier concerns that Ireland was of little interest to readers", a view with which Emer O'Sullivan (2011, 188) concurred.

In writing *The New Policeman*, Thompson's eye seems to have been set more on the British market than on an Irish readership. Just after winning the Whitbread award in 2005, she commented: "I've always felt a bit hard done by in England—you know I've won the Bisto three times in Ireland, but it has felt like nobody has even heard of me in my home country" (Rabinovitch 2006). *The New Policeman* brought her international popular appeal and critical acclaim. English and American reviewers see the Irish setting as integral to the novel's recourse to fantasy and concern with the passage of time. Some of these reviewers comment on the accuracy of the novel's account of Irish history, culture and contemporary outlook, lauding, *inter alia*, the way in which Thompson captures "the buoyant optimism of the craic" (Fairhall 2007) and "the heart of the Irish people" (Shanley-Dillman 2007). In a similar vein, an unnamed Australian reviewer praised "Thompson's use of the fairy tradition", while pointing out that there was "no stage Irish here" (Anonymous 2006, 68). *The New Policeman*, then, presents an idyllic view of Ireland in the English language to international audiences who see it as providing genuine insights into Irish character.

Hurlamaboc, by contrast, provides a more critical account of modern Ireland, but Ní Dhuibhne's Irish-language novel, despite being translated into Scots Gaelic, is unlikely to reach a large international audience. An accomplished writer in both Irish, the language of her father, and English, her mother tongue, Éilís Ní Dhuibhne (2004, 81) has commented on the ramifications for a bi-lingual author to choose to write in either language:

"The fact is that when writing in Irish one feels that one is part of a group—the reality is that one is personally acquainted with many of those who are likely to read the text. In English, one is writing for a large, anonymous audience, for an unknowable entity". When she writes in Irish, her intended readership is Irish. *Hurlamaboc*, funded by the Arts Council of Ireland and written as a result of a commission from Bord na Leabhar Gaeilge, a state agency that aims to assist writers and publishers in producing accessible Irish-language material, was aimed specifically at a teenage Irish readership. Given the treatment of the Irish-language poet who depends on a grant from the Arts Council within the novel, Ní Dhuibhne was clearly taking an ironic approach to her own choice to write for a small audience in that language. In view of the novel's overt criticism of the Irish educational system in general and the Leaving Certificate in particular, it is even more ironic that *Hurlamaboc* now features on the syllabus for that culminating exam (Department of Education and Science 2011), but it ensures that the novel will come to the attention of young Irish readers. Paradoxically, when Kate Thompson writes in English about Ireland for an international audience, her work is perceived as giving authentic insights into her adopted country. By choosing to write in Irish, on the other hand, Ní Dhuibhne gains the freedom to present home truths to a relatively restricted home readership.

The existence of a literature specifically addressed to young readers draws attention to the impact of language on the formation of identity. Since the decline of the Irish language during the nineteenth century, the issue of language has been central to debates on Irish national identity. The existence of two streams of Irish writing for young readers, one in English and therefore accessible to large numbers of readers outside Ireland and the other in Irish and therefore primarily addressed to indigenous readers, highlights one aspect of the diversity that lies at the heart of the ongoing construction of Irishness. That Ní Dhuibhne and the English-born Thompson are both recognized as leading Irish writers of children's fiction similarly underscores the fluidity of Irish identity. Indeed, the publication history of Ní Dhuibhne's fiction for young readers draws further attention to that fluidity. Using the pseudonym of Elizabeth O'Hara, her grandmother's name, Ní Dhuibhne has written a number of children's books in English, including the *Hiring Fair* trilogy published in the 1990s and set a century earlier, which might seem to undermine the argument that she is a progressive writer in tune with modern Ireland. However, writing *Hurlamaboc* under her own maiden name, which she has always used when publishing fiction for adults, she aligned this progressive, young-adult novel with that body of work. Anne Fogarty

(2003, xi) described Ní Dhuibhne's adult fiction as characteristically interrogating "modernity using structures, motifs and influences from folklore", and a similar process is at work in *Hurlamaboc*.

Because both Ní Dhuibhne and Thompson are gifted and prolific writers who have done much to raise the profile of Irish literature nationally and internationally, it would be erroneous to base a judgement of their achievement on an examination of the representation of Ireland in just two works. Nevertheless, the preceding discussion of *Hurlamaboc* and *The New Policeman* points towards an intriguing duality in the development of Irish children's literature in the era of twenty-first century globalization. Thompson's novel, written in English and published by Bodley Head in London and Harpercollins in New York, perpetuates the imperial view of Ireland as a childlike, magical place and presents Irishness as essentially traditional and unchanging. *Hurlamaboc*, written in Irish and published by the Dublin-based firm of Cois Life Teoranta, portrays Ireland as a changing place and presents Irishness as an evolving concept. The recognition that Ireland is coming of age, with all the angst, frustration and compromise that maturation inevitably involves, is reflected in *Hurlamaboc* but not in *The New Policeman*, whose international success shows that old stereotypes of Ireland and Irishness continue to sell well overseas. It is telling that the two sequels to *The New Policeman—The Last of the High Kings* (2007), in which J.J. Liddy is a married father of three, and *The White Horse Trick* (2009), a disturbing futuristic fantasy in which Ireland has become a gloomy, soggy desert— did not enjoy the same international acclaim or popularity as the original novel in the series. New forms of cultural imperialism demand that Ireland, like the fairies who live in Tír na nÓg, should never grow up or change. On the evidence of *Hurlamaboc* and *The New Policeman*, what writers tell young readers at home and abroad about twenty-first-century Ireland varies significantly, reflecting both international market economics and adult perceptions of national identity.

References

Almqvist, Bo. 1977-1979. The Irish Folklore Commission: Achievement and Legacy. *Béaloideas* 45-47: 6-26.

Anonymous. 2011. Irish Magic. *English in Australia*. 41 (1): 68-69.

Ariès, Philippe. 1960. Robert Baldick, trans. 1962. *Centuries of Childhood: A Social History of Family Life*. New York: Vintage Books.

Ashcroft, Bill. 2001. *On Post-colonial Futures: Transformations of Colonial Culture*. London: Continuum.

Carpenter, Humphrey. 1985. *Secret Gardens: A Study of the Golden Age of Children's Literature*. London: George Allen and Unwin.

Coghlan, Valerie. 2009. Questions of Identity and Otherness in Irish Writing for Young People. *Neohelicon* 36 (1): 91-102.

Cosslett, Tess. 2002. "History from Below": Time-Slip Narratives and National Identity. *The Lion and the Unicorn* 26 (2): 243-253.

Curtis, L.P. 1968. *Anglo-Saxons and Celts: A Study of Anti-Irish Prejudice in Victorian England*. Connecticut: Conference on British Studies.

Dégh, Linda. 2001. *Legend and Belief: Dialectics of a Folklore Genre*. Bloomington IN: Indiana University Press.

Department of Education and Science. 2010. *Imlitir 20/2010: Leasú ar Shiollabais Ghaeilge na hArdteistiméireachta (Gnáthleibhéal agus Ardleibhéal)*. http://www.education.ie/servlet/blobservlet/cl0020_2010.pdf?language =EN. Date accessed February 2011.

Dunbar, Robert. 2007. Kate Thompson. *Irish Children's Writers and Illustrators 1986-2006: A Selection of Essays*, eds. Valerie Coghlan and Siobhán Parkinson, 136-143. Dublin: Church of Ireland College of Education Publications & Children's Books Ireland.

Dundes, Alan. 1965. *The Study of Folklore*. Englewood Cliffs, NJ: Prentice Hall.

Fairhall, Anne. 2007. *The New Policeman*. National Association for the Teaching of English. http://www.nate.org.uk/index.php?page=3&rev=111. Date accessed February 2011.

Fogarty, Anne. 2003. Preface. *Midwife to the Fairies: New and Selected Stories*. By Éilís Ní Dhuibhne, ix-xvi. Cork: Attic Press.

Hall, Stuart. 1990. Cultural Identity and Diaspora. *Identity, Culture, Difference*, ed. Jonathan Rutherford, 222-237. London: Lawrence and Wishart.

Haslam, Richard. 1999. "A Race Bashed in the Face": Imagining Ireland as a Damaged Child. *Jouvert: A Journal of Post-colonial Studies* 4. http://english.chass.ncsu.edu/jouvert/v4i1/hasla.htm. Date accessed February 2011.

Hilton, Mary and Jill Sheffrin, eds. 2009. *Educating the Child in Enlightenment Britain*. Aldershot: Ashgate.

Hopper, Keith. 1995. *Flann O'Brien: A Portrait of the Artist as a Young Post-Modernist*. Cork: Cork University Press.

Hutton, Patrick H. 2004. *Philippe Ariès and the Politics of French Cultural History*. London: Eurospan.

Keenan, Celia. 2007. Divisions in the World of Irish Publishing for Children: Re-colonization or Globalization? *Divided Worlds: Studies in Children's Literature*, eds. Mary Shine Thompson and Valerie Coghlan, 196-208. Dublin: Four Courts Press.

Kennon, Patricia. 2011. Contemplating Otherness: Imagining the Future in Speculative Fiction. *Irish Children's Literature and Culture: New Perspectives on Contemporary Writing*, eds. Valerie Coghlan and Keith O'Sullivan, 145-156. London: Routledge.

Killeen, Jarlath. 2011. Evil Innocence: The Child and Adult in Fiction. *Irish Children's Literature and Culture: New Perspectives on Contemporary Writing*, eds. Valerie Coghlan and Keith O'Sullivan, 115-127. London: Routledge.

Mac Murchaidh, Ciarán. 2006. *Hurlamaboc. The Irish Book Review*, Summer 2006: n.p.

Mark, Jan. 2005. Where the Sun Stands Still. *The Observer*, July 2. http://www.guardian.co.uk/books/2005/jul/02/featuresreviews.guardian review34. Date accessed February 2011.

May, Charles. 1999. Chekhov and the Modern Short Story. *Anton Chekhov*, ed. Harold Bloom, 151-169. New York: Simon and Shuster.

Moloney, Caitriona and Helen Thompson. 2003. *Irish Women Writers Speak Out: Voices from the Field*. Syracuse, NY: Syracuse University Press.

Müller, Anja ed. 2006. *Fashioning Childhood in the Eighteenth Century*. Aldershot: Ashgate.

Ní Bhroin, Ciara. 2011. Mythologizing Ireland. *Irish Children's Literature and Culture: New Perspectives on Contemporary Writing*, eds. Valerie Coghlan and Keith O'Sullivan, 7-27. London: Routledge.

Ní Dhuibhne, Éilís. 2011. Borderlands: Dead Bog and Living Landscape. *Irish Children's Literature and Culture: New Perspectives on Contemporary Writing*, eds. Valerie Coghlan and Keith O'Sullivan, 29-39. London: Routledge.

—. 2006. *Hurlamaboc*. Dublin: Cois Life.

Ní Dhuibhne, Éilís, and Marianne Hartigan. 2006. The Tongues of Teenagers. *Books Ireland* 284: 71.

Ní Dhuibhne, Éilís. 2004. Why Would Anyone Write in Irish? *Who Needs Irish*, ed. Ciarán Mac Murchaidh, 70-82. Dublin: Veritas.

Ó Báille, Ruaidhrí. 2006. *Hurlamaboc. Inis* 18: 72-73.

O'Connor, Anne. 2009. With Her Whole Heart: Éilís Ní Dhuibhne and Irish Folklore. *Éilís Ní Dhuibhne: New Perspectives*, ed. Rebecca Pelan, 263-284. Galway: Arlen House.

Ó Dónaill, Éamonn. 2006. Agallamh Beo: Éilís Ní Dhuibhne. *Beo* 58 February. http://beo.ie/alt-eilis-ni-dhuibhne.aspx. Date accessed February 2011.

O'Sullivan, Emer. 2011. Insularity and Internationalism: Between Local Production and the Global Marketplace. *Irish Children's Literature and Culture: New Perspectives on Contemporary Writing*, eds. Valerie Coghlan and Keith O'Sullivan, 183-196. London: Routledge.

Rabinovitch, Dina. 2006. Author of the Month: Kate Thompson. *The Guardian*. January 24. http://www.guardian.co.uk/books/2006/jan/24/booksforchildrenandtee nagers.whitbreadbookawards2005. Date accessed February 2011.

Schacker, Jennifer. 2003. *National Dreams: The Remaking of Fairy Tales in Nineteenth-Century England*. Philadelphia: University of Pennsylvania Press.

Shanley-Dillman, Chris. 2007. *The New Policeman*. teenreads.com. http://www.teenreads.com/reviews/0061174270.asp. Date accessed February 2011.

Thompson, Kate. 2005. *The New Policeman*. London: Bodley Head.

Thompson, Mary Shine. 2009. "That Embarrassing Phenomenon: The Real Thing": Identity and Modernity in Éilís Ní Dhuibhne's Children's Fiction. *Éilís Ní Dhuibhne: New Perspectives*, ed. Rebecca Pelan, 129-150. Galway: Arlen House.

Webb, Sarah. 2003. What's Happening to Irish Children's Publishing? *Inis* 5. http://www.sarahwebb.info/childrens-articles.html. Date accessed February 2011.

Young, Barbara Ann. 2006. *The Child as Emblem of the Nation in Twentieth-century Irish Literature*. Lewiston, NY: Edwin Mellen Press.

Zipes, Jack. 2009. *Relentless Progress: The Reconfiguration of Children's Literature, Fairy Tales, and Storytelling*. London: Routledge.

A TALE WORTH TELLING TWICE: TRAUMATIC CULTURAL MEMORY AND THE CONSTRUCTION OF NATIONAL IDENTITY IN JOY KOGAWA'S *OBASAN* AND *NAOMI'S ROAD*

EIMEAR HEGARTY

Obasan, by Joy Kogawa, was first published in 1981. One of the first fictionalized accounts of the internment of Japanese-Canadian citizens during World War 2, it was published at a time when the facts of this period in Canadian history were not well known. The Canadian government's decision to inter its citizens of Japanese descent and to remove their rights of ownership of their land and belongings resulted in over 22,000 Japanese-Canadian men, women and children being taken from their homes and sent to hastily-organized camps, located in ghost towns in the B.C. interior and in neighbouring Alberta, farms on which they were expected to work as labourers, prisoner-of-war camps, organized road and forestry projects and, for those who could liquidate assets in order to fund their own internment, a number of self-supporting camps. Prior to the publication of *Obasan*, little was generally known about the wartime policies behind this forced migration and a wider consciousness of a long-term impact on Canadian identity remained elusive. The appearance and reception of Kogawa's semi-autobiographical first novel was to change the situation entirely. Not only did Kogawa introduce the subject to a generation of eager readers, her continuing attempts to construct an accessible Canadian cultural memory of this traumatic time have resulted in numerous re-workings of her source material, several of which have evolved as texts for child readers.

Obasan is the story of the young Japanese Canadian, Naomi Nakane, expelled from her family home in Vancouver and sent, with her older brother Stephen, and in the care of her aunt Ayako, the Obasan of the title, to an internment camp. Although the novel is narrated by Naomi and is most evidently her story, it also, by extension, describes the wartime experiences of a number of her family members, including those of her mother, her two aunts, her brother and her uncle. As well as being the recipient of numerous literary awards, *Obasan* was a national bestseller. Thirty years later, it remains one of the most widely-read works of Canadian fiction and has amassed a considerable body of critical and academic attention. It is often taught on Canadian Studies courses, both within Canada and internationally, and is accepted as a key text within the canon of Canadian literature. It is also regularly appropriated by US academics and bent to fit within the field of Asian-American studies. Donald C. Goellnicht describes it as "an excellent text for exploring a number of [...] important issues in Asian American literature" (Goellnicht 2009, 6) and points out that it "is the only Canadian novel to be included in the MLA's *A Resource Guide to Asian American Literature* (2001)" (5). Such rampant de-contextualization of Kogawa's text has forced the novel into an ambivalent state of belonging which denies it a national power at the same time as releasing it from the potential restrictions of those national bonds. The act of appropriation implied in converting it into a cornerstone of an Asian-American canon has stripped it of its Canadian-ness, an act which Roy Miki describes as:

> "[institutional appropriation] by US academics so that the site-specific formation of the Japanese Canadian subject ... tends to become another version of the 'Asian-American' example" (Miki, referenced in Turcotte 2004, 127).

However, treating the novel as an Asian-North American text, rather than a specifically Canadian one, may liberate it from some of the restrictions which that Canadian identity carries with it. This duality of the act of international appropriation is alluded to by Heather Zwicker when she points out:

> "it is important to contextualize Kogawa in terms of ongoing Canadian political and cultural debates because her work is increasingly incorporated into course syllabi and debates in Asian *American* literature at the expense of her status as Japanese *Canadian*. Such absorbent critical moves— offered, no doubt, in a spirit of generous inclusiveness—bear an uncanny resemblance to official multiculturalism's own homogenizing pluralism" (Zwicker 2001, 149).

Obasan was also taken up by those in the public and political sphere and it is credited with breaking the taboo of silence surrounding the internment years and driving forward the redress movement which followed. When the official statement regarding Japanese Canadian redress was made in the House of Commons in September 1988, parts of the novel were read aloud. Kogawa's own thoughts about this use of the text reveal both an awareness of the strategies of appropriation at play and an acknowledgement that, once within such a public forum, the author has little control over the use of her words:

> "*Obasan*'s publication got me into a public realm that I was not used to. [...] I got 'yanked' into the redress movement in Toronto. There are some people who felt the book helped the redress movement, and there are some in the redress movement who feel the movement helped the book. Who knows? At any rate, when redress was announced, a section of the book was read in Parliament and another section in a press conference by, first, the head of the New Democratic Party, Ed Broadbent, and by Gerry Wiener, the Minister for Multiculturalism in Canada" (Kogawa, quoted in Tat-siong 2002, 203).

Obasan has not only fuelled the maintenance and growth of the Canadian canon, but, as a result of the public and official reception of and reaction to the text, it has also been forced to bear the weight of supporting the idealized, yet intangible, multicultural Canadian national identity. Several of Kogawa's own later attempts at addressing what form this identity may or should take have been enacted through the medium of children's literature. Her approach to reclaiming her original minority narrative moved the debate into the field of children's literature, an area of study which has not only been sidelined by mainstream literary critics but within which minority readers will always exist, confined as child readers are by issues of agency, selection and power. Child readers will eventually grow out of their minority condition, but Kogawa has appreciated the importance of addressing them before they leave behind the potentiality of that state. As Naomi herself reflects, "Most of all though, I want to be a child forever and forever" (Kogawa 1986, 5). In order for Kogawa's version of an acknowledged, but un-appropriated, minority national identity to exist, there must be child readers "forever and forever".

It has been argued that by including minority narratives, any canon validates its continued existence. This situation is doubly played-out with the canon of Canadian Literature, forming and defining, as it does, the literary record of the national heritage of tolerance so crucial to Canadian self-identity (See Lecker 1990, 2010). Gerry Turcotte has stated that:

> "one way to shore up both the stability of the canon—and arguably the [peaceable] 'kingdom' [of Canada itself]—is to gesture towards 'challenging texts' without endangering the structure. Indeed, by incorporating such

texts—consuming them in other words—it becomes possible to reinscribe 'relations of internal dominance'" (Turcotte 2004, 128).

Several critics, including Turcotte and Roy Miki (1998), have pointed out this institutional use of *Obasan*, highlighting the ways in which the eager acceptance of the novel into a canon of CanLit reinforces the Academy's own self-defined inclusivity. As a result of these processes of validation, minority narratives and literatures often risk becoming homogenized by their inclusion within the canon, and by their recognition within academic and critical circles. This can be evidenced by the amount of critical work that has continued to concern itself with *Obasan*. In its reception, it has become a supporting pillar within the canon, a position which sets it at odds with the placement of subversive, fringe or cult texts. With its social criticism, minority voice and cultural specificity, *Obasan* might have been seen to fit more easily into this category of fringe texts. The "consumption" of the novel by the CanLit Academy in fact serves to erase Kogawa's truly radical content, an erasure which is fortunately addressed in her later, child-oriented, retellings of her story.

Kogawa has revisited *Obasan*'s protagonist, Naomi, many times. A sequel, *Itsuka,* first appeared in 1992 and was later reworked as *Emily Kato.* Her first revision of the story was in a version for children, originally published in 1986 as *Naomi's Road.* That Kogawa felt a children's book was the most appropriate form within which to initially redress the literary hijacking of her narrative reveals much about the relationship between children's literature and mainstream public and academic perceptions of it. It also serves to acknowledge that children's books were amongst the first texts to address the subject of internment. While it was *Obasan* which brought the experiences of this time to the public's full attention, Shizuye Takashima's *A Child in Prison Camp* (1971) predates that text by a full decade. While the child-oriented versions of Kogawa's narrative do not include some of the more controversial elements of Naomi's story, such as her sexual abuse at the hands of a Vancouver neighbour, they preserve that element of power which had been stripped from the adult text by its reception. Speaking about the moment of redress, Roy Miki observed that:

> "When [redress] was done, there was a loss because that history then got absorbed into the official history of Canada. [...] So here we were in the House of Commons, a group of individuals who had been wronged by the state, in a sense offering up our history to that state so that the state could 'redeem' itself. The state [...] strengthened itself by taking ownership of redress" (Miki, quoted in Beauregard 2009, 73).

Offered up as *Obasan* was, it too had "been absorbed into the official history", and in the process lost an identity which Kogawa then sought to repossess. While some adults may have wondered how suitable the story of internment was for child readers, Kogawa's choice of a children's book format with which to do this rather asserts the unique suitability of that format for her purpose of reclamation. What to tell the child reader is not so much in question, as how to best retell and, in this way, recover the content of her story. If *Obasan* has become a victim of its own popularity, *Naomi's Road* has avoided such a fate. The relative obscurity of the text allows it a life independent of its adult version and gives it a place of potentiality among those "challenging texts" of Turcotte's argument. As such, it allows the reader to re-enter Naomi's world and listen once again to her private story, rather than to simply re-absorb the public narrative created for her.

It is a struggle to find many in-depth critical studies of *Naomi's Road*, its later revised edition (2005) or the most recent reworking of the same material in picture book form as *Naomi's Tree* (2008). This absence of critical attention seems remarkable given the proliferation of critical studies of the source material. In dealing with the same theme and events as *Obasan*, these children's texts offer as much potential for cultural appropriation and national self-validation as the original text. As over twenty five years have passed since the first publication of *Naomi's Road*, one can only conclude that its status as children's literature has somehow rendered it less attractive to critics. Within any national or academic canon, one might struggle to find a less entombed place than that occupied by children's literature. As an area for both publication and study, it has struggled to be accepted as a valid and validated field. Whatever the wider implications of that struggle, its uncertain place offers it, like other fringe or cult texts, a kind of freedom that is not readily, or is no longer, available to other literatures, especially those "challenging texts" which have been neutralized by inclusion in the canon. Children's literature, then, may represent a potential space where subversion *is* possible, and where minority literatures can still exist. In this light, the potentiality inherent within a children's version of Kogawa's story, and in the recognition of the necessity of telling this story to children, should not be underestimated.

Returning to *Obasan* and its relationship to Canadian national identity, Canada, with its official policy of multiculturalism, has constructed a national sense of self which has its basis in the Canadian myth of tolerance, a collective identity built upon the idea of a tolerant nationhood. Multiculturalism became official policy in Canada in October 1971, several months before the opening action of *Obasan*. Yet, despite the officially-promoted policies, which offer reassurance to the contrary, any construction of identity in Canada is unofficially forced to work against what is an unmarked yet dominant, white national identity. This dominant identity is not a stagnant or fixed construction. Rather, it is a social force which is not only engaged in a perpetual mode of self-examination, but which, in fact, draws its strength from being so. Eva Mackey states that:

> "contrary to the common sense that circulates about national identity and cultural pluralism in Canada, national identity is not so much in a constant state of crisis, but [...] the reproduction of 'crisis' allows the nation to be a site of a constantly regulated politics of identity" (Mackey 1999, 13).

The self-examination and resulting acceptance of Canada's treatment of its own citizens brought about by the publication and reception of *Obasan* is one such "reproduction of crisis". The previously un-narrated stories of Japanese-Canadian internment constitute a potential threat to all elements of Canadian society, both for the way in which their narration traumatizes ideas of national identity, and for the risk that they carry of removing the right to claim that trauma and use it to reconstruct the same identity. If *Obasan* cannot be rescued from its minority site of production and reconstructed as a Canadian story, the events within cannot be made to serve the dominant ideology, and the trauma of Japanese Canadian internment cannot be used to buoy an ever-questioning sense of what it means to be Canadian.

In her discussion on national identity in Canada, Mackey points to George Marcus's statement that "any cultural identity or activity is constructed by multiple agents in varying contexts or places" (Marcus, quoted in Mackey 1999, 6). The multiple agents involved in the challenge which *Obasan* and *Naomi's Road* represent are all self-identified Canadians. For the characters within the texts, internment has removed their right to call themselves Canadian, but has, at the same time, forced them into a close re-examination of several key elements of the Canadian foundation myths of identity. They are first stripped of the benefits of democracy, a feature integral to the Canadian vision of self. That which has previously made these Canadians strong now has the power to strip them completely of that strength. Aunt Emily, Naomi's activist aunt, rages against this:

> "'The power of government, Naomi. Power. See how palpable it is? They took away the land, the stores, the businesses, the boats, the house— everything. Broke up our families, told us who we could see, where we

could live, what we could do, what time we could leave our houses, censored our letters, exiled us for no crime'" (Kogawa 1983, 36).

The group is reduced to this state of not-being-Canadian by the decisions of government, but the actual impact of these decisions is carried out by a number of familiar agencies. Most visibly, the rounding-up and removal of many Japanese Canadians is conducted by the RCMP. The image of the red-coated Mountie, upholding the rights of all Canadian citizens, is sacrosanct in Canadian iconography and, as a proud citizen, Emily has early on put her faith in this image and the security it represents. "'The RCMP are on our side. More than anyone else, they know how blameless we are [...] Isn't that encouraging?'" (Kogawa 1983, 81). But this feeling of safety is soon removed. In a letter to her sister she writes:

> "At one time, remember how I almost worshipped the Mounties? Remember [...] how I'd go around saying their motto—*Maintiens le droit*—Maintain the right? The other day there were a lot of people lined up on Heather Street to register at RCMP headquarters and so frightened by what was going on and afraid of the uniforms. You could feel their terror. I was going around telling them not to worry—the RCMP were our protectors and upholders of the law, etc. And there was this one officer tramping up and down that perfectly quiet line of people, holding his riding crop like a switch in his hand, smacking the palm of his other hand regularly—whack whack—as if he would just have loved to hit someone with it if they even so much as spoke or moved out of line. The glory of the Redcoats." (Kogawa 1983, 100).

Similarly, their connection to the land, to that physical element of what it is to be Canadian, is also denied them. Even after the Custodian of Enemy Property has appropriated their right to own land, the group's ability to feel at home in the Canadian landscape is further negated. When an adult Naomi and her fractured family revisit the towns of the BC interior which once housed them, she is filled with a sense of Canadian heritage, of an awareness of her right to inherit the history of a landscape once occupied by Canada's founding settlers. At the same time, she is forced to acknowledge that she no longer has a way to access this inheritance and her place in a wider scheme of belonging is challenged as she considers how she was denied the right to leave her own mark on the land:

> "I drove through what was left of some of the ghost towns, filled and emptied once by prospectors, filled and emptied a second time by the Japanese Canadians. The first ghosts were still there, the miners, people of the woods, their white bones deep beneath the pine-needle floor, their flesh

turned to earth, turned to air. Their buildings—hotels, abandoned mines, log cabins—still stood marking their stay. But what of the second wave? What remains of our time there? […] Where on the map or on the road was there any sign? Not a mark was left" (Kogawa 1983, 117).

This contentious point of a land-based national inheritance forms the central theme of Kogawa's 2008 picture book, *Naomi's Tree*. It revisits Naomi's story but focuses on a tangible element of her sense of place. In it, Naomi's maternal and communal inheritance takes the form of a cherry tree, the seed of which "was carried in the kimono sleeve of a young bride who sailed over the great waters to the Land Across the Sea called Canada" (Kogawa 2008, 5). Planted by her grandparents in the garden of what would become Naomi's childhood home, the tree's presence in her life assured the child Naomi that "all was well" (10). Internment stripped Naomi of the security and identity which the cherry tree represented and the government's post-war dispersal policy meant that it was "many, many years later when Naomi and Stephen were old" (19) before she was once again on the land which the tree continued to occupy. Through her reunion with the tree, Naomi reclaims her maternal identity. "From deep, deep inside her, from a place as quiet as moonlight, she could hear her mother's voice. *Yes, my dear Naomi. You are safe with me. You are at home with me*" (23). While *Obasan*'s Naomi cannot see evidence on the Canadian landscape of her presence there, the Naomi of the children's texts is given this power. At the conclusion of *Naomi's Road*, she gives her own names to the surrounding landscape of her new home and the reunion with the tree of *Naomi's Tree* allows her to actually reclaim an earlier home.

The conflict between the supposed powerlessness of childhood and the fact that it is the children's texts which offer most power to the central character cannot be easily dismissed. It is also interesting to note that, while Kogawa struggled with the impact that the redress movement had on her work, the events recounted in *Naomi's Tree* are intrinsically tied up with that relationship between public and personal spheres. The cherry tree of the picture book is, we are told in the afterword to the text, "grown from the cutting of [the cherry tree]" (Kogawa 2008, no page number) planted in her own childhood home in Vancouver. This house, which Kogawa never returned to after internment, was saved as the result of the Save Joy Kogawa House public campaign. Without the place which *Obasan* came to occupy in Canadian culture, a piece of Kogawa's own childhood would have been lost forever to her adult self. That this act of reclamation was recorded in a children's picture book highlights Kogawa's continued recognition of the importance of child readers and their intrinsic connection to social issues.

The adult Naomi of *Obasan* is a dissatisfied teacher in Cecil, Alberta. She too has not returned to her birthplace of Vancouver, but neither has she established a place for herself in Cecil. In many ways, she is still a migrant, whether self-defined, as she is still moving, frequently travelling between Cecil and Granton, where her aunt and uncle have remained, or labelled as migrant by members of her adopted community, who are ignorant of the reasons that have led to Naomi being there. She offers an example of this external labelling when describing a date with a widower father of one of the boys in her class:

> "'Where do you come from?' he asked, as we sat down at a small table in a corner. That's the one sure-fire question I always get from strangers. People assume when they meet me that I'm a foreigner.
> 'How do you mean?'
> 'How long have you been in this country?'
> 'I was born here.'
> 'Oh,' he said, and grinned. 'And your parents?'" (Kogawa 1983, 7).

Naomi's right to a multi-generational Canadian identity has not just been removed by the official government policies of the past. The un-narrated element of her life-story sets her at odds with those around her, who, because they do not know her history, which is of course their history, further deny her the right to claim her true national sense of self. Multicultural Canada cannot refute Naomi's right to be in this place, but it continues to refuse to recognize that she is actually a product of this land.

Obasan is often read as a narrative of loss. Naomi loses her national identity, her cultural inheritance, her home, her family. In the silence that permeates the text, she loses the thread of her own story, as so many elements of her life remain unspoken and, therefore, unknowable to her. This loss, which belongs not only to Naomi and her fractured family, but also to the wider Japanese-Canadian community, is viewed as a form of traumatic cultural memory and many reactions to *Obasan* have attempted to fill the void left by the loss. Official government moves towards redress can be seen to acknowledge Naomi's material loss and offer some form of compensation for it. Naomi's own decision to tell her story and that of her silenced mother and aunt can equally be seen as an attempt to reconstruct her missing cultural heritage. Her words create a narrative out of the absence of things and become something to offer to the next generation, represented by the children Naomi has in her Albertan classroom. Like Naomi, Kogawa herself chooses to address an audience of children; in a letter preceding the text of *Naomi's Road,* Kogawa directly addresses her child readers, who, though explicitly identified by her as Canadian, are, by their youth, not yet recognized as full citizens. While these readers are not yet capable of tapping into the power of their national identity in the same way as the adult readers of *Obasan* did in their reactions to the text, they will one day be able to and so, for the moment, occupy a unique state of not-yet-being-national. "[W]e are all Canadians together" writes Kogawa (1986, no page number), but her choice to retell her narrative in a children's book acknowledges that silence and untold stories can be a contentious issue in childhood. Just as Naomi does not fully know who she is until she understands what happened to her mother, her own identity will remain forever claimed and reconstructed by those adult readers of *Obasan,* unless her story is heard by those who are similarly not yet fixed into a particular way of being Canadian.

The loss of a national identity, and the very right to claim one, has been treated in a number of ways. The reception of *Obasan* revealed a willingness, even a desire, of Canadians, in general, to help to bear Naomi's traumatic burden and to shoulder the responsibility of what it could mean to be proudly Canadian *and* to acknowledge this shameful episode in one's history. As abject as Naomi's story may seem to a modern Canadian sensibility, any danger which it posed to the dominant national identity of the time of its publication was counteracted by a rush to embrace the most horrific elements of the narrative: the sexual abuse, the hardship, the loss of her mother at Nagasaki. If stoicism and a willingness to recognize past wrongs are desirable qualities in the Canadian character, then the material to sustain this worthy nature must be found somewhere. The Canadian-ness of Naomi's story is readily validated in this way and, through the process of peer recognition of her loss, Naomi's own national identity can also be redressed. By appropriating her story and reworking it into a wider Canadian narrative of self, Naomi once again becomes Canadian.

Many of the most common responses to Kogawa's novel fail to acknowledge that the true trauma of Naomi's experience is not one of loss, but one of theft. Naomi did not lose her identity, rather it was deliberately stolen from her. Readings of *Obasan* which see it as a national text of loss, and which refuse to recognize that an act of theft has been committed, erase the text's true power of subversion. While the characters of the novel are powerless in the face of internment, the decisions and actions which lead to their alienation have been taken by those in various positions of power. There is an identifiable degree of agency within the situation, an agency and power which go unrecognized in those responses to *Obasan* which react solely to the powerlessness of loss, rather than to the power involved in theft. Without recognition of this power binary, the question of who owns, or can own, the trauma of the novel's narrative cannot be honestly answered. A refusal to read *Obasan* as a narrative of what was stolen, rather than what was lost, means the true power of the text disappears. As Aunt Emily bullies Naomi out of her passive sense of loss into an active interest in reclamation, readers of *Obasan* need to relinquish their own active desire to claim the novel's trauma as a source of a national cultural memory and acknowledge that the dominant Canadian narrative of that time was one of empowered theft, rather than the trauma of loss experienced by the Japanese Canadians. By appropriating the story of internment, the trauma experienced cannot be converted to cultural memory because, in this state, it cannot be named as it truly is. As such, there is no traumatic cultural memory to be inherited. What *Obasan* potentially offered then was not memory, but counter-memory, a chance to move beyond the self-perpetuating crises of Canadian multiculturalism and to experience the true trauma of being forcibly deprived of a national identity.

The state of childhood plays an important role in each version of Kogawa's story. In *Obasan* and in *Naomi's Road*, the experiences of early years, those before the departure of Naomi's mother, tell of a small world, a space which is defined by the limits placed upon it. Both texts reveal an awareness that, once left, a child's world cannot be re-entered, as well as acknowledging, at the same time, that much of an individual's sense of identity is born of these years. In their youth, Naomi and her brother, Stephen, were "fed on milk and Momotaro" (Kogawa 1983, 57), Momotaro being the story told to them repeatedly by their mother, of a young boy who appears from within a huge peach discovered by an elderly couple and who is lovingly raised by them. Naomi begs her mother to tell the story on a nightly basis: "'Momotaro. Tell me Momotaro,' I say to Mama almost every night. I love the story of Momotaro. It's my favourite ever since I was a baby" (Kogawa 1986, 4). In these shared moments, Naomi and her mother engage in a level of communication which surpasses narrative. As a child, Naomi's world is both expanded and restricted by the Momotaro story, made manifest by the peach tree which grows outside the bedroom window of her first home. The nightly retellings of the tale are some of Naomi's strongest and most emotive memories from childhood. The story connects her, not only with her family, but also with a secure and unquestioning sense of place over which she once felt, if not ownership, at least guardianship. As an adult, she recalls:

> "[w]hat remains as I remember the story, beyond the rhythm of the words
> and the comfort and closeness, is our transport to the grey-green woods

where we hover and spread like tree spirits, our ears and our eyes, raindrops resting on leaves and grass stems" (Kogawa 1983, 54).

Although Stephen shares in this nightly ritual, Naomi is aware of a difference:

"Secretly, I realize I am more fortunate than Stephen because I am younger and will therefore be a child for a longer time. That we must grow up is an unavoidable sadness" (Kogawa 1983, 55 - 56).

The child reader of *Naomi's Road* is exposed to this same inevitability of leaving behind the pure and treasured state of childhood:

"I'd love to find a peach baby. I'd love to have a dear old grandfather and a dear old grandmother. Most of all though, I want to be a child forever and forever. But children grow up. 'That's the way it goes,' Stephen says" (Kogawa 1986, 5).

A passage in *Obasan* makes explicit the connection between the childhood story of Momotaro and a wider ideology of national identity:

"'Milk and Momotaro?' I asked. 'Culture clash?'
'Not at all,' [Aunt Emily] said. 'Momotaro is a Canadian story. We're Canadian, aren't we? Everything a Canadian does is Canadian'" (Kogawa 1983, 57).

If a childhood story can be used to nurture a Canadian identity, then a story of a Canadian childhood must have a place within wider considerations of a national sense of self. It is in this that *Naomi's Road* offers something new to its readers, something more suitable for their ears and eyes than those of the adult readers of *Obasan*.

Many of the avenues offered to readers of *Obasan* are absent in *Naomi's Road*. The larger social elements of her story, the abuse, the bombing of Nagasaki and the fate of her mother are not included. The structure of an adult Naomi framing her childhood experiences is also removed. Instead, *Naomi's Road* is, in many ways, a much more personal tale than *Obasan*. If Naomi's story first came to life largely in the imaginations of the Canadian public, the conventions of a children's book permitted Kogawa to exercise some control over that appropriation. The inclusion of illustrations by Matt Gould offers a visual representation of Naomi and of her experiences. These black and white illustrations are given a page each and appear mid-chapter, rather than as an introduction to or summary of the action. The narrative pause involved in encountering the drawings encourages the reader to embrace a role as observer, to be a witness to Naomi's experiences but, on this occasion, from a necessarily passive position as viewer, rather than as co-creator of the narrative. The construction of this passive position for the reader of *Naomi's Road,* and the potentiality inherent in occupying it, is a key feature of the re-telling. While the public reaction to *Obasan* resulted in *action,* through recognition and redress, *Naomi's Road* reinstates the vulnerability of its child protagonist. Naomi's own position is one of passivity; she is most obviously held in place by the actions of the government but she is also prevented from moving on as a result of the conspiracy of silence which her family layers around her mother's disappearance. Yet this passive state, while involuntary, is not without potential. While Naomi is kept in a fixed position of inactivity constructed by those decision makers around her, she is also empowered by her motionless nature. As she is the figure standing still at the centre of the narrative, around whom the action revolves, she is uniquely positioned to listen and to tell.

While passivity and silence may seem to go hand in hand, Naomi, although not in possession of all the information she requires, is in fact telling her story. Her act of narration blurs the boundaries of the role created for her, just as it redefines the relationship between (silent) listening and (active) speech. We are told that "somewhere between speech and hearing is a transmutation of sound" (Kogawa 1983, 245). If "hearing" *Obasan* led to an appropriation of the tale to serve the purposes of national identity, then the "transmutation of sound", which *Naomi's Road* makes possible, re-instates its potential to transform that national identity into something new. In many ways, *Naomi's Road* is a call to inaction, a narrative move to counteract what *Obasan* came to be. The letter from Kogawa, which opens the text, offers further guidance to the reader:

> "Naomi's road is a different kind of road. It is the path of her life. If you walk with her a while, you will find the name of a very important road" (Kogawa 1986, n.p.).

The reader is not encouraged here to use the text to walk his/her own path; rather, s/he is being called to a more passive role, that of accompanying rather than leading. By creating a position for the reader within Naomi's narrative, but a position which is not Naomi's, the reader is encouraged to use the narrative as a tool not for self-creation, but rather for self-reflection. In contrast to the contentious choice of a legal memorandum which closes the text of *Obasan,* the inclusion of a personal letter from the author, and an afterword in *Naomi's Tree,* guides the child reader into an awareness of the historical veracity of these narratives. Not only does the story tell us that this happened, but the author has spoken to the readers to reassure them that it is so. In doing this, Kogawa bookends her narrative with indisputable fact, a move which allows child readers to move past the considerations of what is fact and fiction and what their role and responsibility as readers may be in each case. Instead, Kogawa creates an opening, outside of the fictional narrative, but within the physical book, and offers this up as a space for the reader to consider not just the events of Naomi's story, but also the reader's place within her wider narrative. This is not an option which Kogawa sought to present to the adult readers of *Obasan* who attested to the fact that her narrative was a Canadian one. That this potential self-reflection offered to the child reader is necessarily linked to national identity is made clear in the text of *Naomi's Road*. In the closing pages of that story, Naomi is engaged in naming the land around her.

> "'I'm thinking that Mitzi is a good name for a road. But this road we're on, I'll call Mushroom Patch Road. And the swamp will be Mitzi Meadows'" (Kogawa 1986, 82).

Naomi does not share the action of naming her environment with those around her, and the names she chooses are personal ones. As she reclaims her right to stake her own relationship with the Canadian landscape, this avenue is left open for the reader also. The action of doing so carries a sense of power, but also a sense of personal responsibility for one's own relationship with the wider nation. In *Obasan*, Aunt Emily is forced to question, "'*Is* this my own, my native land?'" She continues, "'The answer cannot be changed. Yes. It is. For better or worse, *I am Canadian*'" (Kogawa 1983, 40). While the same question, and a similar response, was enthusiastically echoed by early readers responding to *Obasan*, *Naomi's Road* offers no more resolution than an assurance that Naomi—exiled, traumatized, questioning, different—is Canadian too. There are no maps in this text; there is no key to Naomi's renamed Canadian landscape. While others may accompany Naomi on the road to claiming a national identity, her story is not theirs. Framing such a conclusion in a text for children both re-affirms Kogawa's intent and sustains it for future retellings. Her message is not just one which must be told to children, but one which is perhaps best heard by them.

References

Beauregard, Guy. 2009. After Redress: A Conversation with Roy Miki. *Canadian Literature* 201: 71-86.

Goellnicht, Donald C. 2009. Joy Kogawa's *Obasan*: An Essential Asian American Text? *American Book Review* 31 (1): 5-7.

Kogawa, Joy. 1983. *Obasan*. New York: Penguin.

—. 1986. *Naomi's Road*. Toronto: Oxford University Press.

—. 1992. *Itsuka*. Toronto: Penguin.

—. 2005. *Emily Kato*. Toronto: Penguin.

—. 2005. *Naomi's Road*. Markham, Ontario: Fitzhenry & Whiteside.

—. 2008. *Naomi's Tree*. Markham, Ontario: Fitzhenry & Whiteside.

Lecker, Robert. 1990. The Canonization of Canadian Literature: An Inquiry into Value. *Critical Inquiry* 16 (3): 656-671.

—. 2010. Nineteenth-Century English-Canadian Anthologies and the Making of a National Identity. *Journal of Canadian Studies* 44 (1): 91-117.

Mackey, Eva. 1999. *The House of Difference: Cultural Politics and National Identity in Canada*. London: Routledge.

Miki, Roy. 1998. *Broken Entries: Race, Subjectivity, Writing*. Toronto: Mercury Press.

Takashima, Shizuye. 1974. *A Child in Prison Camp*. 1st US edition. New York: William Morrow.

Tat-siong, Benny Liew. 2002. Writing New and Joyful Songs: Conversing with Joy Kogawa. *Semeia* 90/91: 195-209.

Turcotte, Gerry. 2004. "A Fearful Calligraphy": De/scribing the Uncanny Nation in Joy Kogawa's *Obasan*. *Reconfigurations. Canadian Literatures and Postcolonial Identities,* eds. Marc Maufort and Franca Bellarsi, 123-143. Brussels: P.I.E.-Peter Lang.

Zwicker, Heather. 2001. Multiculturalism: Pied Piper of Canadian Nationalism (And Joy Kogawa's Ambivalent Antiphony). *ARIEL* 32 (4): 148-175.

PART IV

WHAT WAS TOLD TO CHILDREN IN THE PAST?

What Did Advanced Nationalists Tell Irish Children in the Early Twentieth Century?

Marnie Hay

In April 1900 in honour of Queen Victoria's visit to Ireland, an estimated 5,000 children attended a free treat in Phoenix Park in Dublin. On Easter Sunday of that year a group of nationalist women discussed the event and concluded that they should organize "a counter-treat for those children who had not attended Queen Victoria's" (Ward 1995, 48). In deciding to host the counter-treat, they were also responding to an editorial in the *United Irishman* that criticized nationalists for not making enough effort to provide Irish children with a nationalist education, for instance, by holding an outing to a place of national importance. The women immediately formed what came to be known as the Patriotic Children's Treat Committee, with Maud Gonne (1866-1953) as president (Ward 1995, 48). Inundated with donations of money and food, the committee is reputed to have entertained between 20,000-30,000 children in Clonturk Park, Drumcondra, Dublin on 1 July, 1900, the Sunday after the annual Theobald Wolfe Tone (1763-98) commemoration (Pašeta 1999, 494-495; Condon 2000, 173-175). Four speakers, including Gonne herself, addressed the youthful crowd. In her speech she expressed the hope

> "that Ireland would be free by the time they had grown up, so that they could put their energies into building up a free nation and not 'the arid task of breaking down an old tyranny'" (Ward 1995, 49).

Although the event garnered much praise, her admirer W.B. Yeats wondered gloomily: "How many of these children will carry a bomb or rifle when a little under or a little over thirty?" (Ward 1995, 50).

Over the following years some (but not all) prominent Irish nationalists began to recognize the importance of educating children and adolescents for their future role within the Irish nationalist movement. Among them were the women of the Patriotic Children's Treat Committee. Under the nominal leadership of Gonne, they went on to form the nucleus of a new advanced nationalist women's organization called Inghinidhe na hÉireann (Daughters of Erin) in the autumn of 1900. The organization was committed to the re-establishment of Irish independence, the promotion of Irish culture, and the support of Irish manufacturing (Ward 1995, 50-51; Matthews 2010, 34-35). This chapter will highlight the messages that advanced nationalists communicated to Irish children in the early twentieth century by examining some examples of youth-oriented activities and print propaganda generated by Inghinidhe na hÉireann and / or its members.

While Inghinidhe na hÉireann worked hard to push the boundaries of the traditional women's sphere that had kept women in the home and out of public life, its members also recognized that as a result of such confinement, women wielded great power in relation to children. The organization encouraged Irish women to use this power to nationalist ends. Thus, one of its first initiatives was to offer free classes in Irish language, literature, history and music for children over the age of nine, mainly in Dublin and Cork. The Inghinidhe boasted of the popularity of these classes, claiming in *Bean na hÉireann (Women of Ireland,* the monthly publication of Inghinidhe na hÉireann) that hundreds of their former pupils were now working for the Irish nationalist movement (June 1909, 8).

In addition to classes, the Inghinidhe organized events that offered children and adolescents a combination of education and entertainment from an overtly Irish nationalist perspective. Using the surplus money remaining from the patriotic treat, the women held a Christmas treat for the children who attended the organization's evening classes. At this event Gonne extracted "an enthusiastic promise" from the revellers that they would never "join or consort with members of the British army" (Ward 1995, 52-53). In July 1903, Irish children were used once again in the propaganda war between nationalists and imperialists when the Inghinidhe organized another patriotic children's treat in Jones's Road Park to counter the one being held on the same day in Phoenix Park to honour King Edward VII and Queen Alexandra, who were visiting Ireland. This second patriotic treat was less successful, however, having been cobbled together at the last minute and deluged by rainy weather (Ward 1995, 64-65). About fifty students from the girls' classes later visited Wolfe Tone's grave in Bodenstown where Sinn Féin propagandist Bulmer Hobson (1883-1969) delivered a short address on the nationalist icon's life and work. This outing was described as "a merry as well as instructive day" (*Bean na hÉireann* July 1909, 8).

The Inghinidhe's early focus on children was in keeping with similar trends elsewhere. By the end of the nineteenth century many people in western countries displayed a preoccupation with the education, training and moral condition of youth. The Enlightenment had bequeathed a view that childhood was a time of education, particularly for boys. With the advent of Romanticism in the late eighteenth and early nineteenth centuries came "the notion of childhood as a lost realm that was none the less fundamental to the creation of the adult self" (Heywood 2005, 24-25). The editors of the youth paper *Fianna* acknowledged this notion when they (mis)quoted the *English* Romantic poet William Wordsworth on the masthead of their *Irish* nationalist paper, proclaiming that "The child is the father of the man" (sic) (July 1915, 12). As the nineteenth century progressed, many western countries became worried that they were losing their competitive edge in industrial and military affairs and that their populations were declining both physically and morally. For instance, the British Army's poor performance against a force of South African farmers during the Boer War (1899-1902) provoked much concern that British men had become decadent. To arrest this perceived decline, many countries took steps to improve the health, education and moral welfare of the coming generation (Heywood 2005, 29-30). Inghinidhe na hÉireann's work with youth is an Irish example of this phenomenon.

Inghinidhe na hÉireann also addressed issues relating to the health, education and moral welfare of Irish youth in print propaganda that was aimed at children and adolescents or the significant adults in their lives, such as parents, teachers and older siblings. This propaganda reflected an overtly Irish nationalist and anti-British imperialist ideology. As John Stephens has noted, writing for children is usually intended to cultivate in the reader a positive view of shared socio-cultural values. He adds:

> "These values include contemporary morality and ethics, a sense of what is valuable in the culture's past ... and aspirations about the present and future. Since a culture's future is ... invested in its children, children's writers often take upon themselves the task of trying to mould audience attitudes into 'desirable' forms, which can mean either an attempt to perpetuate certain values or resist socially dominant values which particular writers oppose" (1992, 3).

Thus, the Inghinidhe's print propaganda relating to youth was designed to foster in its readers a concern for the underdog (either Ireland itself or disadvantaged Irish children), a love of traditional Irish culture, and a willingness to play one's part in a future war of liberation from Britain. It also urged readers to resist or reject anything British.

In order to explore the messages communicated in such print propaganda, the youth-oriented content in *Bean na hÉireann* will be examined, providing a comparison to similar material contained in other Irish advanced nationalist publications of the time. Four aspects of the paper's youth-oriented content will be discussed: 1) messages related to children that were aimed at adults; 2) reports on the nationalist youth group Na Fianna Éireann; 3) the children's column "An Grianán"; and 4) the provision of Irish alternatives to British popular culture.

Bean na hÉireann appeared between November 1908 and March 1911. Inghinidhe na hÉireann decided to establish the paper in order to spread the organization's views and to fill a perceived gap in the market. Although its members supported certain aspects of Arthur Griffith's (1871-1922), Sinn Féin (which can be translated from the Irish language as "we ourselves") policy, they did not feel that it went far enough. Like other Sinn Féiners, they not only supported anything Irish, such as the Irish language, Gaelic games and home-grown products, but also tried to sabotage and obstruct the British government in Ireland whenever possible. However, they were separatists rather than proponents of a dual monarchy and open to the use of physical force to achieve political aims. The paper's editor Helena Molony (1883-1967) recalled that "there was at that date no paper expressing the view of complete separation from England, or the achievement of National freedom by force of arms, if necessary, and of course no woman's paper at all, except the British 'Home Chat' variety of sheet." A future Abbey Theatre actress and trade union activist, Molony had joined the Inghinidhe in 1903. She took over the editorship after a short-lived editorial committee proved too cumbersome and she later described the paper as "a mixture of guns and chiffon" and "a funny hotch-potch of blood and thunder, high thinking and home-made bread" (Molony no date [circa 1950]).

By the time *Bean na hÉireann* ceased publication in early 1911, two other papers, *Irish Freedom* and the *Irish Citizen*, were in existence. *Irish Freedom* was a frankly republican and separatist organ linked to the Irish Republican Brotherhood, while the *Irish Citizen* was published by the Irish Women's Franchise League. Thus, as Molony explained, "the need for our paper was not so urgent and the strain of getting it out was too much in the midst of other activities" (no date [circa 1950]). The paper had also experienced some financial difficulties, having to take a hiatus from publication for several months in 1910.

In a June 1909 *Bean na hÉireann* editorial Molony asked her readers, "[d]o we seriously consider what a force the children are in the country, or are they thought about at all?" She pointed out that it was not enough to teach Irish language, history and economics in school if children were not imbued with a "National Faith—love of Ireland, of everything great and small, that belongs to Ireland, because it belongs to Ireland, and for no other reason". In order to inspire this faith, she urged Irish women with leisure time "to spare a few hours every week trying to bring some brightness into the lives of the little children of the very poor". As an illustration, she raised the example of a woman who actively promoted Irish material:

> "one young lady, who, although one of the busiest and most hard-working of Nationalists, has a little gathering once a week in her sitting room, where they learn Irish, some simple stories from history, and a verse or two of National songs. This shows what can be done by one earnest woman, but if a number could be got together the work would be easier and more extensive and varied" (8).

Molony's editorial is indicative of the paper's messages regarding children that were aimed at its adult readers.

Members of Inghinidhe na hÉireann concerned themselves with both the minds *and* bodies of disadvantaged Irish children. For instance, in the October 1910 edition of *Bean na hÉireann* Gonne highlighted the issue of Irish children going to school hungry. She praised France's provision of school dinners, arguing that:

> "there is little of that starvation poverty in France that we have in Ireland, because France is governed by the French for the French, and though taxes may be high they do not impoverish people as they do in Ireland; the tax money remains and circulates in France and is not sent to a foreign country…. In Ireland, owing to the extreme poverty which English rule has brought on our nation, the proper feeding of the children is a harder problem than in France, but its importance is even more vital, the need of our children being greater" (6-7).

Gonne, ever the nationalist, blamed the hunger of impoverished Irish school children on the country's subordinate status within the United Kingdom.

Within two months this article had helped to spark the formation of the School Dinner Committee in Dublin and the provision of daily dinners of meat and vegetables to 250 children at St Audeon's National School, which fell under the remit of Gonne's friend Canon Kavanagh, who had spoken at the Patriotic Children's Treat in 1900 (Ward 1995, 81). In December 1910 Molony urged her readers to extend this model to other communities. Not all schools were so welcoming, however. Some rejected the help of such "notorious" women; among the dinner ladies (only some of whom were members of the Inghinidhe) were Gonne herself, Molony,

Countess Constance Markievicz (1868-1927), Hanna Sheehy Skeffington (1877-1946), the Gifford sisters, Muriel (1884-1917), Grace (1888-1955) and Sydney (1889-1974), Kathleen Clarke (1878-1972) and Madeleine ffrench-Mullen (1880-1944) (Ward 1995, 81; Ward 1990, 98-99). Gonne informed a friend that some clergy in Ireland secretly opposed the committee because these priests "seem[ed] to think it dangerous and subversive to feed starving school children" (Ward 1990, 98-99).

The school dinner programme was not designed to be merely an act of charity. Instead its organizers hoped to pressurize the authorities into extending the 1906 Provision of Meals Act to Ireland. This act enabled local authorities in England to provide meals for school children. After much intensive lobbying, particularly on the part of these women, the act was finally extended to Ireland in September 1914 (Ward 1995, 80-82). It appears, however, that the legislation was never implemented. In pushing for British legislation to be extended to Ireland, the women of the School Dinner Committee were willing to put the short-term well-being of Irish children ahead of their own long-term nationalist goals.

The developing minds and bodies of Irish boys were also at the heart of an initiative started by two *Bean na hÉireann* contributors in 1909. Markievicz and Hobson launched the youth organization Na Fianna Éireann (or Irish National Boy Scouts) in Dublin in August of that year as an Irish nationalist antidote to the growing popularity of Robert Baden-Powell's (1857-1941) burgeoning Boy Scout movement and the continuing existence of the Boys' Brigade. Much to the delight of her fellow Inghinidhe members, Markievicz decided to form "a special movement for young boys" after the women's organization "had abandoned its boys' classes because they were too hard to manage" (Molony, no date [circa 1950]). She brought Hobson on board because he had previous experience organizing a boys' hurling club in Belfast, also called Na Fianna Éireann. Their new incarnation of the Fianna offered boys—and later some Belfast and Waterford girls—a blend of scouting, military training and cultural activities. In July 1909 *Bean na hÉireann* announced that the Fianna's promoters hoped to make it "the nucleus of a National Volunteer Army" (8).

From the youth group's inception, *Bean na hÉireann* published monthly coverage of the Fianna's views, activities and growth, making the paper an important primary source for the organization's early history. Most of the Fianna articles were written pseudonymously. In September 1909 a Fianna member reported that "[s]ome Nationalists think that the boys don't count in the nation, but the founders of Na Fianna Éireann rightly consider them of supreme importance. They are the recruits of the future armies of Ireland, and on them the future of Ireland must depend" (8). Pleas for nationalists to support the work of the new youth group appeared in both Fianna articles and Molony's editorials (Nov. 1909; Jan. 1910). Belfast readers were even encouraged to send their younger brothers down to the local Fianna hall to join the organization (March 1910).

The paper's Fianna articles provided readers of all ages with information about how to join local *sluaighte* (branches) as they spread around the country. They also kept readers abreast of events such as classes in military drill, route marches, camping trips, history lectures and concerts. For instance, an early report from September 1909 described a recent camping trip, recording that the "Red Branch" section, which Markievicz set up prior to the official launch of the Fianna, "spent a most enjoyable six days' camping on the slopes of Three Rock Mountain. On Sunday they were joined by the President [Hobson] and some other members, and 'scouting' games were played. The damp evenings were passed quickly with the singing of Irish songs and talks of Irish heroes" (9).

In some cases reports of these events may have been enticing enough to attract new members to the youth group. A report from November 1910 offered a taste of the excitement in store at the Dublin Fianna's forthcoming inter-*sluagh* scouting games:

> "An Chead Sluagh and Sluagh Wolfe Tone will jointly defend the citadel which comprises about 400 square yards of Mr Jolley's land in Scholarstown. The attackers, composed of sluaighte on the north side of the Liffey, shall endeavour to enter the citadel without being captured. When a member of the attacking force enters the precincts of the defender's territory he is free from any molestation from the defenders and cannot be captured. It will be defenders' business to intercept and capture the attackers before reaching the citadel. Marks shall be awarded by the umpires for good scouting work, the capturing of scouts and for those who succeed in entering the citadel uncaptured" (Anonymous 1910, 11).

The article went on to boast of the "steady progress" that the Fianna was making throughout Ireland, claiming that "Irishmen who are alive to the needs of their country are slowly realising the necessity of training the coming generation to be a well-disciplined, strong people, imbued with intense national pride in their country's past, and with the proper sentiments as to their rights of independence" (11).

Such extensive coverage of the Fianna in the pages of *Bean na hÉireann* is not surprising. On one level the youth group was started by Markievicz, a member of the Inghinidhe, with support from Molony and fit in with the women's organization's general ethos and aims. For instance, a pageant and prize-giving at Patrick Pearse's (1879-1916) school, St Enda's, also received favourable coverage and the school was praised as one which would "turn out true Irishmen and true scholars, not mere tape-machines for information" (July 1909, 9). On a more personal level Markievicz, Hobson and Molony ran an abortive agricultural commune at Belcamp Park in Raheny, Dublin, during the late summer and autumn of 1909 that generated a variety of romantic rumours about Hobson's relationships with both women. Markievicz and Molony remained lifelong friends, but later fell out with Hobson over political differences (Regan 2001, 144; O'Faolain 1987, 92; Ó Broin 1985, 37).

Similar Fianna coverage also appeared in other advanced nationalist papers such as *Irish Freedom*, the *Irish Volunteer* and *Fianna*. *Irish Freedom* appeared from November 1910 until its suppression in December 1914. The *Irish Volunteer*, which lasted from February 1914 to April 1916, was the weekly organ of the Irish Volunteer movement started in November 1913. Upon reaching the age of eighteen, Fianna members usually transferred into the Volunteers. Although it was not officially connected with the youth group, *Fianna* was established in February 1915 by Percy Reynolds (1895-1983) and Patsy O'Connor (who died later in 1915), two members of Na Fianna Éireann. It began as a youth paper, but later widened its target audience to include adults. These papers kept current and potential Fianna members up to date on the activities of troops around the country and changes to official policy, with the *Irish Volunteer* also publishing instructional articles on topics such as map reading (22 January -12 February 1916).

In addition to its political content, which remained constant throughout its existence, *Bean na hÉireann* initially published articles on Irish fashion, cookery and housekeeping as well as a regular column for children entitled "An Grianán" (the sunroom of youth). Written under the pseudonym Dectora by Madeleine ffrench-Mullen, the future co-founder of St Ultan's Children's Hospital, this column appeared for about a year between April 1909 and March 1910 (Ward 1990, 96; Bryan 2009). The column's main focus was a monthly competition in which young people no older than their early teens could compete for book prizes, such as *Nuala* (1908) by Lily McManus (1894-1941) and *Old Time Stories of Éire* (1907) by Alice Dease (1874-1949).

The competitions in "An Grianán" were designed to encourage entrants to explore aspects of Irish history and heritage, often by submitting 200-word essays. For example, in May 1909 Dectora asked readers to write about their favourite Irish heroine:

"Some little girls are clever with their needle, and Emer of the beautiful embroideries appeals to them. Others prefer the great Macha who subdued the giants and drew with her breast pin the outline of a great palace she wished them to build for her, or the warlike Grainia Máol (sic). Choose any character you like, and you may search for information about them in histories or other books, or ask grown ups to tell you about them, but you must tell it to me in your own words" (10).

Other essay topics included the feats of Cuchullain, the escape of Red Hugh O'Donnell, and the life of St Patrick (September 1909; December 1909; February 1910). Not surprisingly, the latter subject proved particularly popular with entrants (March 1910). Dectora, however, was unable to award a prize for the best account of a battle fought on Irish soil: two readers "complained that they did not know enough about an Irish battle to write a long account of one", while the only essay deemed worthy of a prize was disqualified because it was written by a girl over the age of sixteen (December 1909, 10).

The competitions also encouraged readers to develop their Irish language skills. For instance, the very first prize that Dectora offered was for the longest list of Irish words formed from the letters making up the paper's title "Bean na hÉireann" (April 1909). A few months later she expressed disappointment after her request for letters written in Irish generated only one missive, which arrived after the deadline. "Perhaps it was too much to ask, as I suppose the majority of you are only beginners", she lamented (July 1909, 5).

Unlike Neasa, the author of *Irish Freedom*'s youth column, "Grianán na nÓg", Dectora rarely dictated ways in which young people could further the struggle for Irish independence. On only one occasion did she suggest a practical way in which her readers could help Ireland and its economy and, by extension, disadvantaged Irish children. She asserted: "I hope all the Christmas cards and presents which are sent out by you will be of Irish manufacture. This is the very best way that little people can help Ireland at present" (December 1909, 10). Dectora's "buy Irish" message was in keeping with Inghinidhe na hÉireann's aim "to support and popularise Irish Manufacture" (*Bean na hÉireann*, March 1911, 14).

Also in contrast to that of *Irish Freedom*, *Bean na hÉireann*'s youth column was occasionally accompanied by children's fiction written by M. O'Callaghan. For instance, a short story entitled "The Land of Why" tells the tale of Katrina, a little girl who annoys people by constantly asking "why". She gets her come-uppance when she has a dream about a land where she is surrounded by dwarves demanding "why" (July 1909, 5-6).

Although written for children, the story may have had more resonance for the relatives of inquisitive three-year-olds.

Another example is O'Callaghan's serial entitled "Campbella: Or the Tale of a Proud Princess", which appeared between October 1909 and March 1910. It relates the exploits of a snobbish princess who learns the error of her ways and attracts a handsome prince, but only after being kidnapped and forced to live like a beggar. Concern for those less fortunate than oneself was a theme that ran through the pages of *Bean na hÉireann*, reflecting the Inghinidhe's (and Molony's) combined national and social conscience.

An examination of the monthly contest winners provides some sense of Dectora's audience, who were most likely the children or younger siblings of the paper's adult readers. Seven prize winners were female, three were male, and one was only identified by a first initial and surname. Eight successful entrants used the Irish version of their names. Six hailed from Dublin, while the others resided in Tuam, Skibbereen, Ennis, Cork, and Co. Wexford. Only the ages of the first two winners—fourteen and twelve—were published. The bias towards girls is not surprising given that the paper was geared towards women, although young men of advanced nationalist views also read it.

Similar children's columns appeared in other advanced nationalist newspapers, suggesting that editors sought to appeal to readers of all ages. As noted earlier, *Irish Freedom* published "Grianán na nÓg", which suggested ways in which young people under twenty could further the struggle for Irish independence and featured monthly competitions. It generated a higher number of winning and commendable entries than "An Grianán", with 82 names being published between December 1910 and 1911, over half of which belonged to boys (Hay 2006, 34). After its re-launch in July 1915, *Fianna* began to publish a column by the same author; "Neasa's Nook: A Corner for the Lads and Lassies" included competitions for youths between the ages of six and seventeen. Competitions were clearly seen as a way of piquing children's interest and generating two-way communication with young readers.

An Gaedheal, a short-lived weekly paper published in early 1916, also included a youth column entitled "Éire Óg" (Young Ireland). Written by someone identified as Maev, its target audience was fourteen to eighteen-year-olds. This paper aimed to reach "the men and women, boys and girls of the country districts and provincial towns whose only literature at present consists of cross-Channel garbage and khaki-tinted West British press" (19 February 1916, 8).

As the previous quotation suggests, Irish nationalists were keen to generate home-grown alternatives to prevalent examples of British popular culture, which, in their opinion, threatened the perceived moral superiority of the Irish people. In producing *Bean na hÉireann*, the Inghinidhe hoped to provide Irish women with a substitute for "the deluge of thrashy [sic] foreign literature in Ireland". "The fact that it is published and printed in England is the least of its faults," asserted Molony in an April 1909 editorial, explaining that there are more insidious dangers:

> "The English atmosphere it brings with it, and the false and mean standard of life that it inculcates is the real evil. The chance of marrying a very rich, and very much titled suitor, the triumph of being able to hold a larger number of fellow creatures in servitude than your neighbour—the dishonest pleasure of having command of a huge income, sweated out of the bones of less fortunate human beings—these are the paltry ideals set before our young Irish women" (8).

This concern for the moral welfare of impressionable Irish readers also led to the establishment of papers aimed at Irish youth. Possibly the best-known and most successful example is the Christian Brothers' *Our Boys*, which combined Catholicism with Irish nationalism (Flanagan 2006, 43-52). Less successful examples include *Fianna* and *Young Ireland*. *Fianna* published fiction, poetry and jokes, articles on Irish history and folklore, and Fianna news and views, though it was not an official organ of Na Fianna Éireann. *Young Ireland* first appeared on 21 April 1917 under the editorship of Aodh de Blácam (1890-1951), who declared that the paper would "always be stoutly Irish and devotedly Catholic from cover to cover" (1). Its content included fiction, poetry, and such regular features as "The Handyman's Corner", the "Cailín's Column" and "Our Professor's Corner by our tame scientist". These two youth papers were later forced to widen their target audience to include adults in order to survive, suggesting that it was extremely difficult to compete with the seductive allure of British youth periodicals such as the *Boys' Friend*. Concern about the reading material available to Irish youth was also expressed in book reviews published in nationalist papers aimed at adults. Writing in *Bean na hÉireann* in January 1909, Máire de Buitléir (1872-1920) heaped praise on *Nuala*, Lily McManus's 1908 novel aimed at teenage girls:

> "Our young people's imagination will be kindled by this tale of gallant deeds and high surprises, and they will find it a rich store of those adventures which are so dear to the hearts of the young and eager. We all remember how we used to revel in 'adventure stories' of red Indians and pale faces. Éire Óg will enjoy still more stories of Irish princesses and

chieftains, for their hearts will leap to recognise the touch of kinship in Nuala, their own charming compatriot" (4).

The importance of providing Irish youth with specifically Irish literature was also highlighted in a 1907 review published in *The Republic*, the organ of the Dungannon Clubs, which promoted the Sinn Féin policy in Ulster and beyond. The reviewer complained about the publication of *A Young Patriot* (1906), an adaptation of the G.A. Henty (1832-1902) novel, *Orange and Green: a Tale of the Boyne and Limerick* (1888), as "a reader for senior standards in Irish National Schools". Although he viewed the book as "harmless" in that "it contain[ed] no immoral tendency", the reviewer (probably Hobson) opined that "surely there are enough writers in Ireland without introducing the inanities of Mr G.A. Henty to Irish boys". He went on to suggest that the publisher should "secure the copyright of some of Standish O'Grady's [1846-1928] stories" because this would offer Irish boys "immeasurably better" books and perhaps lead to higher profits (17 January 1907, 7). Such book reviews highlight the advanced nationalist movement's concern with not only moulding the minds of Irish youth but also influencing their consumer choices.

An examination of the youth-oriented activities and print propaganda generated by Inghinidhe na hÉireann and /or its members provides a sense of what advanced nationalists tried to tell Irish children in the period 1900 to 1917. Members of the Inghinidhe reached out to youth through the organization of the Patriotic Children's Treats, free classes in Irish language, literature, history and music, the youth group Na Fianna Éireann, the school dinner programme, and *Bean na hÉireann* articles aimed at children and adolescents. In doing so, they told Irish youth that their minds and bodies were of supreme importance to the future of the nation. They also told children that their primary allegiance—both political and cultural—should be to Ireland not Britain. They told them to embrace and cherish their unique Irish heritage by learning about their country's history and heroes, speaking its native tongue, reading literature written by and about fellow Irish people, and singing the songs of their homeland. They told them to boost their country's economy and foster the well-being of fellow Irish children by buying only Irish goods. They told boys to join the Fianna so that they could become trained to fight in a future struggle for Irish independence.

Although it is difficult to provide an empirical assessment of the success of these messages, there are some indications that they had a powerful impact. Gonne claimed that even in the 1930s middle-aged men and women were coming up to her in the street and saying "I was one of the patriotic children at your party when Queen Victoria was over", suggesting that participation in the event had made a lasting impression on them (MacBride 1994, 270). In June 1909 *Bean na hÉireann* boasted that hundreds of children who took the Inghinidhe's free classes later began working in the nationalist movement. The truth of this boast is, of course, open to question. That members of the Fianna served as leaders, combatants, scouts and messengers during the 1916 Easter Rising and the War of Independence (1919-1921) attests to the effectiveness of the Fianna's training programme and propaganda. As a result of the Easter Rising, nine Fianna members died, including Con Colbert (1888-1916) and Seán Heuston (1891-1916), who were executed for their roles in the rebellion. Twenty-one others lost their lives during the War of Independence (Holland, no date). Advanced nationalist educational initiatives and print propaganda like those generated by Inghinidhe na hÉireann and / or its members probably contributed to the predominance of young men and women within the Irish Volunteers (later known as the Irish Republican Army) and Cumann na mBan respectively, which has been noted in recent studies of the Irish revolution (Hart 1998; Augusteijn 1996; Coleman 2003; Fitzpatrick 1998; Matthews 2010).

In conclusion, had W.B. Yeats reflected on the messages that advanced nationalists communicated to Irish youth in the early twentieth century, he might have asked himself a similar question to the one he posed after the Patriotic Children's Treat of July 1900: "How many of these children will carry a bomb or rifle when a little under or a little over twenty?" (cited in Ward 1995, 50).

I would like to acknowledge that the Irish Research Council for the Humanities and Social Sciences provided funding that enabled me to undertake research for this chapter.

References

Augusteijn, Joost. 1996. *From Public Defiance to Guerrilla Warfare.* Dublin: Irish Academic Press.

[Anonymous]. 1907. Another School Book. *The Republic*, January 17: 2.

[Anonymous]. 1909. *Bean na hÉireann*, September: 9.

[Anonymous]. 1910. Na Fianna Éireann. *Bean na hÉireann*, November: 11.

Bryan, Deirdre. 2009. Mullen, Madeleine ffrench. *Dictionary of Irish Biography*, eds. James McGuire and James Quinn. Cambridge: Cambridge University Press. Date accessed 28 January 2011.

C. Ua S. [Cathal O'Shannon]. 1910. Volunteers' Branch. *Bean na hÉireann*, March: 8.

Coleman, Marie. 2003. *County Longford and the Irish Revolution*. Dublin: Irish Academic Press.

Condon, Janette. 2000. The Patriotic Children's Treat: Irish Nationalism and Children's Culture at the Twilight of Empire. *Irish Studies Review* 8 (2): 167-178.

[De Blácam, Aodh]. 1917. Editorial. *Young Ireland*, April 21: 1.

De Buitléir, Máire. 1909. The Book of Nuala: A Story for Irish Girls. *Bean na hÉireann*, January: 4.

Dectora. 1909. An Grianán. *Bean na hÉireann*, April: 11, May: 10, July: 5, September: 11, December: 10.

——. 1910. An Grianán. *Bean na hÉireann*, February: 13, March: 11.

Editor. 1916. What About Ourselves. *An Gaedheal*, February 19: 8.

Fitzpatrick, David. 1998. *Politics and Irish Life, 1913-1921*. Cork: Cork University Press.

Flanagan, Michael. 2006. 'There is an Isle in the Western Ocean': The Christian Brothers, Our Boys and Catholic/ Nationalist Ideology. *Treasure Islands: Studies in Children's Literature*, eds. Mary Shine Thompson and Celia Keenan, 43-52. Dublin: Four Courts Press.

Gonne, Maud. 1910. The Children Must be Fed. *Bean na hÉireann*, October: 6-7.

Hart, Peter. 1998. *The I.R.A. and Its Enemies*. Oxford: Clarendon Press.

Hay, Marnie. 2006. This Treasured Island: Irish Nationalist Propaganda Aimed at Children and Youth, 1910-16. *Treasure Islands: Studies in Children's Literature*, eds. Mary Shine Thompson and Celia Keenan, 33-42. Dublin: Four Courts Press.

Heywood, Colin. 2005. *A History of Childhood*. Cambridge: Polity Press.

Holland, Robert. No date. A Short History of Fianna Éireann. National Library of Ireland. MS 35,455/3/12A.

J.B. 1909. St Enda's School Pageant. *Bean na hÉireann*, July: 9.

MacBride, Maud Gonne. 1994. *A Servant of the Queen*. A. Norman Jeffares and Anna MacBride White, eds. 4th ed. Gerrards Cross: Colin Smythe.

Matthews, Ann. 2010. *Renegades: Irish Republican Women, 1900-1922*. Cork: Mercier Press.

[Molony, Helena]. 1909. Editorial Notes. *Bean na hÉireann*, April: 8, June: 8, July: 8.

——. 1910. Editorial Notes. *Bean na hÉireann*, January: 8, December: 8.

——. No date (circa 1950). National Archives of Ireland. Bureau of Military History Witness Statement 391.

Neasa. 1915. Neasa's Nook. *Fianna*, July: 12.

Ó Broin, Leon. 1985. *Protestant Nationalism in Revolutionary Ireland: The Stopford Connection*. Dublin: Gill and Macmillan.

O'Callaghan, M. 1909. The Land of Why. *Bean na hÉireann*, July: 5-6.

—. 1909. Campbella: Or the Tale of a Proud Princess. *Bean na hÉireann*, October: 11, November: 11-12, December: 10-11.

—. 1910. Campbella: Or the Tale of a Proud Princess. *Bean na hÉireann*, February: 13, March: 11-12.

O'Faolain, Seán. 1987. *Constance Markievicz*. 2nd ed. London: Hutchinson.

One of the Fianna. 1909. Na Fianna Éireann (National Boys' Brigade). *Bean na hÉireann*, September: 8, November:8.

Ó Riain, Pádraic. 1916. Na Fianna Éireann. *Irish Volunteer*, 22 January, 29 January, 5 February, 12 February: 8.

Pašeta, Senia. 1999. Nationalist Responses to Two Royal Visits to Ireland, 1900 and 1903. *Irish Historical Studies* 31 (124): 488-504.

Regan, Nell. 2001. Helena Molony. *Female Activists: Irish Women and Change, 1900-1960*, eds. Mary Cullen and Maria Luddy, 141-168. Dublin: Woodfield Press.

Stephens, John. 1992. *Language and Ideology in Children's Fiction*. Harlow: Pearson / Longman.

Ward, Margaret. 1990. *Maud Gonne: Ireland's Joan of Arc*. London: Pandora Press.

—. 1995. *Unmanageable Revolutionaries: Women and Irish Nationalism*. 2nd ed. London: Pluto Press.

"ENJOY THE LAST OF YOUR SCHOOLGIRL LIFE": MAKING TRANSITIONS IN THE GIRLS' SCHOOL STORIES OF L.T. MEADE (1844-1914) AND RAYMOND JACBERNS (1866-1911)

BETH RODGERS

Girls' school stories have not always been taken seriously in literary criticism. Rosemary Auchmuty suggests that this large body of work has been "ignored, dismissed, ridiculed or despised by adult critics, whether teachers, librarians, or literary scholars" (2000, 19). Certainly, early studies of girls' books, such as Mary Cadogan and Patricia Craig's *You're a Brick, Angela!* (1976), frequently judged girls' school stories to be quaint, formulaic, conservative and culturally negligible, while the girls in them were depicted "essentially as passive, domesticated, brainless and decorative" (2003, 9).[1] More recently, school stories of the twentieth century have found advocates among a number of critics, who offer more nuanced readings of the popular series fiction.[2] Yet, in their celebration of what Auchmuty calls the "Big Five" of girls' school story writers—Angela Brazil (1868-1947), Elsie Oxenham (1880-1960), Dorita Fairlie Bruce (1885-1970), Elinor Brent-Dyer (1894-1969) and Enid Blyton (1897-1968)—these critics have confined earlier writers to the footnotes of the genre's history. In her introduction to the *Encyclopaedia of Girls' School Stories* (2000), Sue Sims suggests that a good working definition of the genre might include the following:

> "The story will be wholly or largely set in a girls' school; it is intended for girls, rather than adults, to read; it is written mainly from the point of view of one or more of the girls; the school is seen in a positive light; there is no central heterosexual love interest, and no overt lesbian material; and the school community is the focus of the story" (2000, 2).

This definition is certainly useful, but this tendency to define the school story thematically arguably elides the historical and contextual differences that inevitably exist between works written by a diverse range of writers over a period of more than a hundred years.

This essay offers an alternative reading of girls' school stories written in the period 1886-1906, in particular the work of L.T. Meade (1844-1914) and Raymond Jacberns (1866-1911).[3] In contrast to trans-historical approaches to the genre, I suggest that much of the narrative force of the stories of this era derives from their engagement with changing definitions of modern girlhood and with developments in education for middle and upper-middle-class girls, to which they responded and helped create in the first place. In doing so, I challenge both the sidelined place of these late-nineteenth-century stories in the history of the genre and the assumptions frequently made about the literary value of "formulaic" fiction and what it is presumed to have "told" its readers. Although they do acknowledge that "she was not the first to write about girls' schools as such," Cadogan and Craig argue that "Brazil's early stories indicated the way in which the genre was to develop" (2003, 124). Yet, this acknowledgement does not quite fully represent the fact that Brazil's first school story, *The Fortunes of Philippa* (1906), was published a full twenty years after what is often cited as the first recognizable girls' school story: L.T. Meade's *A World of Girls* (1886). Foster and Simons, in their reading of Brazil's *The Madcap of the School* (1917), suggest that "*A World of Girls* anticipates *Madcap* in a number of significant ways without the radical implications of the later novel" (1995, 197). They indicate that this radicalism lies in Brazil's depiction of "a totally female environment [free] from the prescriptive conditions that determine gendered division in the heterosexual community" (1995, 202). Yet, I take issue with the suggestion that such a world is not already established in the work of Meade and Jacberns. Straddling the turn of the century, the writers of this period arguably represent a singular era in the history of the girls' school story, one that marks the transition between the evangelism of school stories of the earlier Victorian period and the "jolly hockeysticks" girls of Brazil's fiction.[4]

Transition in terms of the history of the genre is not the only kind of transition considered in this essay. The typical school story recounts the process of a new girl's integration into the school community. In depicting this transition from individual to communal identity, I argue that girls' school stories offer readers an alternative mode of self-identification, in which transitions between stages of female identity do not necessarily involve marriage or motherhood. We might make pertinent connections between such literary representations of modern girlhood and specific aspects of late-nineteenth-century feminism. In contrast to suggestions that such stories necessarily capitulate to conservative images of gender, nation and class, I argue that an historicized reading that contextualizes such stories amid contemporary debates about female education and the Woman Question reveals the situation to be rather more complicated. Through close readings of Meade's *A World of Girls* (1886) and Jacberns's *The Girls of Cromer Hall* (1905), I explore to what extent an engagement with contemporary feminist discourse and its interest in communities of women (from the Girls' Public Day School Company to the Pioneer Club) might sit alongside what are often perceived to be the formulaic constraints of the girls' school story.[5] While conceding that there are certainly conservative aspects to these stories, I argue that their formulaic nature also creates a paradigm that renders positive, successful transitions between stages of female identity possible.

Constructing the schoolgirl, 1886-1906

The late-nineteenth-century rush in school stories coincided with changes in the social position of women and the education of girls.[6] Carol Dyhouse has suggested that, "at the risk of over-simplification, three main types of girls' school evolved" in England in the second half of the nineteenth century (1981, 55). The first of these is the Ladies' College, intended to improve the education of governesses, but which often had an accompanying secondary school. Perhaps the most widely discussed of these was Cheltenham Ladies' College, founded in 1854 and led by the much-admired Dorothea Beale (1831-1906) from 1858. The second grouping of schools are those high schools which followed the example of Frances Mary Buss's (1827-94) North London Collegiate School, many of which were members of the Girls' Public Day School Company, founded in 1872 (Dyhouse 1981, 56). The third group consists of the more well-known, large boarding schools, which Dyhouse suggests were intended to be "counterparts of the leading boys' public schools of the time," such as St Leonard's (1877), Roedean (1885) and Wycombe Abbey (1896) (1981, 56). Dyhouse points out that these initial reforms in reality only affected "a very small minority of middle-class girls" (1981, 55). Yet, the introduction of compulsory primary school education for children of all classes following Forster's 1870 Education Act challenged this exclusivity and inevitably broadened the parameters of girls' schools. Alongside this, Dyhouse suggests that these larger, less traditional schools signalled a move away from the purely social aims of small "finishing schools," towards "a formal commitment to academic achievement and meritocratic values" (1981, 57).

It was in this context that the school stories of Meade, Jacberns and their contemporaries became a huge success story in the publishing world. Meade's success is particularly striking: she published upwards of 300 books, mainly for girls, and readers of the popular magazine *Girl's Realm* voted her their favourite writer in an 1898 poll (Mitchell 1995, 14). In her biographical thesis on Meade, Jean Garriock notes that the 1905 edition of *The Bookman*, which drew up a report on the best-selling books for girls in thirty-two towns in England, placed Meade first in seventeen towns and second in ten (1997, 175). These popular girls' books reflected and contributed to discussions about schoolgirls that were taking place throughout the contemporary literary marketplace. *Girl's Realm*, for example, carried a regular feature on "Famous Girls' Schools" towards the end of the 1890s. Featuring Cheltenham Ladies' College and Victoria College Belfast, among others, the articles discussed the daily routines of students in an informative and positive manner. Meade herself produced a pair of articles in 1895 for the *Strand*, entitled "Girls' Schools of Today." It is telling that these articles, which attempt to combine the strong belief in the importance of girls' education with assurances as to the continued femininity of these schoolgirls, appeared in such a popular Victorian family magazine as the *Strand*. Meade's promotion of the benefits of education are balanced with comments about the interior design of the girls' living quarters—"the beautiful drawing-room"—and the feminine pastimes that fill up their non-school hours (1895, 287).

This to and fro between the celebration of social niceties and intellectual accomplishments is, I would argue, typical of the narrative negotiation between opposing positions that characterizes the girls' school stories of the 1890s period, making them sometimes frustrating and often disorientating. But their integral ambiguity also allows for moments of unexpected revelation. One such moment appears at the close of Meade's article on St Leonard's, St Andrew's and Great Harrowden Hall. While some advocates of girls' education attempted to win over the doubtful by arguing that educated girls could still be wives and mothers, Meade focuses on practicality, asking "when all is said and done ... how will girls so educated conduct themselves in the battle of life? How, and in what honourable manner, can they earn their bread?" (1895, 463). Having consulted Miss Beale, Meade answers her own question with a stirring sense of hope for the future:

> "All over the world Cheltenham girls have obtained excellent posts as
> mistresses and teachers. In medicine, in art, and literature, they have also

distinguished themselves. The same may be said of the girls at St Andrew's, and such girls, so trained, must surely be the New Women for whom we long" (1895, 463).

Meade's direct reference to the New Woman, that controversial figure of the 1890s, indicates her interaction with contemporary debates and provides significant evidence to counter her purported anti-feminism. The comment also suggests Meade's awareness that the widening of access to education meant that many of the girls she was writing about and for, both in the *Strand* and in her fiction, were more often members of the lower middle classes, destined to become spinsters and workers, rather than future wealthy wives of the Empire.

The terms of these periodical debates and discussions about schoolgirls were taken further by the various psychological studies that sought to examine the effects of modern education on the young girl in terms of her mental, physical and reproductive health. In his controversial 1897 publication, *Sexual Inversion*, part of his *Studies in the Psychology of Sex* series, Havelock Ellis (1859-1939) discussed the phenomenon of passionate friendships between schoolgirls, known as "flames" or "raves," in Italian, English, American and South American schools. Despite the expected cultural differences, Ellis is keen to point out the universal, cross-cultural nature of these intense friendships:

"These girlish devotions, on the borderland between friendship and sexual passion, are found in all countries where girls are segregated for educational purposes, and their symptoms are, on the whole, singularly uniform, though they vary in intensity and character to some extent, from time to time and from place to place, sometimes assuming an epidemic form" (1933, 218).

Despite the suggestion of an "epidemic," Ellis notes in the study's extended appendix on "The School-Friendships of Girls" that "there is seldom any actual inversion, and on growing up the 'raves' generally cease" (1933, 379). Nevertheless, his language does echo common anxieties felt about the new schoolgirl. His description of their "segregation" from society picks up on the girls' movements between private and public spheres and the uncertainty of this new third space they have entered, this closed world which is all-female but also unavoidably public. His use of the term "borderland" reflects the transitional, colliding identities simultaneously inhabited by schoolgirls: public yet private, innocent yet encouraged to gain knowledge, assumed to be sexually pure yet potentially engaging in "sexually inverted" friendships.

Ellis's concerns may give us pause over Sims's definition of the school story as containing no sexual content, either heterosexual or homosexual. It would be rather far-fetched to suggest that either Meade or Jacberns knowingly depict lesbianism in their fiction at this period, particularly as Sally Ledger points out in her study of the New Woman that "lesbian love did not exist as a discursive construct in Britain until well into the 1890s" (1997, 128). Nevertheless, the intense friendships between characters, such as new girl Priscilla Peel and popular Maggie Oliphant in Meade's *A Sweet Girl Graduate* (1891), for example, clearly have a very real context in contemporary discussions of schoolgirls. When she is informed that yet another "unfortunate girl has fallen in love with [her]," Maggie admits that she has "a perfectly crazy desire to excite love," a comment that is suggestive of Ellis's description of "epidemics" (1891, 47). The great universal admiration for Pollie Quebe, the older adolescent girl in Jacberns's *Cromer Hall*, which will be discussed in more detail later, may also be to some extent a dramatization of Ellis's "girlish devotions". In instances such as these, Meade, Jacberns and their contemporaries demonstrate an engagement with the ways in which schoolgirls and this transitional third space between private and public, and between childhood and womanhood, were being configured in wider discussions.

Setting up the world of girls

In her assessment of Meade's contribution to Victorian children's fiction, J.S. Bratton has argued that:

> "any protracted reading of L.T. Meade leaves one with a sense of distaste bordering upon indignation at the writer's attitude to both reader and material.... Her rate of production, around six books a year, meant that she developed methods of putting together stories from given motifs, characters, incidents and emotions, used as counters to be moved about at will; they call for responses in the reader which are just as easy and undemanding.... [T]here is no questioning or challenging of the reader, morally or intellectually, and certainly no attempt to change either the individual or society by her work" (1981, 207).

The terms of Bratton's criticism of Meade are telling: the assumption that fiction which is formulaic and popular is necessarily always unsophisticated in its methods and plots is one that has plagued the reception of girls' school stories. In this section, I suggest that it is possible to take a more generous position on the formulaic elements of the characters and plots of the girls' school story. The central character is generally a young adolescent girl, usually twelve to fifteen years old, and often recently orphaned and/or impoverished. The new girl will also frequently be a "wild girl" (often a "Wild Irish Girl" in some of Meade's school stories), or there will be an additional wild girl present serving as a foil.[7] The new girl's integration into the school community is often conceptualized in terms of "taming" the rebel, a point which, for many critics, calls into question any potential proto-feminist intention in the stories. As opposed to the assumption that formulaic literature inevitably produces conservative work of little value, I contend that this established formula is key to the ways in which these stories are not necessarily entirely conservative. It is the success of the community by which both the fictional school and the school story as a genre lives or dies, a community that is conjured up and made identifiable by these common generic traits.

Characters are clearly signposted by pointed names or traits so that the reader is in little doubt over what role each is to play. For example, the new girl is invariably utterly miserable about the prospect of attending school, as is Hester Thornton in Meade's *A World of Girls* who "fanc[ies] herself going from a free life to a prison" (1886, 11). In the early stages of the story, the nervous, sceptical protagonist meets and often clashes with the wild girl, who is denoted by her reckless charm, enthusiasm and often deliberate name: Annie Forest in *A World of Girls* or Gypsy Treherne in Jacberns's *Cromer Hall*. Symbolic naming is an important and useful device in the depiction of the school community. Hester finds herself in a school whose name assures her father of the pleasant, feminine and home-like surroundings which will nurture his daughter: Lavender House. Such a name is romantic enough to compete with the grand names of the schools that were being documented in girls' magazines of the time, such as Roedean and Wycombe Abbey, thereby appealing all the more to readers versed in these popular articles. Yet, such names also contain a hint of dramatic irony: their easy, pleasant quality belies the emotional dramas that will occur within them. This symbolic naming works both to create a clearly structured world but also to allow the reader to read between the lines. Rather than being passive, as Bratton suggests, I contend that the reader is called upon, along with the protagonist, to figure out the relationship between reality and appearance and detect the flaws within the school community. In this way, the alert reader knows that the sweet name of a school does not ensure the good nature of all those within it.

In order for new girls like Hester to be fully assimilated into their school community, an incident of great calamity must occur in the narrative. It is only when the community falls apart that the protagonist can finally appreciate the importance of integration and cohesion and desire it for herself. Generally, she is falsely accused of a crime she did not commit and her refusal to confess results in the punishment of the entire school and her banishment from the community. The "crimes" committed are often fairly tame—some hidden belongings and a caricature of the headmistress drawn in Meade's Lavender House and, in Jacberns's Cromer Hall, Monarch the dog is kidnapped. The temptation to read these incidents as trivial, however, distorts what is happening in these stories by failing to read them within the terms of the school story formula. Small though these incidents are, they cause ruptures in the school community that can only be restored by a moment of self-sacrifice and a subsequent scene of public revelation, in which the falsely accused is revealed to be honourable. In the case of the very wild, their eventual self-sacrifice must manifest itself physically in order to signal true submission to the community: Jacberns's Betty must break her arm before she realizes the error of kidnapping Monarch the dog and Meade's Annie Forest is brought close to death after roaming the hills to rescue the baby of the school from the clutches of local gypsies.[8]

In short, the school story formula promotes the transition from the individual to the community, or rather, from the domestic private sphere to this third "borderland" space in which private and public merge. It suggests that a girl's happiness can only be achieved when she surrenders her wild individuality to the community and demonstrates her ability to be responsible and honourable. This "lesson" is not unproblematic. The suggestion that the verve and energy of the wild girl must be subdued in order to ensure the success of a community made up of often much less interesting characters has contributed to the dubious critical reception of these stories. Cadogan and Craig are particularly indignant over *A World of Girls*, noting that Meade has "a great predilection" for "hot-blooded heroines" who are tamed into "acquiescent personalities" (2003, 59). They place particular emphasis on the domestic aspects of life in Lavender House, details which, in their reading, inevitably propagate conservative images of femininity to young readers.[9]

It is true that the domineering headmistresses and neat endings of these stories sometimes make for rather conservative depictions of school life. But Cadogan and Craig's assessment neglects the fact that there may be a variety of ways in which the reader can respond to them. School story writers are, perhaps, saved by their own formula: the wild girl may become the model of virtue and friendship at the end of the story, but she has in many ways already cast her spell on the reader long before this, and this affection renders the success of her taming somewhat questionable. In the course of her research, Garriock was able to procure first-hand accounts of women who had been the readers of Meade in the 1910s and 20s. One anecdote is particularly striking:

> "A woman of 78 who was brought up in a Barrow-in-Furness family that read widely in the classics of English literature was told by her mother to return to the library, at once and unread, the copy of a novel by L.T. Meade she had borrowed from the local public library 'because works by L.T. Meade always have a naughty girl in them'" (1997, 170).

In a similar vein, a contemporary review of *A World of Girls* in the *Monthly Packet* commented that "there is really too much naughtiness, going up to quite an unnatural pitch" (1886, 554). These responses clearly demonstrate that the wildness of the wild girl can survive its apparent taming for readers. Her original naughtiness may in fact be much more persuasive and memorable for readers than the general resolutions of the stories.[10] Mavis Reimer also recognizes this "narrative sleight-of-hand," arguing that Meade's achievement depends on readers recognizing "her negotiation of the conflicting spoken and unspoken interdictions of the culture in which the stories were produced" (2005, 211). Reading turn-of-the-century school stories in the context of contemporary discussions about schoolgirls can help us recognize such "unspoken" elements and re-evaluate them on their own terms.

One particularly incriminating moment in *A World of Girls* has been much commented upon by Meade's critics. The girls are shocked to find their teacher walk to the front of the classroom holding aloft a "neatly bound volume of *Jane Eyre*":

> "There was a hush of astonishment when she held up the little book, for all the girls knew well that this special volume was not allowed for school literature" (1886, 69).

The banning of *Jane Eyre* has been read as clear evidence of the limitation of Meade's vision of progressive education. Deborah Gorham uses the moment to contrast the depiction of female identity in girls' fiction and in works by the likes of Brontë and Eliot, noting that:

> *"Jane Eyre* may have been banned at L.T. Meade's fictional school Lavender House, but the biographical record reveals that many Victorian and Edwardian girls, who in adulthood refused to accept the limitations of conventional femininity, gained the strength that prepared them for their adult choices through reading in girlhood the works of Charlotte Brontë, George Eliot and other writers who presented an analysis of femininity that

was far more complex than that to be found in conventional literature for girls" (1987, 58).

I do not dispute Gorham's comments on the value of reading Brontë and Eliot; however, I would suggest that it is worth rethinking this incident. School life in *Jane Eyre*'s Lowood is portrayed as distressing, unjust and even deadly for the angelic Helen Burns: the utter antithesis of the ethos underlying Lavender House. Interestingly, the teacher does not declare the book depraved or degenerate; rather she twice refers to it as "this special book," an epithet which strikes me as particularly telling (1886, 69; 71). The censorship of *Jane Eyre* is, arguably, motivated by the same impulse that finds the headmistress silencing Annie Forest's prize-winning essay, written after her harrowing experience and described as being:

> "crude and unfinished, and doubtless but for her recent illness would have received many corrections; but these few pages, which are called "A Lonely Child," drew tears from my eyes; crude as they are, they have the merit of originality. They are too morbid to read to you, girls, and I sincerely trust and pray the young writer may never pen anything so sad again" (1886, 287).

The admiration of originality and truth does not, clearly, go hand in hand with a belief that such works should be read by girls, and it is perhaps this reason that a certain admiration of *Jane Eyre* can be implied with the word "special" even while it is definitively banned. These moments of dubious censorship come from the same place as the taming of the wild girl: the need to protect the school community.

"The last of your schoolgirl days"

Annie Forest's time with the gypsies is not the only subplot of danger to be found in the school story. Indeed, I would suggest that, far from rendering the stories unchallenging, the very predictability of the school story plot allows for a certain level of permissible danger to hover around the periphery of the central story, with the knowledge that all will come good in the end. The paradigm of transition set up by the wild girl's move to happy schoolgirl enables other stories of crisis and transition to co-exist. Turning to look more closely at Jacberns's *The Girls of Cromer Hall*, I examine the ways in which the school story formula confronts its inherent tensions and explores more dynamic portrayals of the transition from childhood to womanhood. The central plot concerns the taming and integration of disobedient Betty Lea into Miss Honeysett's school.

Written almost twenty years after the creation of Annie Forest, Betty's reprobate wildness is all the wilder. When Betty arrives at Cromer Hall, headstrong Gypsy Treherne, already established as the school's resident wild girl, declares her intention to "chum with this new girl" and the scene is set for a typical story of bold behaviour and eventual redemption (1905, 32). In the headmistress's concern for Betty's "turbulent spirit," we again see the preoccupation with the need for the girl to undergo a submission of spirit in order to assume her full potential (1905, 14). Unusually, however, these concerns also apply to another character in the story, one who is less predictable: the older adolescent girl. As the story progresses, it becomes apparent that the friendship between Betty and the older Pollie Quebe will form the central relationship, not that between Betty and Gypsy.

Pollie Quebe is introduced to the reader during Betty's first burst of mischief as "a tall, dark, clever-faced girl, who was bending over a book, so completely lost to her surroundings" that she barely notices Betty's arrival (1905, 44). This absorption in her studies is both suggestive of Pollie's intelligence and of the stubborn determination that will figure later in the story. It is soon revealed that Pollie is not only the head girl of the senior school but is also in receipt of the sort of admiration normally reserved for headmistresses:

> "'You can do everything you want to,' pleaded Madge, who, like the rest of the school, believed that there were very few things indeed that Pollie Quebe could not do from gaining a degree to making hard-bake" (46).

There is, it seems, something about Pollie that inspires the younger girls to believe in the co-existence of ambition and femininity. We are told that she "had quick intuitions," "unlimited patience and unlimited energy" and "was a girl who liked to rule, and who knew how to rule," and it is not long before "the universal sway that Pollie wielded" takes its effect on Betty too (1905, 47; 55; 52). As head girl, Pollie is at the apex of the community and of her own girlhood. Her discovery, however, that her father has lost all his money in bad investments jeopardizes her ability to remain in Cromer Hall. This narrative twist signals a rare transition from schoolgirl to the next stage of girl/womanhood that brings the serious subject of how women will go about earning their bread, to paraphrase Meade's *Strand* article, into the arena of the school story. In order to enable Pollie to remain in Cromer Hall long enough to sit university examinations while earning her keep, Madame (as Miss Honeysett prefers to be called) offers Pollie a position as junior governess for the coming term, assuring Pollie that "we workers have the happiest life in the world"

(1905, 93). Noting that Pollie "'has so nearly emerged from the schoolgirl stage,'" Madame predicts that Pollie will be an excellent teacher (105).

This recognition of "stages" of girlhood and Pollie's subsequent painful negotiation of these stages complicates the established closed world of the school story. While other stories rarely allude to life beyond school, Jacberns stretches the boundaries of the school story formula by locating the transition from schoolgirl to young woman within the confines of the school. Pollie's change in status inevitably exposes the temporariness of "the schoolgirl stage." This issue challenges the security of the school community as achieved at the end of the school story plot— Pollie's difficulties indicate the fact that a permanently secure sense of personal identity is not forever achieved by integration into a school community. Nevertheless, Jacberns suggests that the ethos of school life can provide girls with the tools with which to conduct their adult lives after adolescence.

Nervous about the transition ahead, Pollie begs Madame to allow her to begin her role as governess immediately. Advising against her request, Madame's instruction to Pollie to "'Enjoy the last of your schoolgirl life, little one,'" is indicative of her sense of the difficulty inherent in transitions between roles (1905, 109). As well as the suggestion that adult life will contain more serious dilemmas than those experienced by schoolgirls, Madame's advice is primarily motivated by concern over the sheer abruptness of Pollie's transition. Pollie's overnight change from schoolgirl to teacher is responded to with both joy and horror on the part of her former schoolfellows. On discovering Pollie's new role, the whole school erupts into cheers in "spontaneous tribute to her popularity"; yet this initial success is tempered by moments of exclusion, insecurity and self-doubt that plague Pollie's first weeks as governess (133). We see her literally dismantling her former identity as popular, conscientious schoolgirl, "taking pictures down from the study walls... emptying the bookshelves of their contents" (121). As well as causing discipline problems in her classes with the younger pupils, Pollie's abrupt change in status alienates her from her former friends, who tell her:

> "'Things cannot possibly be the same. We cannot talk secrets about Madame and the others if you are one of them now, can we? We cannot have jokes and fun if you are likely to take them all back to the other sitting-room. You can't turn yourself into a schoolgirl for an hour or so every day; you must either be one of us, or what you are now, the junior governess'" (151).

Pollie's predicament seems particularly encapsulated by her change of position in the order of entry to the dining room. Formerly at the head of the line of girls, Pollie now enters at the end of the line of teachers. This change is apparently small but does in fact represent Pollie's crossing of a large social chasm from which she cannot return.

As the story progresses, it becomes clear that Pollie's impatience to make this transition against Madame's advice is fuelled by a fear of failure. This stubbornness to forge ahead becomes intimately linked in the narrative with Betty's refusal to be obedient: Pollie, it seems, is the wild girl in a different guise, one that has tangible consequences for her future career. Although managing Betty's disobedience proves Pollie's biggest challenge, Betty's journey along the inevitable path taken by the wild girl becomes the paradigm by which Pollie can successfully negotiate her own predicament. The juxtaposition of their stories can be seen as an attempt to carry the ethos of the school community further into life. Betty's grandfather's advice to his tearaway granddaughter about not "shirking her fences" becomes a refrain that replays in both Betty's and Pollie's minds throughout the book, inspiring them both to confront and accept their new roles in life. As Pollie announces:

> "'One must grow up some time, and I have grown up in less than twenty-four hours, that's all. Girls, after this I shall be Miss Quebe; now this afternoon I am just your old schoolfellow Pollie, who wants to divide her property before she dies a natural death'" (152).

Yet Pollie's attempt at making a ritualistic split between these apparently opposing identities is not entirely successful at this point. The transition of the wild girl cannot be self-willed: Pollie must and does suffer, as does wild girl Betty, but there is an intriguing sense at the end of the book that their parallel journeys have not produced identical endings. Some transitions, it seems, are never complete, but always to an extent unresolved. Speaking to Betty in the closing pages of the book, Pollie's words attest to her pleasure at her new role in the community, but also allude to her greater understanding of the inherent confusions of identity and a sense of weariness over the difficulties that her transition has incurred:

> "'I tell you what it is, Betty. I shall be glad, really glad to come back to Cromer Hall next term as Miss Quebe, the governess, and you will be glad to come back as Betty the schoolgirl—that is about it, I think'" (255).

Conclusion

In their preface to the 2003 edition of *You're a Brick, Angela!*, Cadogan and Craig respond to the growth of interest in girls' fiction since the first publication of their book. They suggest that:

> "Nowadays, it is taken seriously—sometimes *too* seriously! It's important to remain alive to the merriment of the genre, as well as its various sociological implications" (2003, 14).

In this discussion, I have suggested that the seriousness and merriment of the girls' school story genre in the late nineteenth and early twentieth century are, in fact, intimately related. Although school stories were certainly intended to entertain, by the very nature of their subject matter they cannot be divorced from the reforms in girls' access to education that were occurring in the second half of the nineteenth century. The extent to which school stories supported, promoted or, indeed, hindered these educational opportunities for girls has been subject to much debate, but the assumption that light fiction for girls necessarily capitulated to conservative attitudes fails to read the stories in the context of the complex and often conflicting negotiations between definitions of femininity and feminism at this time. The importance of contemporary communities of women co-operating together to achieve lasting social change at this period, such as the Girls' Public Day School Company, sheds considerable light on the context for and preoccupations of the school story. While the methods by which the community of schoolgirls comes into being are sometimes not entirely unproblematic, the attempt to reconcile competing images of girlhood is certainly there to more of an extent than is often recognized.

These tensions are not lost on the writers themselves. There were, I have shown, moments in which school stories self-reflexively discussed the problematic nature of their constructions of girlhood. Jacberns's Pollie finds herself pushed out of the school community in a very final way, beyond the situation of the wild girl. Nevertheless, the spirit of schoolgirl life, conjured by the generic traits common across these stories, is shown to provide a paradigm of transition with which these characters can forge ahead in their future womanhood, even if Pollie's experience suggests that the certainty a girl feels in her identity as a schoolgirl (whether wild or simply new) will never quite be hers again. By considering the contexts in which contemporary readers would have read these texts, this essay has challenged assumptions about the value of popular, formulaic fiction. One such reader was, interestingly, the nine-year-old Virginia Woolf. In the correspondence section of the December 1891 edition of their mock newspaper, *The Hyde Park Gate News*, Virginia and her sister Vanessa hint at potential Christmas gifts: "Reader: If the child is a girl 'A World of Girls' or the 'Girl's Own Paper' would be suitable gifts" (2005, 11). The use of a rare footnote to inform "the reader" (that is, their parents) that L.T. Meade is the author of *A World of Girls* suggests that this is a genuine request from the sisters not permitted to attend school themselves but deeply interested in the comings and goings of their schoolboy brothers. Such readers challenge Bratton's assumptions about the supposedly passive and unreflective readership of girls' school stories. That the future author of *A Room of One's Own* (1929) desired knowledge of these communities of girls creates a serendipitous link between the fiction of this period and the feminism of the early twentieth century.

Notes

[1] Cadogan and Craig reconsidered their discussion of school stories in their new preface to the 2003 edition of their study, published by Girls Gone By. Cadogan writes: "Yes—in retrospect we might have been slightly tough on, or frivolous about, certain aspects of the school stories; but I believe that, at the very least, we succeeded in presenting these, for future mainstream literary critics and social historians, as a suitable and worthy subject for treatment" (2003, 12).

[2] See, for example, Auchmuty's *A World of Girls* (1992); Gill Frith's essay "'The Time of Your Life': The Meaning of the School Story" in *Language, Gender and Childhood*, eds. Carolyn Steedman, Cathy Urwin and Valerie Walkerdine (1985): 113-37; and Sheena Wilkinson's *Friends in the Fourth: Girls' School and College Friendships in Twentieth-Century British Fiction* (2007).

[3] L.T. Meade was born in Bandon, County Cork, in 1844. She was an immensely successful and prolific writer, editor and journalist, publishing upward of 300 books across her career, mainly for girls. For further biographical information, see Mitchell (1995) and the entry in the *Encyclopaedia of Girls' School Stories* (2000). Raymond Jacberns is the pseudonym for Georgina Mary Isabel Ash (1866-1911), the daughter of an Anglican minister who was born in France and lived mainly in Sussex. She wrote approximately fifteen school stories, as well as many other children's books. Very little is known about her life, but it is suggested in the *Encyclopaedia* that she may have worked as a teacher.

[4] Gillian Avery notes that "Angela Brazil is usually credited with creating the school story as it is parodied by its detractors; larky and slangy accounts of whoops in the dorm and tussles on the hockey pitch" (1975, 207).

[5] The Pioneer Club was an organization of professional women who met to debate social, educational and political topics. Meade was on the club's managing committee and regularly led debates (Mitchell 1995, 10).

[6] Some useful discussions of the history of female education include Joan N. Burstyn, *Victorian Education and the Ideal of Womanhood* (1980); Joyce Senders

Pederson, *The Reform of Girls' Secondary and Higher Education in Victorian England: A Study of Elites and Educational Change* (1987); and Ellen Jordan, 'Making Good Wives and Mothers': The Transformation of Middle-Class Girls' Education in Nineteenth Century Britain. *History of Education Quarterly* 31.4 (1991): 439-62.

[7] For a fuller discussion of Meade's "Wild Irish Girls," see Carole Dunbar's 2005 essay, The Wild Irish Girls of L.T. Meade and Mrs George De Horne Vaizey, in *Studies in Children's Literature, 1500-2000.*

[8] Mavis Reimer interestingly proposes reading this incident in the context of contemporary debates raised by W.T. Stead's exposé of child prostitution in the "Maiden Tribute to Modern Babylon" articles which appeared in the *Pall Mall Gazette* in 1885, a year before the publication of Meade's book. Reimer suggests that Meade "read another figure in Stead's narrative, that of the schoolgirl" and suggests that, although the kidnapping of baby Nan recreates the anxieties of Stead's article, we might read Annie's courageous rescue of Nan as a recreation of a romantic quest narrative that represents a different response to the threats identified by Stead than simply fear and acceptance of female adolescent vulnerability (1999, 47). Such a reading exemplifies the rewards of contextualizing writers such as Meade in their historical moment.

[9] Similarly, Kimberley Reynolds suggests "these reformed rebels not only revitalised the domestic angel in the house, but in the process, created an audience which colluded in its own containment and a reader who reacted against change, adhering to—or even reverting to—her place in the home and a moral ambience based on feminine idealism" (1990, 138).

[10] My argument here echoes Janice Radway's conclusions about the potential complexity of the reading experience. In her work on the readers of romance fiction, Radway points out that "[c]ommodities like mass-produced literary texts are selected, purchased, constructed, and used by real people with previously existing needs, desires, intentions, and interpretive strategies" (1984, 221).

References

Anon. 1886. Conversation on Books. *The Monthly Packet*: 553-5.

Auchmuty, Rosemary. 1992. *A World of Girls*. London: The Women's Press.

—. 2000. Critical Response. *The Encyclopaedia of Girls' School Stories*, eds. Sue Sims and Hilary Clare, 19-33. Aldershot: Ashgate.

Avery, Gillian. 1975. *Childhood's Pattern: A Study of the Heroes and Heroines of Children's Fiction, 1770-1950*. London: Hodder and Stoughton.

Bratton, J. S. 1981. *The Impact of Victorian Children's Fiction*. London: Croom Helm.

Brazil, Angela. 1906. *The Fortunes of Philippa*. London: Blackie and Son.

—. 1917. *The Madcap of the School*. London: Blackie and Son.

Burstyn, Joan N. 1980. *Victorian Education and the Ideal of Womanhood*. London: Routledge.

Cadogan, Mary and Patricia Craig. 2003. *You're a Brick, Angela! The Girls' Story 1839 to 1985*. 2nd ed. Bath: Girls Gone By.

Dunbar, Carole. 2004. The Wild Irish Girls of L.T. Meade and Mrs George De Horne Vaizey. *Studies in Children's Literature, 1500-2000*, eds. Celia Keenan and Mary Shine Thompson, 38-43. Dublin: Four Courts Press.

Dyhouse, Carol. 1981. *Girls Growing Up in Late Victorian and Edwardian England*. London: Routledge.

Ellis, Havelock. 1933. *Studies in the Psychology of Sex. Volume II: Sexual Inversion*. 1897. 3rd ed. Philadelphia: F.A. Davis.

Foster, Shirley and Judy Simons. 1995. *What Katy Read: Feminist Re-Readings of "Classic" Stories for Girls*. Macmillan: London.

Frith, Gill. 1985. "The Time of Your Life": The Meaning of the School Story. *Language, Gender and Childhood*, eds. Carolyn Steedman, Cathy Urwin and Valerie Walkerdine, 113-37. London: Routledge.

Garriock, Jean Barbara. 1997. *Late Victorian and Edwardian Images of Women and their Education in the Popular Periodical Press with Particular Reference to L.T. Meade*. Dissertation, University of Liverpool.

Gorham, Deborah. 1987. The Ideology of Femininity and Reading for Girls, 1850-1914. *Lessons for Life: The Schooling of Girls and Women 1860-1950*, ed. Felicity Hunt, 39-59. Oxford: Blackwell.

Jacberns, Raymond. 1905. *The Girls of Cromer Hall*. c. 1905. London: Thomas Nelson.

Jordan, Ellen. 1991. "Making Good Wives and Mothers": The Transformation of Middle-Class Girls' Education in Nineteenth-Century Britain. *History of Education Quarterly* 31 (4): 439-62.

Ledger, Sally. 1997. *The New Woman: Fiction and Feminism in the Fin de Siècle*. Manchester: Manchester University Press.

Meade, L.T. 1895. Girls' Schools of Today I: Cheltenham College. *The Strand* 9: 283-8.

—. 1895. Girls' Schools of Today II: St Leonard's and Great Harrowden Hall. *The Strand* 9: 457-63.

—. 1891. *A Sweet Girl Graduate*. Chicago: M.A. Donohue.

—. 1910. *A World of Girls*. 1886. London: Cassell.

Mitchell, Sally. 1995. *The New Girl: Girls' Culture in England, 1880-1915*. New York: Columbia University Press.

Pederson, Joyce Senders. 1987. *The Reform of Girls' Secondary and Higher Education in Victorian England: A Study of Elites and Educational Change*. London: Garland.

Radway, Janice. 1991. *Reading the Romance: Women, Patriarchy, and Popular Literature*. Chapel Hill: University of North Carolina Press.

Reimer, Mavis. 1999. "These Two Irreconcilable Things—Art and Young Girls": The Case of the Girls' School Story. *Boys, Girls, Books, Toys: Gender in Children's Literature and Culture*, eds. Beverly Lyon Clark and Margaret R. Higonnet, 40-52. Baltimore: John Hopkins University Press.

—. 2005. World of Girls: Educational Reform and Fictional Form in L.T. Meade's School Stories. *Culturing the Child, 1690-1914: Essays in Memory of Mitzi Myers*, ed. Donelle Ruwe, 199-217. Lanham: Scarecrow.

Reynolds, Kimberley. 1990. *Girls Only? Gender and Popular Children's Fiction in Britain, 1880-1910*. London: Harvester Wheatsheaf.

Sims, Sue. 2000. Introduction. *The Encyclopaedia of Girls' School Stories*, eds. Sue Sims and Hilary Clare, 1-18. Aldershot: Ashgate.

Sime, Sue, and Hilary Clare. 2000. *The Encyclopaedia of Girls' School Stories*. Aldershot: Ashgate.

Wilkinson, Sheena. 2007. *Friends in the Fourth: Girls' School and College Friendships in Twentieth-Century British Fiction*. London: Bettany Press.

Woolf, Virginia and Vanessa Bell, with Thoby Stephen. 2005. *Hyde Park Gate News: The Stephen Family Newspaper*, ed. Gill Lowe. London: Hersperus.

PART V

WHAT ARE THE CHILDREN HEARING AND WHAT ARE THEY TELLING US?

"Here's Looking at You, Kid". From Big Brother to Big Brother: Teenagers and Surveillance

Kay Sambell

Introduction

This chapter discusses the ways in which the young adult author, Melvin Burgess, engages with the theme of surveillance. It will focus on his 2006 novel, *Sara's Face*, arguing that this novel critically explores discourses regarding teenage girls' relationships with the media and celebrity culture. In so doing, Burgess moves away from Orwellian narratives which overtly warn children about the invasiveness of surveillance as a means of totalitarian control. Instead, he represents the teenage protagonist, Sara, as capable of manipulating what John Edward McGrath (2004, 2) calls "surveillance space." Here such a space is situated in people's consumption of mass entertainment and popular media texts. Burgess argues that young people are aware of the tensions around media and are capable of understanding and manipulating such spaces themselves. In this assertion, Burgess is offering an innovative approach to articulating the relationship between young people and contemporary media forms.

Surveillance states and surveillance space

In *Loving Big Brother: Performance, Privacy and Surveillance Space*, McGrath (2004) suggests that, given the extent to which surveillance has been adopted by contemporary Western society, it is important to discuss and develop ideas about surveillance as a field of experience. He argues that, in recent years, "surveillance has proliferated not least because we desire it—we enjoy it, play with it, use it for comfort" (2004, vii). However, according to McGrath, newly emerging ideas which associate surveillance with pleasure and playfulness stand in stark contrast to the dominant ways in which surveillance has tended to be framed since Orwell's seminal masterpiece, *Nineteen-Eighty-Four* (1949).

McGrath asserts that whilst surveillance has undergone a massive and profound explosion in contemporary Western society, most discussions of it remain ideologically framed by the dominating conceptual framework of regulation and discipline. He notes, too, that the term surveillance "comes pre-loaded with negative imagery and chilling emotions" (2004, 1) which owe much to the Orwellian imagination. From this standpoint, the expression "Big Brother" has become negatively associated with the notion of the surveillance state and the ways in which an all-seeing totalitarian eye represents the invasion of individual privacy and the systematic removal of personal freedom and control. According to McGrath, the shocking denouement of Orwell's novel, in which Winston finds he is compelled to love Big Brother, acts as "a chilling prophecy of the complete destruction of the self by the surveying state" (2004, vii).

Anders Albrechtslund (2008, 4) also notes that, in an Orwellian sense, surveillance often becomes imaginatively associated with the horrifying destruction of the subjectivity of those under surveillance. Like McGrath, he argues that conventional understandings of surveillance have largely become established within a hierarchical system of power and repression. Albrechtslund refers to the ways in which, for theorists of surveillance, the idea of Big Brother has come to be associated with Foucault's metaphor of the panopticon. As such, he notes, both metaphors have been interpreted as representing a vertical, hierarchical power relationship in ideas around surveillance, in which the gaze of the watcher controls the watched. He argues that, as a result, the visual metaphor associated with the practice of "watching over" has become an extremely potent one. It implies a spatial hierarchy where the watcher is positioned *over* the watched. In other words, Albrechtslund, like McGrath, draws attention to the dominance of a reading of surveillance which places power in the hands of the watcher, while those being observed are more or less passive subjects of others' control.

It can be argued that the recent explosion of critical interest in the relationship between surveillance and childhood has tended to draw heavily upon discourses which frame surveillance in terms of the adult control of the young, with the issues of safety, privacy and crime prevention being foregrounded. For instance, Valerie Steeves and Owain Jones (2010, 187) assert that young people today are watched and monitored to such a degree that the experience of being perpetually watched has become a central, and oppressive, feature of modern youth. These researchers importantly draw attention to the ways in which this raises disquieting questions about young people's rights, freedom and the notion of adult control of young people. Similarly, Allison James (2000, 28) suggests that the pervasiveness of the adult gaze and adult ordering of children's lives and bodies is significant, and Steeves and Jones assert that the "increasing normalization of surveillance technologies in the social spaces that young people inhabit raises alarming questions about the potentially negative effect of intrusive surveillance on their everyday lives, their sense of identity and their social relationships" (2010, 188).

Further, it can also be argued that Orwell's explicitly political model of tyrannical, sinister and repressive state surveillance, in which Big Brother is always watching, has become a dominant discourse in children's novels since the 1970s. Many writers have warned young readers about an adult world which seeks to over-control and restrict them. Authors have suggested ways in which monitoring can threaten both actual children and romantic constructions of childhood in starkly admonitory fictions like John Christopher's *The Guardians* (1970), Robert Westall's *Futuretrack 5* (1984), Lois Lowry's *The Giver* (1994), Tim Lott's *Fearless* (2007) and David Thorpe's *Hybrids* (2007). Common to all of these texts is an emphasis on child protagonists escaping surveillance to avoid discipline, repression and enforced conformity.

McGrath, however, argues that we need new ideas which will help us better understand the multifaceted and potentially participatory ways in which "we experience surveillance...and ourselves within surveillance, that are quite different from the common ideological understandings" (2004, 2). His aim is to offer an alternative approach to thinking about surveillance which might help us to deal in novel and complex ways with the fact that the relevant question today is not *whether* we should live in a surveillance society, but *how*. He uses the term surveillance space to refer to a radical new reading of surveillance which focuses partly on the lived experience of surveillance and partly on the cultural products that reveal our lives under surveillance. For McGrath, new ideas about surveillance are epitomized by the ways in which the popular television programme, *Big Brother*, repositions the Orwellian metaphor, situating it firmly within the field of experience associated with mass entertainment. Nowadays, he observes, we "find ourselves in a society in which watching ordinary people do not much on television has become a popular past-time" (2004, vii). For him, this represents a shift in which, within our mediated world, surveillance offers new possibilities for participation and communication.

To make his case, McGrath highlights how, for example, in the television show, *Big Brother*, ordinary people scramble for five minutes of media fame. He argues that, contrary to the disapproval routinely expressed by the upmarket press, this desire for fame can be seen positively, as an act of self-reproduction in the mass media. McGrath's theoretical approach, then, throws an unfamiliar light on surveillance. His notion of surveillance space sets out a surprising alternative in which constant scrutiny is not framed as an Orwellian invasion of privacy or an infringement of human rights, but as a radical new space in which individuals have much to gain, as well as lose, from the experience of being watched.

Mark Andrejevic (2003) also notes a shift in contemporary notions of "Big Brother". Similarly, for him, the popular television show *Big Brother* heralded a new, gentler way of thinking about surveillance. He argues that for what he describes as the media-savvy, post-war generation (2003, 136), in television's *Big Brother* the totalitarian spectre suddenly shifted to became a figure of fun, heralding the development of a perception that there was "nothing particularly frightening about perpetual monitoring, nor the commodification of young people's private lives for mass consumption" (2003, 96).

Furthermore, according to Albrechtslund (2008, 4) these new theoretical approaches reposition surveillance within a "flat," or more equal, relationship between watcher and watched, or even one which favours the person under surveillance. He, too, argues for a new reading of surveillance that is empowering and which offers new ways of constructing one's own identity. He suggests that, in this context, the visual metaphor which relates to the practice of being watched offers a space in which individuals may claim "copyright" (2008, 5) of their own lives by engaging in the self-construction of identity, which becomes exhibited to others via surveillance space. For Albrechtslund, this allows the possibility of changing the role of the person under surveillance from passive to active, since surveillance, in this context, offers new opportunities to take action. Visibility becomes a tool of power that can be used, for instance, to rebel or challenge the status quo.

Such theoretical frameworks, then, challenge the traditional model of surveillance as a hierarchical power relationship in which the watcher controls the watched. In what follows I will argue that, in *Sara's Face,* Burgess explores the issue of surveillance, framing his exploration, importantly, within the context of surveillance space. Rather than delivering a lecture to young readers on the perils of a surveillance state, as Orwellian narratives do, he takes a different approach to this theme, emphasizing the ways in which contemporary children (particularly teenage girls) watch and perceive themselves as watched. By exploring ideas about surveillance space, Burgess posits a more ambivalent relationship between power, youth, surveillance and media than that indicated by previous texts.

Sara's Face and celebrity culture

Burgess positions *Sara's Face* firmly within the context of surveillance space. To achieve this he draws upon several manifestations of contemporary surveillance culture in his novel. Sara yearns, like many teenage girls as argued in the popular press, to be famous. This is presented as much more than a vapid or vain desire. Sara tells us from the outset that she does not simply crave to be pretty, or to have talent. Instead, she wants people to see her as "a blessing" (2006, 10). In the first few pages of the novel we see her reflecting on the meanings of fame. It is clear that she has highly-developed ideas about the topic, and her motivations to become famous are complex, rather than purely reactionary or shallow. She defines fame, for example, as having "something about you that inspires" people who look at you "to be more than themselves....It's not about who knows you or who you are. It's not what you do—it's about what you make other people do" (2006, 11). This, importantly, introduces the idea that Sara believes she can achieve a high degree of power by being watched, and suggests that, rather than effacing or destroying the self in an attempt to conform to others' ideals of fame and beauty, she might use surveillance space to build subjectivity.

Moreover, on an important level, Sara's desire for fame ties the novel in firmly to ideas about celebrity status and mass entertainment. Sometimes the novel's allusions to celebrity culture are "real", and sometimes fictional, but all serve to frame Sara's story in terms of surveillance space and present her as someone who is acutely aware of how the space operates. For instance, at times the narrative explicitly builds up references to actual cultural productions which are drawn from the reader's world, such as *OK!* or *Heat*—magazines which focus on celebrities' lives. These publications use magazine photography as surveillance in continually recording and revealing the changing bodies of predominantly female celebrities, often criticizing them, and they form Sara's staple reading material. Furthermore, "real" television chat shows are directly referred to, such as *The Jonathon Ross Show* (28), which delve into the private lives of celebrities. The narrative world of *Sara's Face* is also fleshed out with concrete examples of specific tabloids—the *Daily Mirror*, the *Sun* and the *News of the World* (190)—and examples of actual celebrities, such as Michael Jackson and Cher, who both achieved notoriety within popular media for literally as well as metaphorically manipulating their image by allegedly using cosmetic surgery.

These direct references to celebrity culture are used to build up a sense of the popular media which routinely construct celebrity pin-ups, such as the imaginary Jonathon Heat, the pop idol with whom Sara's life becomes fatally embroiled. In this way Burgess deliberately blurs the boundaries between the "real", the embodied and the fabricated celebrity culture created within the novel. On one level, this means that, while the powerful narratives which fuel Sara's imagination and actions may seem absurd and grotesque, they find their roots in the lives and bodies of actual celebrities in new forms of surveillance space. On another level, it highlights the extent to which Sara is utterly immersed in, and aware of, the power afforded by the potent sets of media images which saturate her imaginative world. It also means, as the novel's opening frame narrative establishes, that the ways in which the reader knows Sara are "filtered through opinion and memory, and of course by how much other people want you to know" (2). This draws the reader's attention, right from the start of the novel, to the complex ways in which public images are manipulable and potentially deceptive and offer characters the opportunity to exert power over others by being watched. In other words, it emphasizes how far people like Heat and Sara, both of whom have achieved celebrity status, have honed the capacity to weave powerful fictions about themselves by actively using contemporary media practices.

At other times the novel's references to surveillance culture serve to underline the domestic and participatory ways in which individuals can use surveillance space. *Sara's Face* also draws upon blogging/video diaries, in which traditionally private thoughts become public documents, encouraging those who create them to see themselves as surveilled and monitored, but also offering the potential for manipulating public perceptions of the private individual. Tellingly, several chapters of *Sara's Face* are written as if the reader is watching Sara's video diary. On the one hand, this narrative tactic appears to allow Sara to "speak directly to us" (3), allowing us voyeuristic access to her personal thoughts and motivations. However, it is abundantly clear that Sara is extremely conscious of being watched whenever she makes a video entry. Her first piece of video footage, for instance, is introduced by an omniscient narrator, who carefully describes the way in which Sara has set up the camera, and speculates about her reasons for acting in the way that she does:

"(Sara is sitting in a chair looking off to the side of the camera, as if someone else is sitting there talking to her. But hers is the only voice we hear. In fact, she's pretending to be interviewed for the TV. Occasionally she glances at the camera and examines something—she can probably see herself on a monitor. At other times, she forgets where she is and seems to be talking almost to herself. It's as if she's working out her own thoughts and feelings through this pretend interview)" (2004, 4).

This narrative tactic explicitly draws attention to the diverse ways in which Sara might be using surveillance space. Thus, we are invited to speculate about whether Sara's film is produced by her in a knowing way (with Sara carefully orchestrating and manipulating the ways in which her image is published) or in a wholly innocent way (with Sara naively spilling her thoughts as she plays childishly at being interviewed as a "wannabe" (11) celebrity). Both interpretations are plausible, meaning that this space, too, potentially represents a shift in representations of young people, who become framed as confident and knowing consumers of and participants in surveillance space, rather than innocent victims suffering constant scrutiny.

In overall terms, then, Burgess's allusions to celebrity culture systematically place emphasis on the deeply ambiguous ways in which celebrities are positioned and constructed in popular media practices. In some ways the novel acknowledges that celebrity culture affords the celebrity an element of power and influence. In other ways celebrity culture positions the celebrity as a victim who is trapped by the ideals of the watchers. In what follows I will demonstrate how Burgess creates Sara as a deeply ambiguous and "elusive" (2) character, in order to systematically explore the issues, ideas and pleasures of these shifting sets of experience.

Sara: innocent victim (or in control)?

The novel is predominantly preoccupied with exploring Sara's complex and contested relationship to surveillance space. While Burgess sees young people like Sara as able to work with this complex cultural space and not as cultural dupes, the novel does not ignore the idea that some teenage girls may seem dangerously and helplessly addicted to celebrity culture and the popular media texts which confer celebrity status. Of particular interest to Burgess is the idea of identity formation and the notion that informed teenagers can encounter and manipulate their popular culture environment in diverse and contradictory ways. However, rather than simply warning young readers to reject celebrity culture, Burgess is keen to understand and engage with its appeal. This drives him to document and report it in an extremely even-handed way, by showing multiple perspectives on the issue.

The novel announces from the outset that it is important to speculate about whether Sara, embroiled in the celebrity lifestyle of the legendary rock star Jonathon Heat, has been "in control the whole time" or is "just the innocent victim of Heat and his surgeon, Wayland Kaye" (2006, 1). This central question, posed on the very first page, invites the reader to consider whether these adults seek to cherish and help Sara, making her dreams come true, or whether they plan to steal her face in order to rejuvenate Heat's public image. It is arguable that Burgess has systematically constructed the novel so as to deliberately encourage interpretative ambiguity and in so doing he offers a huge spectrum of possible readings of Sara. These range between two extreme interpretations: one in which Sara is a powerless victim of celebrity culture, the other in which she plays, knowingly and in a calculating way, with survelliance space.

Sara can be read as a powerless and tormented victim of celebrity culture's messages about what girls should be like. Burgess's narrative engages extensively with the teenage protagonist's obsessive concern about her appearance, her fixation with her weight, her dissatisfaction with her body, her desire for physical perfection and cosmetic surgery. This ties in with public angst about girls supposedly falling prey to the ill-effects of the media (Tiggemann and Pickering 1996; Brumberg 1997; Harrison and Cantor 1997; Hargreaves 2002). Within these discourses girls are believed to internalize the overwhelming presence of idealized representations of the female form in the beauty industry and the mass media, to the extent that they learn to monitor themselves and their own bodies (Younger 2009). From this point of view Sara's behaviour exemplifies a subtle form of self and peer surveillance, in which the teenage girl is consistently positioned as consumed by the controlling gaze of the outside world.

Even so, the novel is not judgemental about, or dismissive of, Sara's fixation with media representations. Instead, her desires for fame and beauty dominate her thoughts and direct her behaviours in apparently self-destructive and alarming ways. It is clear that it might be extremely frightening to be Sara, and to experience the world as she sees it. Thus the reader is offered a serious, authentic and sympathetic representation of narcissistic self-loathing (which, because of its associations with exhibitionism and egocentricism, is often mistaken for self-loving). For instance, Sara often expresses neurotic concern with her own appearance, as follows:

"Look at this flab, ugh!... I look like the blubber bunny. And for the other
stuff, the stuff you can't fiddle with, I've already got that booked in...The
nose is going to be straightened. You can see. There. Like a bulbous—
well, like a bulb...I wanted them to suck out some of my lard, but they
won't do that. They say I'm thin enough....So what's this, then? ...it's fat.
You need to do that sort of thing in today's entertainment world. .." (2006,
65).

The violent way in which Sara speaks about her own body suggests a
deeply disturbed way of seeing herself. In passages like these it seems that
Burgess is keen to acknowledge the appalling potential consequences of a
culture which endorses self-alteration and cosmetic surgery. We see this
distaste, too, in the graphic description of the destructive outcomes of
Heat's cosmetic surgery:

"...under the mask, the wreckage was terrible. The skin had peeled off, the
blood supply dried up, the nervous system gone haywire. Flesh had begun
to die and to grow and to bleed without order..." (2006, 30).

In this way *Sara's Face* does not shy away from telling young readers
about the potentially destructive power of media narratives of fame and
beauty.

However, Burgess is keen to ensure that Sara is not simply read as a
passive victim. He persistently draws attention to the ways in which Sara
explicitly resists being framed in such ways. She derides the many
characters in the novel who worry for her, pity her and try to help or
rescue her from what they see as her helplessly addictive behaviours. Most
characters regard Sara as ill and in need of treatment. In so doing they
construct her as a powerless victim who is deeply unstable and spiralling
out of control. They fear her self-destructive urges and, in their concern,
they monitor her every move in order to control her. However, Sara deeply
resents being watched in this way. She rails angrily at the intrusive gaze of
those who seek to control her body by checking her eating habits and by
trying to force her to eat. She lashes out when people suggest she's "mad"
(85), delusional (81), or imply that they believe her "accidents" (39) are
actually episodes of intentional self-harm. She actively hides the
behaviours others disapprove of, becoming secretive and deceptive. On the
one hand, this might be seen as a form of denial, representing Sara's
inability to resist the contemporary standards of the "thin ideal" (Younger
2009, 3). On the other, it illustrates Sara's profoundly expert capacity to
manage other characters' impressions of her.

This capacity affords Sara the possibility of literally constructing her own identity. By altering her own physical appearance she can be regarded as making choices which enable her to determine for herself what she wants to be and how she wants to be known. She achieves this because she is so capably conversant with the possibilities for agency that surveillance space offers. At one key point in the novel, for instance, Sara has a serious "accident," when she trips and presses a scalding iron to her face (37). It is never clear whether she engineered the situation deliberately, or why or how it really happened. But different characters in the novel read the significance of the scar differently. Some people, like Heat, see the blemish on Sara's face as a flaw. He assumes that Sara must want to rid herself of it, and he offers to pay for the restorative operation himself. However, while Sara may indeed see her scar as a blemish, in an important sense she also seems to admire it. She turns the scar into her brand—in the sense of a trademark—an image to which she becomes particularly attached, and which she subsequently uses to manipulate other people. Sara's attitude towards the scar, and her motivations for harming herself, then, cannot be taken at face value, just as Heat's real motives for wanting Sara to submit to surgery are ambiguous and unknowable. Perhaps he genuinely wants to help her, but perhaps he deviously wants to steal her face to restore his own.

We never know the truth of any situation in the novel, because Sara's story is being pieced together retrospectively by Burgess, who, we are told, has been commissioned by Sara, following a gruesome operation, when her face was transplanted onto Heat's. We know from the outset that Heat was committed to prison for his part in what the papers and courts perceived as a monstrous crime, but Sara's fate, we are told, is more open to "endless speculation" (1). In fact, she remains "a mystery, a figure without explanation" (1). In compiling Sara's story, Burgess (as narrator) tells us that he has spoken to almost all the people involved in the events, bar Sara herself. And, the opening frame narrative reveals: "Sara has proved to be incredibly elusive" (2). In fact, unable to speak to Sara directly, the narrator has had to make do with trying to understand the "versions" (2) of her that she, and other people, have told him, have told each other, and have told the paparazzi. And Sara has "told so many versions of what was going on to so many different people, it's as if she has done her best to extinguish her real self in favour of her own legend" (2).

In an important sense, then, Sara has written herself into being by using surveillance space so skilfully. The narrator guides us to see that Sara is a "master dissembler," with only a very "shaky idea" of who she really is or what she wanted to become (2). She has a talent for telling vivid stories, which she makes other characters, and possibly even herself, believe, despite their clichéd absurdity. These tactics all explicitly call attention to the skill with which Sara manipulates surveillance space. For instance, she seems responsible for spreading the idea that Heat is trying to steal her face. She spreads wild stories about a girl who has previously gone missing in Heat's house, whose photograph she has seen in the hallway, but who appears to Sara as a ghost whose face has been stolen by Heat. One of Sara's video-diary entries focuses on a patch of blood smeared on the wall where, she claims, the ghost passed by. Yet no one but Sara sees the ghost and we never know whether she placed the blood there herself, as an elaborate hoax, to manipulate other people's readings of Heat and orchestrate his downfall. Indeed, the narrative world being pieced together is, quite possibly, wholly engineered by Sara, who uses her skilful manipulation of surveillance space to conjure the whole story, making everyone believe what she wants them to believe.

Tellingly, in the video-diary episodes of the novel, Sara controls the camera, choosing to film herself and construct images of herself for future public consumption. The video-clips she creates are, in fact, the narrator's only way of knowing Sara. But Sara's video-diaries might be carefully fabricated to narrate herself into being in a way which ensures her story will arrest attention and press itself on the public imagination. Her knowledge of surveillance space and the fictional worlds of images and appearance allows her to control all the characters in the novel, including the journalist/novelist, Burgess, who ostensibly narrates her story. In short, Sara recreates herself in sensational ways and gains a considerable measure of control by manipulating fictional worlds and mobilizing complex media practices. Above all, she understands the power of her image to influence, persuade and even hide in plain sight. This is indicated by the way that her best friend, Janet, tells stories of the ease with which, since childhood, Sara has amused herself by playing different characters.

Thus, in contrast to the notion of Sara as feeble victim, one can also read Sara as a knowing, media-literate individual who understands, and hence can exercise, agency via surveillance space. Ultimately, perhaps, she gives her public the spectacle they crave. She secures herself a global audience by cleverly arranging for the paparazzi to be present when the police storm the operating theatre where her face is being transplanted onto Heat's. This means that the film crews and photographers are there to capture and publish the very moment at which Sara and Heat are wheeled out of Heat's mansion on theatre trolleys. This is the precise instant when Sara's face, now on Heat, became a notoriously famous image, "revealed to us through a thousand newspaper headlines, magazine articles, news bulletins, TV shows and an endless commentary on the radio" (1).

Sara's motives for this shocking exposé remain deeply ambiguous, so Sara is unknowable to the end. Perhaps she sought revenge for the ways Heat mistreated her, or perhaps she staged her shocking eviction from the house as a publicity stunt to shore up her own faltering identity. However, the novel also offers the possibility that Sara might have been driven by a desire to use surveillance space, and her celebrity status, to make people think and change the world. She had, after all, staged a similar exposé while still at school, when she used the local press to blow the whistle on an instance of alleged sexual bullying.

Ultimately, Sara comes across as a tangle of contradictions, and the young reader must decide, based on the diverse images offered by the characters within the text, what to think about the part that Sara, and others, have played in the novel. It is all a matter of how Sara, and different stories about Sara, are interpreted. This is as true for the reader as it is for the characters in the novel. The writing's rich complexity always suggests a wide range of interpretative possibilities. The effect is that any reading of a given character is never as simple as it may at first appear. The polyphonic nature of the novel ultimately refuses to allow a single vision of Sara. Critics have often called attention to Burgess's fondness for this narrative tactic, noting how, in other novels, such as *Junk* (1996), he switches point of view between characters in order to establish moral complexity and relativism (see, for instance, Thomson 1999; Rudd 1999). This might also be true of *Sara's Face*. The novel does not condone or condemn Sara's fascination with celebrity culture, but seeks to explore and understand it in context.

However, I have shown how, in this novel, polyphony is also used to draw attention to the way in which Sara's world is entirely embedded in the fantastic fictions of surveillance space. These—not real life—provide the fictional concepts and codes through which the young spectator or reader views the characters. Eager consumers of such fictions, the text implies, might be best placed to appreciate the different ways stories and fictional concepts can be used. For Sara, rather than influencing her or simply defining who she is, the popular media fictions she consumes help her realize how she will be watched. They give her power by helping her know that "It's not what you are, it's what people think you are that matters" (11). That power, in Sara's world, depends on one's capacity to play with, and subvert, surveillance space. These features all serve to underline the point that *Sara's Face* is not intended as convincing social realism, with a view to counselling or cautioning the young reader about celebrity culture or particular media practices. The novel is consciously stylized, underlining, instead, the need to examine and remain wary of fictional systems which transform and filter reality.

References

Albrechtslund, Anders. 2008. Online Social Networking as Participatory Surveillance. *First Monday*. 13, 3.
http://firstmonday.org/htbin/cgiwrap/bin/ojs/index.php/fm/article/view Article/2142/1949#author. Date accessed September 2011.

Andrejevic, Mark. 2003. *Reality TV: The Work of Being Watched*. Lanham MD: Rowman and Littlefield.

Brumberg, Joan Jacobs. 1997. *The Body Project: An Intimate History of American Girls*. New York: Random House.

Burgess, Melvin. 1996. *Junk*. London: Penguin.

—. 2006. *Sara's Face*. London: Andersen Press.

Christopher, John.1970. *The Guardians*. Harmondsworth: Puffin.

Hargreaves, Duane. 2002. Idealized Women in TV Ads Make Girls Feel Bad. *Journal of Social and Clinical Psychology* 21: 287-308.

Harrison, Kristen and Joanne Cantor. 1997. The Relationship Between Media Consumption and Eating Disorders. *Journal of Communication* 47: 40-67.

James, Allison. 2000. Embodied Beings(s): Understanding the Self and the Body in Childhood. *The Body, Childhood and Society*, ed. Alan Prout, 19-38. Basingstoke: MacMillan Press.

Lott, Tim. 2007. *Fearless*. London: Walker Books.

Lowry, Lois. 1994. *The Giver*. London: Harper Collins.

McGrath, John Edward. 2004. *Loving Big Brother: Performance, Privacy and Surveillance Space*. London: Routledge.

Orwell, George. 1949. *Nineteen-Eighty-Four*. London: Martin, Secker and Warburg.

Rudd, David. 1999. A Young Person's Guide to the Fictions of Junk. *Children's Literature in Education* 30 (2): 119-126.

Steeves, Valerie and Owain Jones. 2010. Editorial: Surveillance and Children. *Surveillance & Society* 7(3/4): 187-191.

Tiggemann, Marika, and Amanda S. Pickering. 1996. The Role of Television in Adolescent Women's Body Dissatisfaction and Drive for Thinness. *International Journal of Eating Disorders* 20:199-203.

Thomson, Stephen. 1999. The Real Adolescent: Performance and Negativity in Melvyn Burgess's *Junk*. *The Lion and the Unicorn*. 23 (1): 22-29.

Thorpe, David. 2007. *Hybrids.* London: Harper Collins.
Westall, Robert. 1984. *Futuretrack 5.* London: William Morrow and Co.
Younger, Beth. 2009. *Learning Curves: Body Image and Female Sexuality in Young Adult Literature.* London: Scarecrow Press.

WORDS, WOUNDS AND CHINESE WHISPERS: THE COMPLEX HEARING-TELLING DYNAMIC OF WRITING FOR AND BY YOUNG ADULTS

KIMBERLEY REYNOLDS

The question "what do we tell the children?" begs another: "what do the children hear?" How different telling and hearing can be, especially when the tellers are adults and the listeners are young people in the throes of adolescence, was demonstrated during a panel discussion in 2007 following two short plays commissioned for an education programme run by the National Theatre in London. The plays, *Chatroom* (2005) by Edna Walsh and *Citizenship* (2006) by Mark Ravenhill, were performed to groups of students between 15 and 18 who were exploring how and where young people's views are expressed in culture: the places where they get to do the telling. Performances were supported by a series of events of which the panel discussion was one. *Citizenship*, which deals primarily with sexual experiments and developing personal relationships, provoked verbal interactions and collective belly laughs from the engaged and focused teenage audience. *Chatroom*, a piece about self-harm and suicide, was watched in the kind of intense silence of concentration that is rare among large groups of any age. Particularly during the post-performance discussion with the panel (comprised of a playwright, actors from the company, a counsellor and myself representing children's literature), it was evident that the young people in the audience had heard something in both plays that was important to them. What also became clear was that what they were hearing was rather different from what the members of the panel thought they were being told through the plays which were, of course, conceived, mounted and performed by adults.

Chatroom introduces six young people who meet in two internet chatrooms: one designed to help people who are having suicidal thoughts, the other targeting teenagers from the London suburb of Chiswick. It is a dark piece that follows the actions of the Chiswick group as some of its members encourage Jim, a depressed working-class boy, to commit suicide in public. When Jim instructs the other members of the chatroom to meet at the Chiswick MacDonalds, it seems inevitable that he will either kill himself amidst the families and French fries or embark on one of the mass shootings that have become too familiar over the last decade. In fact, the episode is defused by laughter. When Jim, dressed in a cowboy outfit, climbs onto a table and starts to twirl two pistols to the *Rawhide* theme song that is playing on his ghetto blaster, bemused youngsters start to applaud and enjoy the spectacle. Their recognition and appreciation settle the doubts, anxieties and self-loathing that Jim has been confessing to in the chatroom; as he rides the laugh it becomes clear that the pistols are only toys and the threat was never real.

Jim's story addresses the difficulties associated with maintaining a sense of self amidst the personal and social changes associated with adolescence. His need to be recognized and affirmed comes from the sense that he is being socially "disappeared" by former friends, who no longer seem to be interested in him, and a family in which he feels himself to be the odd one out and possibly responsible for his parents' divorce. Although both the adult panel and the young people in the audience had a shared understanding of what Jim was going through, as listeners they were positioned and responded differently. *Chatroom* was telling the young people in the audience, who were themselves in the process of negotiating adolescence, about what that experience might involve. Since all the adults attending the performances were there in professional capacities, they were positioned alongside the tellers rather than the listeners. For the panel, then, Jim's story represented a problem to be solved and a cautionary tale about the stresses experienced by contemporary youth. As well as being positioned differently, there were significant differences between how the adolescent target audience and the adults on the panel understood the issues explored in Edna Walsh's text. These differences reflect the way the telling-hearing dynamic affects meaning and changes according to who is listening. Responses diverged around key areas; notably in how what was being said about the Internet and constructions of adolescence was understood.

For the panel, *Chatroom* seemed to be designed to tell its audience that the Internet can be a dangerous space where they may encounter people and situations that are beyond their experience; that young people themselves can be dangerous and untrustworthy, and that many of them are stressed, unhappy and engaging in behaviour which may be risky to themselves and others. From this perspective, in *Chatroom* the Internet appears to be a forum for risky behaviour, a view underlined for the panel because Jim's "cure" is associated with him leaving the chatroom and going out into the world. Implicit in this reading is the recognition that many adults would be more comfortable if the young were reading books and spending time in face-to-face encounters with people their own age rather than spending time online with people they don't know and who may not be what they seem (Applebaum 2009).

Significantly, while these negative messages spoke loudly to members of the panel, in the post-performance discussion none of them was raised by the young people in the audience. The key points they identified were the way *Chatroom* dramatized the volatility of interactions between young people, and its characterization of young people as potentially dangerous members of society. So, while the panel thought the play was telling its young audiences about the potential risks of the Internet, the pupils heard *Chatroom* adding to the negative discourses and representations around young people in contemporary culture. A substantial part of the post-performance discussion consisted of members of the audience pointing out the extent to which the media concentrate on reporting stabbings, shootings and other kinds of violent incidents involving teenagers (most recently during the 2011 riots in Britain's cities), instead of the positive things that young people do and achieve. The young people in the audience also voiced the suspicion that they are subtly discouraged from becoming engaged with social and political issues, not least through the books they are given to read; in other words, by children's literature.

The frustrations of fantasy

At one level *Chatroom* is a kind of children's literature in that it features juvenile characters and was written and performed by adults for young people. Significantly, however, Edna Walsh attempts to distance her play from the genre of children's literature; *Chatroom* begins with one of the characters attacking Roald Dahl's *Charlie and the Chocolate Factory* (1964) and through it books for children generally. The attack is part of a chatroom exchange between Jack and William, both members of the Chiswick set. Jack asks William why he dislikes the story so much:

> "Jack: It's only a children's story.
> William: It's a lie! What's the point? What are they telling us?
> Jack: What are who telling us?
> William: The writers! Our parents! Harry Fucking Potter!?! In the real world he's still under the stairs. He's a thirty-year-old retard who's developed his own under-the-stairs-language!
> Jack: The point is… is that children don't want to read the true stories. What child wants to read the news?! It's just escape. It's important that we dream of other things.

William: Fuck off! Life's too short. If the world is going to evolve in
any way... children should be told what's really happening. Cold, clear
facts... that's what's taken us down from the trees, that's what powers the
economy.... They're trying to keep children young! Adults. Publishers.
Fucking writers. They don't want children thinking for themselves. They
see children as a threat. They want to keep everything 'fantasy'" (Walsh
2005, Scene 1, n.p.).

William's attack on children's literature gives voice to a set of ideas that
many who value children's books might want to contest, but which
nevertheless need to be considered, especially with regard to what
children's books tell their readers. These ideas include the belief that
young people shouldn't trust children's books because they do not show
the world as it is and children's writers are trying to coerce child readers
into thinking and behaving in ways that suit adults but which are
disenfranchising and forestall the transition into adulthood. If children's
literature as a medium is discredited with adolescents, a potentially
important vehicle through which adults can share information gained
through experience and study of the world is being lost. Adults do have
valuable things to tell, but these are of no account if they are not heard or
are misinterpreted. *Chatroom* endorses William's suspicions about
children's literature by claiming that, unlike children's books, it does tell
the truth and reflects the world as teenagers know it. Paradoxically, one of
the truths it tells is that when faced with ethically challenging issues,
young people as represented by its characters, lack the maturity and
experience necessary to deal responsibly with the situations they have
created.

As well as attacking children's literature, William's outburst implicitly
compares children's literature and the Internet. During the post-
performance discussion it was clear that for the young people in the
audience, this comparison was one of the aspects of the play they heard
most clearly and which they endorsed. While many adults may regard the
Internet with dubiety, what William is suggesting is that the Internet is
preferable to fiction in books because it is a forum where real
conversations are had, real information is found and real opinions are
formed. Moreover, unlike the children's books that he attacks, it offers the
opportunity for young people to construct independently images of
themselves rather than having these constructed for them by writers and
the media. The Internet also allows them to experiment with different
voices and opinions instead of being required to take up positions created
for them on the page by adult writers. In cyberspace, children and young

people can themselves become tellers rather than always being required to listen.

Disembodied voices

Arguably one reason why the Internet appeals so powerfully to the young is because, in addition to giving them opportunities to speak, it separates voice from body at a time in life when bodies can seem particularly problematic. In cyberspace the extent to which selves are discursively constructed is total, providing temporary respite from clashes between inner and outer selves. This raises the possibility that, far from being a place of danger, the Internet may help prevent despairing adolescents from harming themselves. But the Internet alone cannot resolve these tensions. Because it is so dominated by language, the Internet requires its users to be able to verbalize their feelings. This is where, despite William's accusation, children's literature has a role to play and where young adult fiction in particular is working to give its readers both some of the truths William demands and strategies for engaging with them. Listening to what they are being told in fiction featuring characters who resort to harming themselves may help teenage readers articulate their feelings, including through the Internet.

Being able to speak about what they are feeling is important because when words fail, the body may be used to express and relieve feelings. Fiona Gardner, a psychoanalyst specializing in self-harming adolescent girls, explains that self-harming behaviour occurs when:

> "patients have no words for feelings….It is in these sorts of states of mind that people can either harm themselves and experience *no* pain, or harm themselves *in order* to feel pain. To reconnect, the person has to begin to imagine and create some way of representing their sensations, feelings and perceptions so that this can be thought of, recognised and integrated" (2001, 97, my emphases).

Speaking through the body may take the form of piercing, tattooing or injurious behaviours including eating disorders, cutting, burning, head-banging, scratching and overdosing. Some of these may temporarily provide relief, but they do not substitute for being able to express and explain emotions. Fiction can help young people verbalize their feelings because it is able to document, explore, explain, and provide models, metaphors and vocabularies for doing so.

The subgenre of books—both fictional and autobiographical—that feature characters who deliberately harm themselves has expanded considerably since the turn of the twenty-first century. The kinds of self-injury most commonly featured are cutting, starving and purging, refusing to speak and substance abuse, sometimes in combination. The incidence of such behaviour in society and on the page has become so familiar that there are now texts in which it is taken for granted: for instance, readers of Meg Rosoff's *How I Live Now* (2004) gradually become aware that the focalizing character, Daisy, has an eating disorder bordering on anorexia, but this is only a facet of her character—it is not at the centre of the novel or what defines her. In Tabitha Suzuma's *From Where I Stand* (2007), disturbed teenager Raven regularly cuts himself, including unintentionally in front of his five-year-old foster sister Ella. His behaviour is not sensationalized; it is presented as what he does to cope. Uncertain but not particularly bothered about what she has seen, Ella intuits that it is to do with his unhappiness; she offers him a plaster and goes back to her drawing. No one takes him to the hospital or dresses his cuts, although his foster family and classmates know about them.

In *Citizenship*, the companion play to *Chatroom*, Amy is a cutter. Again, this is presented in a matter of fact way, and captures particularly well both Amy's inability to articulate what she feels and her reliance on other ways to communicate—in her case, through attacking her body. Her friends know that she cuts and she talks to them about it openly, though without much insight, as is apparent in an exchange with her friend, Tom. Tom, who is uncertain about his sexuality, also expresses himself through his body more effectively than he does in language, though his chosen medium is fashion rather than flesh. Tom has come to Amy's to ask her to help him dye his hair blonde, but she says she is supposed to be doing her affirmations:

> "TOM: What's that? [the affirmations]
> AMY: I'm supposed to write out a hundred times 'I'm surrounded by love'.
> TOM: Why?
> AMY: Cause I cut myself again last night.
> TOM: Why?
> AMY: I dunno. I was bored. Or something. Or stress. I dunno.
> TOM: You gotta know.
> AMY: I don't. Mum took me down to the healer and she told me I had to do the affirmations.
> TOM: You can do them later. Do my hair" (Walsh 2005, Scene 5, n.p.).

"Dunno" illustrates Amy's inability to put into words the feelings that drive her to communicate through marking her body. As with Rosoff's *How I Live Now*, Amy's behaviour is not presented as bizarre or life-threatening, but as part of a recognized spectrum of adolescent behaviour. The emerging tendency for YA fiction to normalize self-harm raises some practical and ethical questions. Might it, for instance, encourage readers to start harming themselves or to ignore a friend's self-injurious behaviour? Possibly, but literature's ability to stimulate insights and suggest ways of talking about the self and self-harming behaviours make this a risk worth taking. Clinical bibliotherapists have for long argued that books can provide "a mode of intervention in aiding persons severely troubled with emotional or behavioural problems" (Lack quoted in Doll and Doll 1997, 7). They do this through a combination of integrating new knowledge, offering insights into the self and facilitating articulation. Just as importantly, bibliotherapists have also found that books can trigger a catharsis through empathetic recognition of aspects of the self in characters (1997, 7–8).

Recent work by the Reader Centre at the University of Liverpool also suggests that reading poems, plays and novels that explore the darker emotions can help alleviate mental distress and other kinds of pain. The project involves creating reader groups for people who have a variety of personal problems, from recovering addicts through prisoners, to those with a wide spectrum of mental health problems. Just as Bruno Bettelheim argued that children need fairy tales to be unadulterated to help them work through such powerful feelings as rage, fear, and anxiety, so these groups use literary works such as Thomas Hardy's *Jude the Obscure* (1895), the Psalms, and Dante's *Inferno* (c. 1314) to help readers externalize and work through their feelings. Writing about the Liverpool project, Blake Morrison explains: "By attending to the cry of another, we articulate our own cries, frame them, contain them, and feel less stranded" (Morrison 2008). One thing that young readers need to be told, then, is where to find the cries of others in the fictions that feature people like themselves. This also requires them to accept that children's literature is not a duplicitous medium.

The cries of others

Joanna Kenrick's *Red Tears* (2007) does a particularly good job of offering readers the cry of another. The novel is based on interviews with a number of young women who self harm and professionals who work with them: manifestly, then, it demonstrates adults both listening to young people and telling them the truth as far as they understand it. The many testimonials included in the preliminary matter for the book and available online suggest that it maps the motivation and progress of the behaviour accurately; so accurately, in fact, that it is prefaced by a warning that self-harmers may find it contains moments that can trigger the desire to cut. *Red Tears* tells the story of Emily, an English middle-class teenager from a happy family with a strong friendship network and a history of academic excellence, during the year of her GCSE [General Certificate of Secondary Education] state examinations. This makes Emily a "typical" twenty-first-century self-harmer; previously cutting was associated with poor educational achievement, dysfunctional families and often a history of sexual abuse. The book plots changes in Emily's life as she starts to find it difficult to cope with the pressure of school work and changes in her friends, who have begun to experiment with sex and socializing of a kind her family won't permit and which makes Emily nervous. They begin to ignore her and eventually she is ostracized.

Like Jim in *Chatroom*, when her friends desert her Emily starts to feel she is becoming invisible; even the teachers seem no longer to notice her. Emily's misery at school and her anger at her mother's obsession with exam success and failure to respect her privacy provoke Emily into an outburst during a family outing. As a consequence, her mother also ignores her, leaving Emily to wonder whether, "eventually there will be no one left who will acknowledge my existence," and, "If that happened, would I cease to exist, too?" (115). In four months Emily goes from being top of the class, popular and lively to wondering whether, if she were to die she would "leave a hole in the world? Or would it simply close up like a wound? Heal itself and grow over the top" (154). The wound metaphor is not accidental because, like many young people who go through similar changes and sometimes become clinically depressed, Emily has begun to cut herself. Although a fictional character, Emily's behaviour corresponds closely to that of many of Fiona Gardner's patients, who are not refusing to tell others about their problems but fear both that they do not know what to say and that they will not be heard. Cutting is the beginning of attempting to speak since, as Gardner explains:

> "in performing these private attacks [of cutting], the young women gradually found a public voice. The silent actions, which took place in such secrecy, became the route into the public domain and eventually into the world of words" (2001, 146).

In a coda to her study, Gardner compares forms of self-harm, and cutting in particular, to culturally-approved traditions of marking the body through recognized rites of passage. She speculates about whether the loss of many of the official moments of transition that signalled the process of growing up has contributed to the increase in self-harming behaviours, which she suggests can be understood as faulty initiation rites. Because they have no cultural status and are not validated, these self-directed behaviours cannot help young people gain a sense of recognition and self-control and so they offer only a temporary sense of achievement. This may explain why behaviour such as cutting needs to be repeated until a way forward is found.

In Emily's case the text makes it clear that at some level she wants her parents to know what she is doing, despite the fact that she carefully conceals her cuts and scars. When after many months her sleeve slips back while she is washing the dishes and her mother sees one of her arms, Emily is both exhausted and relieved, though she is still lost for words.

> "'Well?' [my mother] says loudly. 'I'm waiting for an explanation.'
> I stare at the floor. What can I say that would explain anything?...
> Dad suddenly breathes in through his nose. 'Oh God,' he says.
> I know he knows. And actually, the fog starts to clear a bit. Because now – he knows. They will know. I know. You know. He/she/it knows. We know. You know. They know. And so the telling of them is done. I'll never have to tell them again. I'm very tired" (Kenrick 2007, 159).

This scene instigates a series of decisions in the family that see Emily embark on work with a therapist. In this way she commences the process of moving from silent actions to the world of words. The importance of this transition is something books about self-harm regularly seek to tell their readers.

Truthful fictions

Parallels have often been drawn between therapeutic processes and reading. Psychoanalysis in particular functions like reading, with patients making use of metaphors, symbols, gaps and other strategies that demand interpretation from analysts. Gardner, for instance, classifies cutting as a metaphoric representation in which "actions have to carry the direct meaning, and represent the inner state of mind" (2001, 147). The comparison between reading and therapy works both ways, so readers are like therapists; they learn to understand characters through interpreting what texts reveal. The strategies required to analyze characters' behaviour can also be applied to the self, and this is precisely what YA fiction about self-harming encourages. Books such as *Red Tears* tell readers about the experiences of others in an attempt to help them help make sense of their own feelings and actions. Understanding the situations and feelings that trigger self-harming behaviour is the first step to managing them. The books do not purport to be cures; rather, they almost always end with the self-harming character(s) seeking and accepting professional help, having recognized that they are trapped in self-destructive cycles and need to be shown how to move forward.

Although they tell readers about self-injurious behaviour, like *Red Tears*, most books about self-harm involve adult authors listening to and learning about young people's experiences and incorporating their voices and views in the texts. Such fictions do not conform to the version of children's literature put forward by William in *Chatroom*. Like most books that deal with self-harm, *Red Tears* tells its readers "what's really happening. Cold, clear facts...." Its aim is to get "children thinking for themselves," and in doing so it works to unpick the fantasy of childhood innocence that so enrages William. William's charges against children's literature should not be discounted, however; neither should the ability of the Internet to enable young people to participate in telling as well as listening be forgotten. Forging an alliance between fiction and cyberspace offers the prospect of communication which combines telling and hearing on the parts of both adults and children. The question then would no longer be, "what do we tell the children" but "what are children and adults telling each other?" Such a dialogue holds the promise of more effective telling and better listening across the generations.

References

Applebaum, Noga. 2009. *Representations of Technology in Science Fiction for Young People*. London and New York: Routledge.

Bettelheim, Bruno. 1986 [1976]. *The Uses of Enchantment: The Meaning and Importance of Fairy Tales*. New York: Vintage.

Doll, Beth and Carol Doll. 1997. *Bibliotherapy with Young People*. Englewood, CO: Libraries Unlimited.

Gardner, Fiona. 2001. *Self-Harm: A Psychotherapeutic Approach*. London: Routledge.

Kenrick, Joanna. 2007. *Red Tears*. London: Faber and Faber.

Morrison, Blake. 2008. The Reading Cure. *The Guardian*, 5 January. Accessed online 19 December 2010.

Ravenhill, Mark. 2006. *Citizenship*. London: Methuen.

Rosoff, Meg. 2004. *How I Live Now*. London: Penguin.

Suzuma, Tabitha. 2007. *From Where I Stand*. London: Bodley Head.

Walsh, Edna. 2007 [2005]. *Chatroom*. London: Samuel French. Please note: quotations were taken from the unpublished performance text.

CONTRIBUTORS

Jane Suzanne Carroll teaches at the School of English, Trinity College Dublin. Her research interests include landscape, children's fantasy, picture books, Old Norse literature, and Vikings in children's literature. She has published articles on Susan Cooper, children's ghost stories and on mindscape in children's literature. Her first book, *Landscapes in Children's Literature,* was published by Routledge in 2012.

Norma Clarke is Professor of English Literature and Creative Writing at Kingston University, London, where she teaches children's literature. A specialist in the eighteenth-century, her books include *Dr Johnson's Women*, *The Rise and Fall of the Woman of Letters*, and *Queen of the Wits, a Life of Laetitia Pilkington*. She has also published five novels for children.

Shehrazade Emmambokus recently completed her doctoral thesis, entitled 'Contemporary Adolescent Fiction from the South Asian Diaspora', at Kingston University, London. Engaging with cultural studies and sociological investigations, she offers readers a renewed way of understanding cultural identity development for South Asian diasporic youth as represented in the novels that she explores. She has published in *Bookbird* and in the essay collection *Postcolonial Spaces: The Politics of Place in Contemporary Culture.*

Michele Gill studied for her PhD at the University of Newcastle-Upon-Tyne with a project that explored representations of boyhood in YA fiction published in the UK, Australia and the USA around the new millennium. Her current work includes a study of changing portrayals of the male in Carnegie Medal winning novels since the 1930s and research into the impact of ideological understandings of childhood on YA fiction. Michele teaches children's literature to undergraduate students at The Open University in London.

Marnie Hay is the author of *Bulmer Hobson and the Nationalist Movement in Twentieth-Century Ireland* (Manchester University Press, 2009). In addition to lecturing in Modern Irish History at University College Dublin and Trinity College Dublin, she is the Academic Director of the Parnell Summer School (2011-12).

Eimear Hegarty is completing her doctoral studies at St. Patrick's College, Drumcondra. Her research interests are focused on postcolonial theory and the representation of forced migration in contemporary children's literature in English.

Patricia Kennon is a lecturer in English Literature at Froebel College of Education, County Dublin. She is editor of *Inis: The Children's Books Ireland Magazin*e and president of the Irish national section of IBBY. In 2010 she won an Excellence in Teaching Award from the National Academy for the Integration of Research, Teaching and Learning. Her research interests include gender in children's literature and popular culture, visual culture, transmedia storytelling and Victorian literature.

Nora Maguire completed a PhD in German studies at Trinity College, Dublin. Her thesis examined the narrative functions of tropes of childhood in post-reunification German historical fiction for adults. Her wider research interests include children's literature and culture, contemporary Germanophone literature, Holocaust studies, notions of nationalism and cultural memory, comparative studies and translation studies. Nora currently teaches in the German Department at the National University of Ireland, Maynooth.

Kerry Mallan is Professor and Director of the Children and Youth Research Centre at Queensland University of Technology. Her main areas of research are in children's literature and film, with specific interest in gender and sexuality. Her publications include *Gender Dilemmas in Children's Fiction* (2009) and an edited book (with Clare Bradford), *Contemporary Children's Literature and Film* (2010).

Anne Markey is a Teaching Fellow in Foras Feasa, National University of Ireland, Maynooth, and on the staff of the School of English, Trinity College Dublin. Her research focuses on intersections between Gaelic traditions and Irish writing in English and on literary representations of childhood from the seventeenth century to the present day. She is editor of *Patrick Pearse: Short Stories* (2009) and *Children's Fiction 1765-1808*

(2011), and author of *Oscar Wilde's Fairy Tales: Origins and Contexts* (2011).

Ciara Ní Bhróin lectures in English Literature in Coláiste Mhuire, Marino Institute of Education, an associated college of Trinity College, Dublin. She is a founder member and former president of the Irish Society for the Study of Children's Literature. Her areas of special interest are identity and ideology in Irish children's literature, Irish mythology and the representation of the past in Irish children's fiction. She has published on the work of Maria Edgeworth, Lady Gregory, Standish O'Grady, Eilís Dillon, Elizabeth O'Hara and on the young adult novels of Robert Cormier.

Kimberley Reynolds is Professor of Children's Literature in the School of English Literature, Language and Linguistics at Newcastle University. Recent publications include *A Very Short Introduction: Children's Literature* (OUP, 2011); *Children's Literature Between the Covers* (Modern Scholar, 2011) and, co-edited with Matthew Grenby, *Children's Literature Studies: A research handbook* (Palgrave, 2011). She currently holds a Major Leverhulme Research Fellowship investigating Modernism, the Left, and Progressive Writing for Children 1910 - 1949.

Beth Rodgers is a doctoral candidate in the School of English at Queen's University Belfast. Her thesis explores constructions of adolescent femininity in the literary marketplace of the Victorian fin-de-siècle period. She has presented papers on children's literature and Victorian periodicals at a number of conferences and is currently working on an article on the Irish children's writer, L.T. Meade.

Kay Sambell currently works as a Professor at Northumbria University, in the School of Health, Education and Community Studies, where she teaches on the Childhood Studies degree. She specializes in constructions of childhood and youth in literature for young people and is widely-known for her research on dystopian and futuristic fiction for young readers.

INDEX